The
Garland
CLASSICS OF FILM LITERATURE

REPRINTED IN PHOTO-FACSIMILE
IN 32 VOLUMES

ROTHA ON THE FILM

Paul Rotha

GARLAND PUBLISHING, INC. • NEW YORK & LONDON • 1978

Library of Congress Cataloging in Publication Data

Rotha, Paul, 1907-
Rotha on the film.

(The Garland classics of film literature ; 27)
Reprint of the 1958 ed. published by Essential Books, Fair Lawn, N.J.
Includes indexes.
1. Moving-pictures--Addresses, essays, lectures.
I. Title. II. Series.
PN1994.R573 1977 791.43'015 76-52126
ISBN 0-8240-2892-9

Printed in the United States of America

ROTHA
on the
FILM

other books by Paul Rotha

*

THE FILM TILL NOW
(1930, *and with Richard Griffith*, 1949)

CELLULOID: THE FILM TODAY
(1931)

DOCUMENTARY FILM
(1936, 1939, *and with Richard Griffith and Sinclair Road*, 1952)

MOVIE PARADE: A Pictorial Survey of the Cinema
(1936, *and with Roger Manvell*, 1950)

WORLD OF PLENTY
(*the book of the film*, 1945)

*

PORTRAIT OF A FLYING YORKSHIREMAN
(*the letters of Eric Knight to Paul Rotha*, 1952)

*

Editor of
TELEVISION IN THE MAKING
(1956)

Studio Impression, Elstree (1928)

ROTHA
on the
FILM

A Selection of Writings about the Cinema

1958

ESSENTIAL BOOKS, INC.

FAIR LAWN, NEW JERSEY

Printed in Great Britain

To
the Memory of
RICHARD WINNINGTON
who saw it all through
and saw through it all
but still loved what
was left of the real
Cinema

Acknowledgments

My thanks are due to the Editors of the following journals for permission to use articles which first appeared in their pages: *The Times*, *Manchester Guardian*, *New Statesman and Nation*, *The Spectator*, *Reynolds News*, *Public Opinion* (*The Daily Mirror*), *The Connoisseur*, *Cinema Quarterly*, *Sight and Sound*, *Theater Arts Magazine*, *Tribune*, *Films and Filming*, *Picturegoer* (incorporating *Film Weekly*), *World Review* and *The Leader* (Hulton Press), *Museums Association's Journal*, *Close-Up*, *Documentary News-Letter*, *British Film Academy Journal* and *The Living Cinema*.

Also to Longmans, Green & Co. for permission to reprint the chapter on *Earth* from *Celluloid: the Film Today*, now out-of-print; the Educational Foundation for Visual Aids for the piece *History on the Screen*; Triangle Publications Inc. for the articles that appeared in the *Philadelphia Public Ledger* and the *New York Post*, and the Edizione Dell' Ateneo, Rome, for the survey of British Films in *Twenty Years of Cinema in Venice*.

Stills reproduced are acknowledged individually to their production companies, but my thanks are due to the National Film Archive, London, for making available the photographs that appear facing pages 80, 92, 108, 109, 144, 145, 160, 161, 192, 193, 208.

The drawing by the late Richard Winnington on page 298 is reproduced by kind permission of the Editor of the *News Chronicle*. The drawings facing pages 48, 49 and 64 first appeared in *Film Weekly* (now incorporated in *The Picturegoer*) in 1929, and later in *Close-Up*, Vol. V, No. 1, of the same year. The frontispiece was drawn at Elstree, 1928, and has not been reproduced before.

My thanks, as in so many things, are also made to my wife who aided greatly in the preparation of the text for the press.

P.R.

Contents

IV. THE CONSTANT CRISIS

INDEXES

Illustrations

Foreword

To excavate and republish old writings about the cinema without refurbishing is no doubt asking for trouble. Those young tyros who are now just discovering it all as some of us discovered it years ago will disdain my eager approach when the screen was still a rational size and good films had to be searched for. That is a penalty of middle-age. But to have grown up with the cinema, to have seen the Delhi Durbar in Kinemacolor and a John Bunny comedy (in which the mice bit his feet in bed) as my first movie programme, to have gone to the pictures often as many as four times a week in the jovial company of wounded soldiers (and thus be let in free) during the last half of World War I, to have been unfit for 'games' for some years and thus able to spend two afternoons a week at the local picture-palace, to have been at the first performance of the Film Society in London in 1925, these are events for which I would not exchange a later birth-year.

Nostalgia plays no part in this. Having decided at an early age to make films my life, I am fortunate to have grown up with them. But I am ever grateful that my sensible parents, and especially my brother, encouraged my enthusiasm. If today my youthful adulation of the senior Fairbanks, or my passionate plea for better set-designing in British studios, seem naïve I can only say that it is how I thought then—and wish it had been better written! May the pomposity and dogmatism of a young man not mask his enthusiasm and love for the cinema, which latter exist in him just as strongly today.

Writing about films, however, has never been my first aim. Making them has always been my major wish. But to gain access to the ways and means of production, however modest, is not continuously easy and there have been times in the past thirty years when writing about the cinema has been a first necessity. *The Film Till Now*, for example, was written during the long spell of unemployment which was had by most workers in the British film industry when our studios were changed over to sound in 1929. This explains, too, why the film reviews in Part II fall into three groups coinciding roughly with years when there was least demand for my film-making talents, such as they may have been.

To select from more than 1500 articles and lectures is a job I never want (nor am likely to have) again. If the selection is disparate, at least it has a common theme. I have tried to make the choice as wide as possible in order to show that it is the cinema in *all* its forms and aspects which has held me in its spell.

Some will note that in the '20s and '30s I was what today they call angry. I still am. And I hope, if necessary, I shall continue to be. So far as cinema is concerned, I am angry when I see this magnificent medium—which I believe to be the most exciting and imaginative so far available to an artist in this century—misused and abused for the sake of material profit alone. Heaven knows, pictures must make money in most countries or they couldn't go on being made, but for the profit motive to be the *sole* arbiter of a film's shape and subject, style and stars seems to me to be a shocking abuse of a great medium.

While it is true that the majority of entertainment films are made by producers, writers and directors who are frit (as our local word is) of committing themselves to any kind of outlook, or to any kind of place in the fabric of society, fortunately there are film-makers who use their art as a means of interpreting their outlook on life. Cinema today is comprised of those many who are content to be 'entertainers', absorbed as often as not in the technique of making films *per se*, and those few who are prepared to struggle to say something purposeful in their work, something which is at least a contribution to our times. An artist does not have to join a political party—any party—or a church to be committed to a viewpoint. His commitment will appear in his work whether he paints, writes or makes things. It is symptomatic of our era, alas, that so few artists are prepared to commit themselves to anything other than an interest in their technique of producing. This is more true of films than of any other medium, partly no doubt because the tools of the craft are so expensive and because access to audiences, so far as this country is concerned, is restricted.

Yet if I have learnt one thing about the cinema over the years, it is not to be cynical. When the public screens are filled with an endless stream of meretricious floss, suddenly from somewhere —and it can sometimes be Hollywood—comes a lively, exciting, unheralded picture to reaffirm all one's belief in the cinema. It is only infinitely regrettable to me that such a film so seldom comes from England.

From that esoteric and cultish quarterly of the British Film Institute, I note that my post-war activity is written-off as what it likes to call my 'belabouring of the iniquitous industry'.[1] This inaccurate and damaging reference (by a journal whose editorial board should know better) presumably applies to the kind of piece which makes up Part IV of this book.

It will, I hope, be obvious to those who read what I have called 'The Constant Crisis' that what I have always had at heart is a British film industry which is not only economically healthy but is also an honest reflexion of contemporary life and thought and artistry. Any 'belabouring' that my analyses of the industry's problems may represent has been inspired by that urge alone. I can appreciate that some of the things said in this book will not endear me to those who pay lip-service to the betterment of British films, or to those whose main anxiety is to make a good living out of film production. But to those who are sincerely and seriously concerned with the present and future of British films, in so far as a nation's cinema is a reflexion of its character and outlook, I hope some of my comments and conclusions will be thought worth consideration and discussion.

The National Film Finance Corporation, whose work is dealt with at some length later in this book, brought about a much-needed curtailment of the extravagance associated with the British film industry before, during and immediately after the War. At the same time, the N.F.F.C. has not tackled the basic problem of the British independent producer—freedom of distribution for his films without terms, artistic as well as financial, being dictated by the all-powerful cinema circuits in the United Kingdom. The healthiest thing which has ever happened to

[1] *Sight and Sound*, Vol. 27, No. 2, Autumn 1957, p. 73.

American cinema is that of nearly 300 feature films estimated for production in 1957, some 40 per cent is independent of the major studio concerns.[1] This situation has come about by the divorcement by law of American production companies from cinema-ownership. For this reason more than any other, American talent has been freed to give us such interesting pictures as *The Young Stranger*, *Twelve Angry Men*, *Marty*, *Bachelor Party*, *A Man is Ten Foot Tall*,[2] and others of the same outlook. The fact that some of these subjects were first television plays has little to do with their social realism, contrary to some English critics' belief.

It is my belief that we shall never have a virile, imaginative, artistically and socially meaningful British cinema until the independent producer is given his rightful status of real independence. I admit no compromise in my attitude that the film-makers of this country should have the right of access to cinema-screens at least as freely as in any other country. Thus to those who denounce me for 'belabouring' the industry, I say that as the years have passed I have unwillingly but perforce become more and more concerned with the 'politics' of the cinema, in the main as an objective observer on the sidelines. The main impulse that has sparked my writing—other than critical reviews—has been to see created conditions in which the unique qualities of the film medium can be used to their full so that a creative contribution can be made to the world in which we live—the interpretation of life so that the community of mankind may gain aesthetically and socially from that interpretation.

For films are a part of life. Sometimes they are life itself—as is that masterpiece *Umberto D.* And all great films are an interpretation of life as seen by the film-maker and his writer.

As the story-film has followed the path of social realism and the documentary film has been broadened to include human beings 'in the round', so their roads have converged. I refer now not to their different methods of financing but to their social and aesthetic purpose. In *Umberto D*, or in *Bicycle Thieves*, De Sica asked the spectator to share in an experience which is as

[1] *Variety*, September 4, 1957.

[2] *The Edge of the City* in the U.S.

near to a real experience in life as a work of art can be. In *Louisiana Story*, Flaherty tried the same endeavour. The former we call story-films; the latter documentary. But, in point of fact, there was as much fiction and 'contrivance' of realism in Flaherty's depiction of the story of the Cajun boy's first experience of the civilizing technological world as there was in De Sica's story of the aged and lonely civil servant. If achieving 'nearness to life' in expressing a point of view towards that life is the ultimate aim of cinema, then films such as *Umberto D*, and more recently Bresson's *Un Condamné à Mort s'est Echappé* and Dassin's *Celui Qui Doit Mourir* are far along the road to that end.

The spokesmen of the Free Cinema group in England claim that their documentary films are 'concerned with basic human relationships and the problems of establishing communication on a human level . . .' and that 'this marks a distinct change from the temper of the '30s'.[1] How far this 'discovery' is from being new may be noted from the following 22-year-old quote:

'. . . Clearly a full and real expression of the modern scene and modern experience cannot be achieved unless people are observed in accurate relation to their own surroundings. To do this there must be establishment and development of character. There must be the growth of ideas, not only in theme, but in the minds of characters. Your individuals must be of the audience. They must be familiar in type and character. They themselves must think and convey their thoughts to the audience because only in this way will documentary succeed in its sociological or other propagandist purpose. Documentary must be the voice of the people speaking from the homes and factories and fields of the people.'[2]

In no way do I denigrate the Free Cinema boys and girls and their 'discovery'. Some of them have real talent and worthwhile viewpoints. *Every Day Except Christmas* and *Thursday's Children* are two of the best pieces of social observation in film terms to come out of England in recent years. My main concern is that the most creative and socially committed of this new group should successfully find ways and means to develop their con-

[1] *Sight and Sound*, Vol. 27, No. 2, Autumn 1957, p. 73.

[2] *Documentary Film* (1936 edition), p. 113.

tribution. British cinema badly needs it. Some of the problems facing them—unless they compromise and become 'entertainers'—are dealt with at length in the third and fourth parts of this book. They will need to be tough negotiators, patient promoters, persuasive talkers and tolerant critics—as well as talented film-makers with views about life.

While in the United States this summer I was fortunate in being allowed to read in MS. the greater part of Dr. Siegfried Kracauer's new book on Film Aesthetics. I also talked with him at length in the convivial surroundings of Wilmington, Vermont. His thesis begins with the important, but till now underestimated, part played by still-photography in the birth of the cinema and thereafter traces the path of the film as a 'true record' of life up to the neo-realists and documentary exponents. By happy coincidence, we were able to find an illustration of certain aspects of his thesis in the National Film Board of Canada's brilliant short film *City of Gold* (by Walter Koenig and Colin Low) which combines still-photographs of the '90s with cinematography of the same locations half a century later. (This was one of many interesting films projected at the third seminar of the Robert Flaherty Foundation at Brattleboro, Vermont.)

Kracauer and I agreed about the basic aim of the film artist being to invite his audience to share in a participation of life to ultimate social benefit of that audience. We agreed, too, that the methods used to achieve such realism are becoming more and more practical as cinema's technological production processes are perfected—not fiddling around with screen-sizes or spatial sound but the introduction of magnetic reproduction on tape, midget microphones unimpeded by cables, and the like. These new technical devices are a thousand times more important and valuable to film artists than mail-box screens and freak new lenses because they permit a closer, more intimate *selective* observation of reality—even if that reality be partial reconstruction. They allow an intermixing of actors and non-actors in actual surroundings and an enactment of preconceived situations that were impossible a few years ago.[1]

[1] The only point on which Kracauer and I did not reach full agreement was my theory (I was in a purist mood that day) that music in the form of accompaniment

Foreword

The taking of film-making equipment to actual locations has become increasingly popular since the last War. There is nothing new about it. It has been done since cinema began. What is new and challenging is the discovery of an aesthetic of filming amid actuality—the discarding of the studio mentality, with its artificiality, and the discovery in its stead on the real location (both indoors and out) of a quality that becomes an integral creative part of the film and not merely 'scenery'. By 'scenery' I mean the use of real surroundings as found in such recent films as *Boy on a Dolphin, The Pride and the Passion* and *Island in the Sun.* Those films used the real location as a backdrop is used in the theatre. Compare them with such pictures as *Un Condamné . . .*, *The Quiet One*, or *Terra Trema* and you will see at once what I mean by the film's story and its interpreters having a sense of 'belonging'. The film-makers and the actors derive their inspiration from their environment and do not superimpose themselves upon it. This quality, it may be observed in passing, has often a great deal more to do with what is called 'national character' in films than the story itself.

There is an obvious reason why this striving for realism and actuality is not liked by the conservative among film executives, especially those with capital invested in studio-plant. In the latter, production can be rigidly controlled and disciplined; so many shots-per-hour, so much cut screen-time-per-day, every aspect of the picture as far as humanly possible taped, scheduled and card-indexed so that if the film is to breathe and have life at all, its makers must have tremendous strength to break these chains. I am not suggesting that schedules, planning and discipline are not necessary; of course they are—within reason, because the film is an industrial art. And they too can be intelligently applied to location work. It is when they are allowed to take command and dictate a film's shape and style that I object. It is the kind of psychology which permeates the all-studio-mind that I deplore and suggest is alien to good picture-making. How

to realist story-films—no matter how well composed and written—is an anachronism, a hangover from the silent cinema which few film-makers are brave enough to discard. I argued that the only music justified is that which logically has its source in the story—a street-band, a song, a radio, a café musician. All non-source music is an artificial aid to stimulate the emotions of the audience and not an integral and valid part of film aesthetic.

often have I heard it said, 'It's easier in the studio!' So it is for the lazy, and for the perfectionist who worries about the quality of the sound or the photography but forgets that what is recorded or photographed is what matters most.

Many exceptions can be found to this argument for the real as opposed to the synthetic. It takes all kinds of films to make up cinema as a whole. *Casque d'Or*, *La Ronde* and *Gervaise* were essentially creative products of the studio, just as *Terra Trema*, *On the Bowery*, and *A Girl in Black* were works of the street and country which would have been impossible of studio production if they were to have achieved sensitivity to life as it is lived and not fabricated. On the other hand, musicals are fundamentally studio-conceptions, just as cartoon films come from the specialized studio of the animators.

But cinema has entered, I believe, a new era of extreme realism and interpretation of the living world, leaving to television the role of the photographed play—the photoplay of old—whether it be prefilmed or 'live'. Television, too, has its interests in actuality as we know so well, but it can never find the time for careful selection and contemplation and the presentation of isolated significant detail that help to make up the art of the cinema amid actuality. By its very 'liveness', television is denied an aesthetic. The true film that uses all the real assets of the medium must always be the first choice of the artist. What is needed by the world's film industries right now—especially the British and the American—is a relook at what those assets are: one of them, the most valuable, is the *creative* interpretation of reality around us in human terms.

Much of my work, though by no means all, has been with the documentary approach in the cinema. These days most of what is labelled 'documentary' in the film and television worlds is what used to be known as *reportage*, journalistic, general interest, business or industrial film-making. Serious critics call 'live' TV programmes which interview the man-in-the-street, or visit Top People in their comfy homes, 'documentary' programmes. They are nothing of the kind. To be preferred is the American term 'public affairs', or even the BBC's 'features', to this growing misuse of the word documentary. Nothing is precious about restricting the term documentary to the use to which we originally put it in the '20s and '30s. It might even help to remove some of the mud which it has been smart to sling at documentary during the past twelve years in the mistaken belief that everything in the cinema which was not a story-film or a cartoon was a documentary! Some of the young men today who write brashly about documentary, probing its weaknesses and abusing its early exponents, might spend some time usefully researching into the documentary films and writings of the pre-war years. I quote again from the B.F.I.'s quarterly from a piece called 'Looking for Documentary' by a Mr. David Robinson.[1]

'In the '30s, the impulse for documentary was strong and unmistakable and irresistible—or *so it now seems* (my italics). The tasks were obvious. The "Projection" of Britain and the Empire soon became subsidiary to the business of hastening the process of socialization and of fitting people for life in a technologically controlled and socialist society. . . . The War began, and the documentary machine was "geared to total effort". The War ended; and incidentally the socialist state had been won. The old jobs were finished . . . the new ones seemed obvious. "internationalism" was the watchword. . . . The Impulse *somehow* (my italics) petered out. . . . It is hard, now, to argue why British documentary of the "interpretive" type ran suddenly into artistic—as well as economic—doldrums in the period after the war; why it seemed to lack any real sense of direction, a sense of the needs and tone of the time. . . .

'It may be that the film-makers (and immediately after the War almost all the leading documentarists were old Griersonians), trained so hard to respond to one impulse, could not easily have adapted themselves to another even if they had been able to discover it.'

The investigator then quotes that delightful critic Miss Dilys Powell, as saying, in 1953: 'In the best days the British documentary was an attacking cinema; something, it said again and again, had got to be done. We have the Welfare State—and the belligerent documentary makers had lost their subject. It is no longer quite so obvious that something has got to be done in this country.'

[1] *Sight and Sound*, Vol. 27, No. 2, Autumn 1957.

Mr. Robinson continues:

'Her view—that the Old Documentary had lost its subjects and with them its vital impulse—is echoed by almost all the surviving first generation, many of whom will tell you: "There are no social problems now; the work we set out to do is finished!" '[1]

If the journal which published this article had not an influential circulation both in this country and abroad, I should not bother with it. But misrepresentation of British documentary's past and present can do harm if left uncorrected. As one who was not inactive documentary-wise in the period in question (and who has miraculously survived), I make the following observations for the record:

1. Few of the 'famous' documentaries of the '30s were actually concerned with attacks on social problems. To take six 'classics' of the period—*Drifters, Song of Ceylon, Night Mail, North Sea, Aero-Engine* and *Pett and Pott*—only Wright's Ceylon film had any remote connection with the exposure of social problems. No film made officially by either the E.M.B. or the G.P.O. Film Units (under a Tory Government recall) did anything whatsoever to hasten 'the process of socialization'. Of the main films that did tackle social problems—*Housing Problems, Enough to Eat?, Today We Live, Eastern Valley, Children at School* and *Face of Britain*—only one was produced under Grierson's aegis. Not all the old documentary group committed (as the word is these days) themselves to a social purpose and were prepared to take the consequences. It is interesting that the record shows so few of the films in the '30s to have been socially attentive.

2. It is news to me—and no doubt to many others—that when World War II ended 'the socialist state had been won'; and that 'the Old Documentary had lost its subjects and with them its vital impulse'. If Mr. Robinson had read the pieces in Part III of this book, especially those written in 1946–47, when they were first published, he would have observed that there was a very alive awareness that most of the 'battles' some of us tried to fight in the '30s had (and have) still to be fought and won.

3. 'Internationalism was the watchword. . . . The impulse

[1] Not this baby!

somehow petered out.' This curt dismissal of those of us who for many years tried to get documentary established on an international level is not only inaccurate reporting but downright bad manners. It fails to recognize that the first film contribution to the United Nations conception was made as early as 1943 by Britain; and that even before the War, Alex Shaw's *The Future's in the Air*, Cavalcanti's *We Live in Two Worlds* (with J. B. Priestley) and Stuart Legg's two films for the League of Nations promoted the theme of internationalism. It ignores the fact that a blue-print for the U.N. film information services and for those of its Specialized Agencies was prepared by British documentary people in 1945. It was beyond our control that the concept was side-tracked. Nor can those whom Mr. Robinson calls the 'first generation' be held responsible for the Labour Government of 1945's mishandling of its film information services, as the widely-circulated memorandum on page 236 of this book makes clear. (If he was not around at the time, he could have found pertinent references to it in the Foreword to the last edition of *Documentary Film* in 1952.)

4. It was not, as our misleading young investigator suggests, because any of us had been 'trained so hard to respond to one impulse' (trained by whom, incidentally?) that we 'could not have easily adapted' ourselves 'to another even if' we 'had been able to discover it' that British documentary declined in the post-war years. It was, as Part III of this book reveals, because *the economic basis of British documentary production which had been made secure by the Government over five years vanished almost overnight*, and because little if any educational and promotional work had been done during the same war years to encourage and develop non-governmental sponsorship.

The United Nations failed utterly to grasp the concept of imaginative documentary at an international level; the Labour Government quarrelled internally over it and failed to understand the importance of information services at a national level; and non-governmental sponsorship—except for Shell—had neither been educated nor promoted widely in the documentary idea. In retrospect, the critical year was 1946–47, when British documentary as a whole suffered a set-back from which it has never recovered and for which it was not itself responsible, except in so far as we were wrong to assume that our educational work in the '30s had taken root.

The politicians and the civil servants paid lip-service to the documentary idea and to its exponents but as time passed it became all too plain that they had not grasped the first principles either of information service needs in general or of the documentary idea in particular. (An exception was Stafford Cripps but these matters were officially outside his field of operation at that time.) Thus the way was left wide open for the Tory Government to annihilate the Crown Film Unit in 1952 and the Colonial Film Unit a year or two later. Of all these happenings which deeply affected British documentary at every point both then and since, young gentlemen like Mr. Robinson apparently know nothing and take no trouble to find out.

A misconception which appears to be held these days is that in the '30s sponsors and would-be commissioners of British documentary films queued at our doors to have films made. The exact opposite was the fact. When the E.M.B. Film Unit was axed in 1932, Tallents and Grierson will tell you what a struggle it was to have the tiny unit and its film library taken over by the Post Office. Non-governmental sponsors had to be found, educated in the *idea* of documentary and persuaded of its value as public relations long before any films could be made. In those days some of us spent far more time in promoting films-to-be-made than in actually making films! One great neglect in British documentary's post-war years has been promotion and education in the documentary concept, as a result of which sponsors have taken the easy course of having made publicity, industrial, tourist or just plain advertising films. Few of the younger generation of British documentary-makers have troubled themselves with the arduous, difficult and often unrewarding task of promotion. They only want the jam of the film-making. The memorable campaign in 1938, about which films were sent from Britain to the New York World's Fair, dealt with several times in Part III of this book, was a united effort by *all* the major British documentary people at the time. Nothing of the kind has taken place about the forthcoming Brussels Exhibition in 1958.[1]

[1] Cf. pp. 241–245.

Still another factor seriously affecting British (and other) documentary today is cost. As far back as 1936, as I have pointed out, I was making the plea that our films needed humanizing. But the more this plea is met and the more people in films are invested with character, the more complex becomes the technique of production with an inevitable steep rise in cost. If we remember also that every other item in film-making has increased in step with the national economy, it is plain that documentary of the maturer type has largely outpriced itself. With rare exceptions, sponsors have not this kind of money to spend on film-making. Thus if directors want to develop their talent in this direction, they must perforce turn to the feature film with all its frustrations and hazards.

Seen in this perspective, the failure of the Group Three project promoted by the National Film Finance Corporation takes on its full tragic aspect. 'In England, many hopes are that the Group Three scheme of the N.F.F.C. will bring forth fresh inspiration. With public finance to produce six moderate cost pictures, with ample talent on which to draw, Grierson is in a unique position to do something of lasting importance for British films. Without flouting commercial requirements, he can develop the documentary idea in fictional form in a series of films in a way that no one else has had the chance to try. It is an opportunity that has long been awaited and, if it fails, may never come again.'[1] That was written almost exactly six years ago. No one, certainly not our young investigator from the B.F.I., has made the effort to analyse why Group Three failed, and how with it so many bright hopes faded.[2] Its output far exceeded the six films first planned. Its cost must have run to over half a million pounds. Yet today its films are largely forgotten. It is not a happy story on which to dwell.

In all, except in England, it is an inspiring picture of cinema as a whole that faces us today. Stimulating work is coming from new names in countries which are comparatively new to good cinema—such as India, Spain, Poland, Greece and the Argentine—as well as from those with a long tradition of fine film-

[1] *Documentary Film* (1952 edition), p. 37.

[2] In addition to John Grierson (Executive Producer), the directors of the board were Sir Michael Balcon (Chairman), John Baxter and J. H. Lawrie (of the N.F.F.C.)

making—Japan, Sweden and France. In a year that has brought to England such remarkable feature films as *Pather Panchali*, *Throne of Blood*, *Kanal*, *The House of the Angel*, *The Seventh Seal*, *Four Chimneys*, *Ugetsu*, *Un Condamné . . .*, *Gran' Rue*, *The Unvanquished*, *Celui Qui Doit Mourir* and, at a lower level of assessment, *The Bridge on the River Kwai*, *Bachelor Party* and *Sweet Smell of Success*, we have no cause to complain of the lack of virility or progress in world cinema. I just deplore the fact that only one picture from my own country can, with any real honesty, be included in the list and even that was made for an American producer and distributor! The fact is, however unpleasant it may be for some of us to stomach, that we have learned less how to equate art with industry in the cinema in this country than in any other, including the United States. We have rich potential talent, of that I know. What we have not is the means to let it flower.

But our time will come. The fifty-year-old habit of regular film-going without thought of what picture is playing is disappearing as a result of television in the home. This can only mean that mass-production methods of film-making in order to keep so-many screens filled for so-many hours, so-many weeks a year, are also doomed in the long run. In the United States, always more alert to the public need than we are, this is already recognized. Hence, the great increase already referred to in independent and less factory-made production. It will not be long before the Pinewood rose-garden (just now celebrating its 21st birthday, for what it is a little hard to discover) and the Elstree cabbage-patch in England will, as always, be compelled to follow the American example and give freer opportunity to the independent film-maker, the non-conformer, the guy who'll take a chance with imagination and ideas and an urge to say something other than what the middle-class, suburban-minded, conservative fellows think is entertainment. Then perhaps we shall have British film artists working freely to place pictures alongside those of other countries by directors like Kurosawa, Fellini, Bresson, De Sica, Kazan, Becker, Visconti, Bardem, Clément, Andrej Vajda, Sjöberg, Clair, Bergman, Ray, Dassin, Cayette, Zinnemann and the other really interesting film-makers in the world. Why is it that our two most acclaimed directors—Carol

Reed and David Lean—work for American interests today? Why does such a good young director as Sandy McKendrick make his best film to date in the United States? The answer is too patent to state again here; Part IV of this book should make it clear, as it made it clear a decade ago.

A last word about the illustrations. Here, I confess, some nostalgia has crept in. In one piece I refer to the collection of film-stills that I began at an early age, the great majority of which are now in our National Film Archive. I have, however, found a few old favourites still in my possession, such as those of the senior Fairbanks, Garbo, Hessling and Negri to remind us of those wonderful days, and some moth-eaten old drawings of my own done for fun at Elstree.

And now I must hasten away to finish the script of that suspense-thriller I'm making and which 'they' hope will get an 'X' certificate. . . .

P.R.

Cuddington, Bucks.
October, 1957.

Foreword

RICHARD WINNINGTON REFLECTIONS[1]

'The film critic cannot look at a film as if it came spontaneously from nowhere, a finished creative work. He must take in economic and political factors that govern the making, marketing and exhibition, factors that often divert or destroy ideas and soil talent. He must identify the many separate elements that flow into a film. And he must very soon recognize that the hucksters of the cinema, the middlemen and monopolists, have a lower set of values than the public whose pulse and pocket they have their fingers on and in'—December 27, 1947.

'The power of the screen to unify, coerce, stupefy, enthral and mesmerize audiences in every country of the world is either sinister or miraculous according to how it is used, or even, if you like, according to the progress or otherwise of humanity. Certainly a world that does not pretend seriously to make peace, that is incapable of feeding itself, that lives fearfully from day to day, cannot be expected to exploit the dynamic art of the screen. For the screen realized and released is both pacifist and universal. It identifies man with man and place with place, it is a medium of poetry, compassion and illumination. It is an art that nobody will let grow up. . . . The creator of the grown-up film must see in the cinema his only means of expression, and he must see his material as something far richer than the actual, as something far removed from the literal: the paradox of the cinema is that it is anything but photographic. . . .

'No art is served without endless battle, and indeed the opposition to the smallest advance of the film has all the appearance of invulnerability. Yet it can and will be fought and circumvented. . . .'—May, 1948.

[1] Taken from his book *Drawn and Quartered* (Saturn Press, 1948) now out-of-print and scarce. A copy is given, however, each year to the winner of the Richard Winnington Award, signed by the members of the committee—Michael Ayrton, Nicolas Bentley, Paul Dehn, Alan Rawsthorne, Michael Redgrave, Paul Rotha, Rex Warner, Norman Wilson and Basil Wright. Winners to date are: 1955, Mark Donskoy for the *Maxim Gorky* trilogy; 1956, Denis and Terry Sanders for *Time Out of War*; and 1957, Robert Bresson for *Un Condamné à Mort s'est Echappé*.

I
BETWEEN THE REELS

Sixty Years of Cinema (1956)

To equate the freedom of the artist with the economic discipline required by a vast industry is a problem that has bedevilled film-making since the turn of the century. Before then, the cinema was an inventor's playground for the honoured names of Reynaud, Muybridge, Edison, Friese-Greene, Paul, the Lumières and Méliès. Their apparatus and celluloid snippets fascinate us today by their simple ingenuity. From the first accepted story-film in 1903, Edwin S. Porter's *The Great Train Robbery,* inspired by the trick-effect fantasies of the Frenchman, Georges Méliès, to this week's mammoth-screen spectacle, it has been a long restless marriage between those who have wanted to interpret life through this inexhaustible medium and those who have owned its complex, mechanical means of manufacture and exhibition.

When the bioscope became the universal recreation before World War I, it was inevitable that the mass-production of films to fill the world's screens would increasingly limit the individual artist's opportunity. The respected names of the early silent days—Méliès, Griffith, Ince and Chaplin—are with us yet (Chaplin is indeed at work in Europe now) and their films are reshown to a new generation, but one doubts if a Griffith or a Chaplin could again achieve independent status in the industry as it is now organized. From a happy-go-lucky investment by small-time *entrepreneurs,* the cinema has in sixty years become a matter of gambling with public taste on the grand scale, with investment mainly restricted to those controlling other great international manufactures. Governments have become involved at every point, be it trade, prestige, taxes, censorship, finance or political ideology.

While the commercial expansion of the cinema has become big business, so its technological developments have always been ahead of the use made of them. No creative film-maker asked for the talking-film; trade economic problems gave the screen its tongue. No film-maker asked for three-dimensional photography, or wide and panoramic screens; they were the businessman's reply to television. Of the handful of distinguished film directors alive today—De Sica, Donskoy and Kurosawa, to name but three—one doubts if any one of them is dissatisfied with the medium as he knew it ten years ago. It is difficult enough, they would say, to master and employ fully the subtleties available from the normal cine-camera and orthodox proportioned screen, plus the complexities of speech, sound and music, without being complicated by further technological developments. An easy confusion to have made down the decades is to mistake operational technical skill in film-making for creative artistry.

In sixty years, the film has been explored along roughly four paths: the great welter of fiction story-films, the films of fact from the newsreel to the documentary, the animated film with its hand-drawn and puppet techniques, and the experimental or *avant-garde* film of which, because of the expensiveness of the medium, there have been relatively few. The sponsors of the story-film for entertainment have always sought to have films made which would, they hoped, appeal to the largest public in order to recoup eventually a big return on outlay. Thus inevitably the subjects chosen have been believed by precedent to have the most appeal to the adolescent minds that have comprised the bulk of world film-going audiences. Within those limits, certain outstanding films of adult appeal have been made in many countries as the result of a working compromise reached between the film's maker and the film's producer. (*Where, on the other hand, the film industries have been under State control and gain from exhibition has not been the first motive, there has been the risk that the film artist's personal creative aim might have conflicted with the current ideology of the government. The more the film has become a factor in world trade and politics, the more assiduously must the search be made for its creative impulses.*)[1]

Despite these production problems, the cinema has from time

[1] Deleted as published.

to time reflected the social thought and background of successive generations in various countries. (*The short-lived vitality of the British film during the last years of World War II; the explosive, technically brilliant period of the Soviet cinema in the mid-'20s; the sombre, introspective but pictorially superb 'golden age' of the German film in the early '20s; the dynamic phase of 'neo-realism' in the post-war Italian film; the urge of the British documentary school before and during the last war; the reflection of the Depression and the New Deal in Hollywood films of the '30s; all these suggest that the cinema is sometimes a mirror to our lives. At the same time, the cinema could have been consciously used much more to promote international understanding and goodwill. It has been easy to harness the film in the cause of war; less so to let it interpret peace.*)[1]

In style, the story-film has ranged from the theatricalism of the filmed photoplay to the fresh naturalism of the epic Western; from the sophisticated comedy to the slapstick knockabout. But all the time the basic principles of the film as a means of creative expression have remained the same.

Fundamentally, film is an art based on observation guided by poetry. True observation is only obtained at first-hand. A film significant and affirmatory of life is a microcosm of a microcosm. The great films have been those nearest to life as it is lived and not imagined.

Moreover, the years have shown that the basis of all film aesthetic is movement. From the film's power to present movement through and by the camera arises the illusion of reality that gives cinema its very existence.

Although in recent years many film directors have relied on the spoken word to tell their story or make their pictures clear, the films that matter, that catch hold and excite and stay in the mind over the years, are those that visually have moved. For that reason one remembers *Intolerance*, *Greed*, *Moana*, *The Gold Rush*, *Potemkin*, *The Last Laugh*, *Kameradschaft*, *Bicycle Thieves*, *Open City* and *Rashomon*. Speech has contributed much to cinema, when used selectively and with significance, but speech can never take the place of action in the true film any more than 'back-projection', however skilful, can be a convincing substitute for the real location. Too few films, one may also

[1] Deleted as published.

remark, have been made from stories written for the screen; too many have been adapted stage-plays or novels, especially if these have had prior success. Above all, one notes, the true film is a virile art with its roots firm in contemporary life.

So the great names of cinema arise for the record—Méliès, Murnau, Chaplin, Carl Mayer, Griffith, Stroheim, Pudovkin, De Sica, Clair, Garbo, Eisenstein, Vigo, Carl Dreyer, Donskoy, Renoir, Dovjenko, Flaherty, Pabst and Lubitsch—each of us has his own list.

Slowly evolving over the years has been what has been called The Other Cinema, the serious use of the film in the service of education, science, research and public information. Britain's distinction in the documentary *genre* is world-acknowledged but in the past fifteen years she has been joined by some of the Commonwealth countries, notably Canada, and by such nations as the United States, Denmark, Holland and France. (*Documentary has opened up a new method of financing films. Special films for children have come belatedly to cinema but their need is now recognized. Less-developed than other forms, the animated cartoon and the experimental film have been restricted by the medium's expensiveness. Disney is ubiquitous but represents only one style; others remain to be tried as the UPA group in Hollywood and the Czech puppet films have shown, while Mr. Norman McLaren's animated pattern pictures disdain the use of a camera at all.*)[1]

As the cinema has struggled into adolescence, so have been set up bodies and organizations, both official and trade, employer and employee, to regularize its growth and conditions and promote certain trends. Institutes, academies, film archives, and training schools have appeared of varying merit and authority. A world-wide movement of film societies for the special screening of 'unusual' films has grown steadily since the original Film Society was inaugurated in London in 1925. A small body of serious criticism and literature has evolved; distinguished critics like Louis Delluc and Richard Winnington are commemorated by special awards made in their names. A whole new generation of filmgoers has grown up to whom a silent film is an unknown experience except at such a special house as the National Film Theatre in London or the Museum

[1] Deleted as published.

of Modern Art in New York. Those who grew up with the red-velvet curtain and wooden tip-up seat look back with respect at the 'masterpieces' of the silent days when without doubt the spectator's imagination was allowed more play than with the speaking films of recent years. But films recollected in memory are apt to be biased by nostalgia.

Now television has shot up overnight to offer a new mass-entertainment for the pleasure-seeking public. Shrinking cinema audiences have already led to second thoughts on economics. This could be for good. The film may at length reach adulthood by a more discriminate financing, by the public's discarding of the cinema-going habit irrespective of what film is showing, by a less rigid system of distribution and by a greater independence of production without distributor control. Much is to be done, especially in Britain. There is as yet no Chair of Cinematography nor a proper training school; no focus point of films in the public service has replaced the much-missed Crown Film Unit; and, above all, there is urgent need to finance more creative experiment without which the cinema could perish as an art and only the industry remain.

—THE TIMES, *June* 7, 1956.

Technique of the Art-Director (1928)

Three men are required, all working in perfect harmony and rhythm with one another, to make a film that is of high artistic merit. The Director. The Cameraman. The Art-Director.[1] Of these, the first in late years has had world-wide publicity: the second has assumed the cloak of a magician and is regarded as such; while the art-director remains the unknown quantity, taken for granted, unmentioned by all save the student of the cinema. And yet he is the vital figure in the composition of the picture. How many art-directors can the ordinary person name off-hand? How often does one see their names in the press? And yet it must be realized that those great sets with polished floors and marble columns are conceived, designed and built by an artist. He it is, too, working in an obscure corner of the studio, who arranges the model shots, the miniature work, the glass shots, and designs the accurate models for use in the Schufftan Process. Nevertheless his work goes almost unnoticed by both the public and the critics. Save for an occasional credit title, often as not deleted from the film after its pre-release, he remains the unknown worker.

His work is as hard as that of anybody in the film business. The qualifications alone required by an artist to fill the post of a competent art-director for a motion picture are many, and impose a severe strain on the mentality of the artist. They may briefly be set out as follows:

He must possess—

(*a*) a deep appreciation of line, form, proportion and composition

(*b*) a knowledge of architecture in all its branches

[1] The omission of the writer is reprehensible; *pace* all screen-writers!—P.R. (1957).

(*c*) an expert understanding of camera angles and perspective
(*d*) a knowledge of colours and their photographic values under panchromatic and ordinary film stock
(*e*) a working knowledge of lighting, and the use of light and shade, and tone values
(*f*) a definite knowledge of such side-lines as furniture, pictures, costume design, materials, etc., and he must be competent enough to design any of these if necessary
(*g*) a practical experience of plaster-work, carpentry, painting, varnishing, stone-work, joinery, etc.

He must be able to work in complete unison with his director, fulfilling his ideas, anticipate the necessary action entailed so that the set is practical, and agree with the cameraman as to the most effective lighting for both set and players. He must study the make-up of the latter so that the photographic tone of the walls of his set provides a suitable background for their faces. His work is always ahead of time. His proposed sketches of the sets should be in the hands of the director before the picture is begun. Once these sketches are approved he settles down to make detailed working drawings, elevations and plans which can be read with ease by the carpenters, plasterers and painters. Where it is possible to incorporate the use of stock fireplaces and windows possessed by the studio in which he is working he does so, for economy is a god to be served. The work is then put in hand, the set is built, allowance being made for lighting, the plasterers do their stuff, the painters succeed them, the sprayer dirties down the finger-plates on the door, and cobwebs are specially prepared for the ceiling. Finally it is dressed with carefully chosen furniture under his direct supervision.

The difficulties to overcome are innumerable. He has the eternal problem of finding sufficient floor-space for his sets, fitting one in with another; of working to scheduled time so that shooting may not be held up; of estimating the cost of his sets and the amount of time needed by a number of workmen to build them; of matching up the exteriors of houses shot on location with the interiors he builds in the studio. He must be able to have access to books of reference, for he may be called upon to erect the most out-of-the-way scenes imaginable. He must be assured of being accurate in his facts for surely his critics number the largest in the world for the arts. Above all his mind should be capable of superb creative work, for there are films that call for settings of a fantastic nature such as *Caligari* and *Waxworks.*

The true aim of the art-director is simplicity. In the same way as a great artist achieves his effect by as few lines as possible in a drawing, so should an art-director be able to create the impression he desires with as little material as is necessary. Paul Leni achieved this in *Waxworks.* Unless the script definitely calls for spectacular sets, there is no call for them. They are waste of good money and material. It is well to bear in mind that Manet once said that three people make a crowd—if used in the right way. In such cases as the *Nibelungen-Saga,* however, large sets were justified; in *The Student of Prague* they were not needed and were not used. The highest art of the film designer is the decorative motion picture, where traditional motives are employed with the additional individual creative work of the art-director. *Warning Shadows* exemplifies this. Here the costume designs were traditional *Directoire* with an added exaggeration on the part of the designer that lifted them from the rut of orthodox historical costume to the realm of fantasy.

Costume design in itself is a vast subject, as yet almost unexplored on the screen as Romanticism is out of fashion. There has been little achieved successfully in what has been done in this manner. Even historical costume has been badly ill-treated. There have not been half a dozen costume films made that are satisfactory, despite millions of dollars spent on them by American producing companies. *The Man Who Laughs* is an example of this. Never have there been such bad period sets and costumes as in this film, and yet they were supervised by Paul Leni, who achieved excellence in this respect with *Manon Lescaut.* The costumes failed in *Casanova* because the skirts of the men's coats were cut too short, and thereby threw out the proportions of every figure. Too much attention cannot be paid to details such as these because they can so easily damn the whole. Walther Röhrig was most successful in his designs for *Tartuffe;* Rudolph Bamberger in *A Glass of Water* was adequate. *Federicus*

Rex was as historically accurate as has yet been seen. One remembers Claude Autant-Lara's work in *Nana* as being charming.

In England there is little creative set-designing. The type of films produced in British studios does not demand this treatment. They require strict realistic detail in a conventional manner and such work is being admirably done by J. Elder Wills and Norman and Wilfred Arnold. The only creative work being executed in this country is by Alfred Jünge, for E. A. Dupont's *Piccadilly*, and is amongst the best yet done in any studio. Jünge's knowledge of modern design is superb, his method of utilizing the camera as showman for his work subtly clever. He recently designed a set with the most delightful mural decorations that have been seen for a long time. Jünge is a brilliant artist who realizes all the possibilities of the cinema.

There is, however, one thing that must be realized. Every film cannot be a *Caligari*, or the screen would become dull. But there is no reason why just as much design and composition cannot be used in a kitchen set for a slapstick comedy as in an expressionistic setting. Neppach realized this in *The Edge of The World* and Söhnle and Erdmann in *The Joyless Street*. The dressing-table in *Bed and Sofa* contained as much arrangement as the Feast of Belshazzar in *Intolerance*, and was a great deal more praiseworthy. This clever arrangement of detail is marked in Pabst's *The Loves of Jeanne Ney*. Henrik Galeen has been seen to arrange an inkpot and two brass ashtrays on a table as carefully as Cézanne arranged a still-life.

The time will undoubtedly come when the importance of the art-director will be appreciated as is that of the *metteur-en-scène* in the ballet. But how much greater is his scope! The film, the newest art that contains all the other arts, offers a vaster canvas to the artist than could ever have been found in the past. The limitations are practically nil. He loses indeed his colour, but gains in every other conceivable way. It is surprising that more artists have not turned to the motion picture as a means of self-expression. It is without question the greatest art-form yet discovered for the pleasure of mankind.[1]

—FILM WEEKLY, *November* 12, 1928.

[1] The appearance of this article caused the author's instant dismissal from the British studio in which he was then working as an assistant art-director.

The Art-Director and the Film Script (1930)

The era of the creative studio production may be said to have been at its zenith during the best period of the German art film, from the eventful years of 1920 to 1925, when the cinema was still closely allied to the theatre and its painted decoration. We know that at that time the decorative setting was the binding element of completeness to the thematic narrative. The Germans were (as Mr. Harry Alan Potamkin has pointed out) essentially film craftsmen rather than film creators, and it was only to be expected that painted scenery usually connected with the theatre should have played a large part in their film development. By their essential mysticism and fantasy, the German themes at that period demanded the decorative setting. We can refer to the key-films of the time, viz.: Wiene's *Caligari*, Kobe's *Torgus*, Lang's *Siegfried*, the same director's *Destiny*, Berger's *Cinderella*, Robison's *Warning Shadows* and *Chronicle of the Grey House* and Leni's *Waxworks*. These were all pictures in which the decorative environment was the binding element of the realization, against which the thematic narrative moved with a slow, psychological deliberation. These films ended in themselves. They were supreme instances of the painter's cinema. The names that mattered were Walther Röhrig, Robert Herlth, Walther Reimann, Rudolph Bamberger, Andrei Andreiev, Erich Kettlehut, Otto Hunte, Paul Leni, Alfred Jünge, Albin Grau, and later Neppach and Werndorff.

Since that time, the film has progressed to find its true realization in an environment of reality. Through the work of the neo-realists[1] and naturalists, Pabst, the Soviet left-wing directors, the stumbling methods of Dziga-Vertov, the open-

[1] I wonder if this is the first use of the term 'neo-realist', to become so widely used in post-war cinema, especially in Italy?

airness of Epstein, Flaherty, etc., there has been achieved the true cinema. No longer is it possible to feel that we should like to take down each image from the screen and hang it on our wall as we should a painting. This was so damning in Dreyer's *La Passion de Jeanne d'Arc*. Instead, we have learned that each visual image is but a fragmentary contribution to the whole composition of the film's unity. It is the film in its entirety that we frame and hang in our minds, where it is linked by a universal idea with other films, to become emotions remembered in tranquillity.

There is no place for the painter in the film studio. He is accustomed to think in broad terms of pigment and sentimental decoration (viz.: *The Little Match Girl, Le Voyage Imaginaire*, etc.), a habit of mind which is useless in the detailed building of a film. We know that a filmic mind is essentially one that thinks in terms of building; I call it arithmetic architecture. We know that Eisenstein has admirably compared the construction of a film to playing with a child's box of tricks. We have only to contrast the analytic and synthetic methods of Pudovkin with the Chauve-Souris decorative direction of the late Paul Leni in order to realize the value of constructivism.

The art-director has developed from a decorator into a technician, whose main work entails a strictly organized structure of settings at the will of the director. The setting, instead of being the binding environment dictated by the creative imagination of the art-director (such as it is in the ballet or the expressionist theatre) has become a part in the whole concatenation of events, alongside the technical accomplishment of the camera and the three stages of the organization of the film material. It follows, conclusively, that art-direction must take its place in the construction of the script as an integral part of the preconception of the film in literary terms before its realization on the studio-floor, on location, or in the cutting-room.

*

The process of script organization, which is the first act of montage in the construction of a film, is familiar to all film-makers. It is divided into three sections: one, the selection of the theme, environment and rough action and characterization of the protagonists; two, the filmic treatment in narrative form of this theme, indicating its future visual and aural possibilities; and three, the preparation of the detailed shooting-script, which we may also call the script-plan. This latter consists, as far as is possible, of a complete literary expression of the film *as it will appear* when realized, and is divided and sub-divided into sequences, scenes and shots with the appropriate sound images. Further, we know that the script is welded into a whole by the constructive editing of shots into scenes, scenes into sequences, sequences into the film composition as a unified whole; a living, pulsating, throbbing thing. We anticipate the script to be built out of a thousand or more separate shots that are dependent one on another for their effect. It is by means of this composition of shots which is eventually achieved by editing (the final act of montage) that the film is made to come alive, thus giving rise to emotional and intellectual audience reaction.

We are aware, of course, that a script-writer selects his shots from an unlimited number available to him, and it is assumed for the purposes of argument that there is no angle or position from which an object, a person or a piece of action cannot be photographed, both terminals of the shot (the object and the camera) being either static or in motion. It is the obligation of the writer to select from the shots in his imagination those which are the most vividly dramatic in order that they may bring out the full significance of the content of the scene as required by the narrative. These selected shots he describes in his script by words, for want of better means, although obviously the words themselves are of little interest as compared with the visual images, as well as the sound images, that they represent. The procedure of the script-plan is the preliminary representation on paper of the eventual visual images on the screen and the sound images on the film strip or on disc, as the case may be. In the hands of the script-writer, the camera and the microphone dig down deeply into the inner reality of everyday life, bringing consciousness of inanimate things to the spectator. The whole aim of the film lies in the representation of unnoticed things and motives for the living and the unliving, presenting them filmically for the pleasure or boredom of the spectator, according to his receptive interest.

The Art-Director and the Film Script (1930)

The incorporation of draughtsmanship is of the greatest importance for the clarity and perfection of representing visual images in the shooting-script. I believe that not only should the script be written but it should also in part be drawn.

In the first place, purely architectural diagrams of the lay-out of sets, mobility of the camera (travelling shots, panning shots, etc.) should be included in order that a clear visualization of the action of the characters in relation to the movement of the camera may be possible from the script. Added to this, the shooting angles and set-ups of the camera can be indicated, as conceived in the imagination of the writer, based, of course, on his *first-hand* filmic knowledge and studio experience as well as his creative faculties. Secondly, it is possible to emphasize the literary description of the selected visual images by means of drawings which will be clues, as it were, to the actual shots on the floor or on location. Here, obviously, a difficulty arises. The literary descriptions in the script are usually concerned with movement of acting material, which is difficult if not impossible to convey by the means of a drawing, the nature of which is static. For this reason, therefore, I suggest that the drawings should be in the nature of footnotes, clues to the actual realization, while the necessary movements can be fully indicated by diagrammatic plans.

The script-writer, as we know, visualizes the complete film in his imagination before it ever enters the studio to be fixed on to strips of celluloid. It is only logical that there are many aspects of the visual images that he cannot incorporate in his script in word form. It is, then, at this failure of the literary medium that the writer could turn to draughtsmanship for a clear expression of his ideas. In other words, the director should be able to work from drawings as well as from text in the realization of the script.

It will at once be remarked that this method indicates that the script-writer should possess another qualification other than the many already necessary to him. . . . It is obvious that he must have a specific knowledge of all the filmic methods of expression. Every property of pictorial composition, of symbolism and suggestion, of contrast and similarity in the association of ideas and shapes, of the drama of camera angles, of the rhythm achieved by editing and cutting, of the technical accomplishment of camerawork, trick devices and studio architecture, shall be in his mind to be employed in order to express the dramatic content with the greatest possible effect.

It is for the essential reason of simplifying the task of the script-writer that I suggest that draughtsmanship should be included in the script. It need not necessarily be the work of the writer himself. I put forward the argument that three or four persons could have the organization of the shooting-script in their control. The writer, the director, the art-director and the cameraman. Their work would proceed as follows: The selection of the theme by the writer and director and its treatment in narrative form. Then, the preparation of the shooting-script during which the art-director shall contribute diagrams and plans with his special knowledge of sets and their construction for emphasis of content by distortion and illusion. On these the cameraman shall suggest in collaboration with the director the movements and set-ups of his equipment in accordance with the lay-out of the sets. Meanwhile, the art-director shall, in collaboration again, scatter the text which is being composed with small drawings of individual shots, showing the proposed schemes of lighting, arrangement and contrast of masses, etc. In this way there will result the nearest approach to a complete film preconceived and set down on paper. The script will thus be the collective work of the four most creatively-important film-makers. Both pictorially and textually the script will indicate the exact course of the events in the studio, on location and in the cutting-room. . . .

There is, however, one danger to be avoided in this proposed method. That is the tendency it will carry to regard each visual image as a thing by itself. That is, of course, in direct opposition to the welding together of the script as a whole. It is fatal to think of a scene in terms of isolated shots. Rather, we must always visualize in a series of shots with their eventual screen realization (as well as the symphony of sound images) uppermost in the mind. We must continually be conscious of the varying relations of the visual image lengths, for it is their rhythmic tension which ensures the increasing interest of the audience in addition to the action of the characters. The draw-

1. Film Psychology (1928). *What it is really meant to express is best explained in paragraph 2, page 46: what some aestheticians call the "space-time continuum" of the film medium*

2. *Star in a Studio* (1928)

ings in the script must be clues to the progress of the film itself; a graphic commentary on the unfolding continuity of the visual images. Although the drawings themselves are static, even as the words in the descriptive text, they are to be regarded as but the suggestion of their future filmic realization.

Note.—It will be appreciated, of course, that the above suggestions apply to the general production of studio-made films and would be antagonistic to the naturalistic methods of film-makers who aim at using only actual material. It is a plea for the closer cooperation between the script and art-departments in producing concerns, in particular in England where such cooperation might bind together the loose methods of working that at present exist.[1]

—CLOSE-UP, *May*, 1930.

[1] The ideas set out here have, of course, been put into practice many times in later years but such teamwork as proposed would have been a novelty in British studios at the time the article was written. A well-known example of preplanning with drawings was in David Lean's production of *Oliver Twist* (1947) with art-director John Bryan; and, although the existence of this article had long been forgotten, I used much the same method when directing *No Resting Place* (1950), with art-director Tony Inglis.

A Painter Looks at Films (1934)

London, April 10, 1934

One day this week I was called on the telephone by a man whom I had not seen for eight years and who, when I last heard of him, was on the eve of making a successful career for himself in the world of painting. Within a few minutes of our conversation, we were buying beers at the nearest pub to my cutting-room.

My friend, it appeared, had succeeded well with his painting. He owned a spacious studio overlooking one of London's most glorious heaths, he painted when and where he desired, and he sold almost every canvas of which he cared to dispose. Yet he was morose, obviously under a cloud of deep depression. Gradually the reason came out.

Painting, he had decided, had reached a state of stagnation. From earliest times, through Byzantine eras and Italian Renaissance, through French court-painters and Flemish schools, the economics of painting had been solved through patronage—either by the Church, the Court or the rich bourgeoisie. Painting had flourished as a means to an end, as a method of education, as a recorder of events and persons and scenes, as a symbol of inspiration to the ignorant masses. Photography had displaced all this. For the last sixty or seventy years, painting had become a needless luxury, a method of individual expression which was selfishly personal and wholly uneconomic in its production.

'The time has come,' continued my friend, 'when we must make an important decision. Personally, I think it is useless to continue to paint easel-pictures. There is no purpose in it save self-pleasure, which inspired no man to do good work. It is a dead pursuit and can lead nowhere. In ten years' time I shall be painting, probably better than I do now, pictures of things I like and selling my work where and when I choose. But even if I should become a great painter, my pictures cannot do anything which has not already been done. You cannot excel a Degas, a Leonardo or a Manet. So why go on? Painting today no more reflects our present existence than do these beer mugs. You see what I am driving at? Only one medium today offers expression to a creative mind to reflect existence as it is. That medium is the film.'

So it has taken him twelve years of hard labour before his easel to come to that decision, I said to myself. Aloud I told him something of the movie-racket, of the narrow limits within which film can progress, of the commercial ends that must be served and of the utter impossibility of achieving anything above craftsmanship in movies as they are made under the present dictates of big business. I told him of the vicious circle that exists between the producer, the renter and the exhibitor; of the complete fallacy of the film trade's slogan—'We give the public what it wants!' Of the puerile mentalities that govern the destiny of a film into which you may have poured a year's solid work; of the petty jealousies, corruptions and moral indecencies that decide whether this or that picture shall be made or shown and whether this or that director shall make it.

But he would have none of it, or rather dismissed my summary with a sweep of his hand.

'I know and appreciate all that. But by the very way you have spoken, you have convinced me of the vitality of the film. You talk of all these obstacles but the very enthusiasm of your words betrays that you are fighting for something worthwhile, something which you are certain will happen. Every day you are probably wrestling against a hundred prejudices, meeting a hundred set-backs to your work, but still you go on because you believe that one day you will win and films will be made as you believe they should be made. That is impossible in painting. There is no vitality, no purpose. There is nothing to fight against. There is nothing to win which has not been won before. In architecture, in writing and above all in films there is an awareness of modern existence, a common enthusiasm that makes everything significant.

'Granted that your creative mind cannot carry out the themes it wishes, that a truthful statement of fact is as impossible in cinema as it is in literature, but even then you can get part of the way. And you have years and years of experiment ahead. You have the sounds of the earth with which to orchestrate your ideas. You can play with space and time. You can reproduce the most beautiful movements of natural life, speed them up, slow them down, hold them in suspension, as you please. You can compare the shape of this with the shape of that. You can present a thing from a dozen different points of vision in as many seconds. And when you have played with only the fringe of these astonishing possibilities, ten, nay, twenty million people at least will see what you have done no matter how poor you may think it is or how you may dislike the theme of what you have done.'

There was a long silence. Then added my friend:

'So I have finished with painting. Now, tell me, where can I take hold of my first piece of film?'[1]

—PHILADELPHIA PUBLIC LEDGER and NEW YORK POST.

[1] After a brief but rewarding spell in films, my friend returned to his painting. Today he is among Britain's most distinguished and respected painters and teachers. This little piece is here reprinted with his agreement.

A Museum for the Cinema (1930)

No more suitable time than the present could be found for the formation of a museum to meet the requirements of the student of the cinema and to create interest in films as objects of collectable value. The cinema has been in existence for roughly thirty-five years, during which period it has suffered shifts and divergences in natural accordance with the rapidity of its scientific, commercial and technical developments. But only in the last few years, up till the opening of the second cycle of its career marked by the introduction of mechanically-reproduced sound, has the film itself shown any qualifications that cause it to be considered as a potential work of art.[1] The early days, however, were distinguished by innumerable although crude experiments in both America and Europe, and these, such as they are, now assume definite value as primitive examples of cinematic art.

The problem of collecting such objects may be regarded from two points of view. Firstly, there are articles of purely scientific interest relating to the evolution of the instrument itself, including early examples of cinematograph cameras and projectors, as well as various types of lighting apparatus, used by the pioneers, Edison, the Lumière brothers, Friese-Greene, Robert Paul and Thomas Armat. Secondly, and of more general interest than the mechanical side, there is at present the opportunity for the collection of actual films themselves, beginning with the 'primitives', now somewhat rare, and proceeding down the years to the scarce remaining copies of films of comparatively recent make, the rarity of which is due to the destruction of the original master negative, either by fire or by copyright laws. Few copies remain, for instance, of the short freak films with

[1] I should point out that this piece was published in a dignified journal devoted to reverence of the antiquities, hence its pomposity.

'magic' effects made and shown by Georges Méliès at the *Théâtre Robert Houdin* in Paris during the late '90s; whilst little product of the old London Film Company, which was making films up till the time of the outbreak of the Great War, still exists, most having been burnt under copyright agreements and still more destroyed accidentally by fire. Early films made in America, by such men as D. W. Griffith and Sydney Olcott, during the first and second decades of this century, are also difficult to obtain.[1]

Apart from the obvious necessity that these early efforts should be gathered together, it is important also that some source of reference should be accessible to the student and the collector in order to keep check on the course of the development of the film as an art. What actually is needed is a library of films, representative of all countries, each exhibit marking a new phase in the growing aesthetic significance of the art, being examples of the ever-increasing schools of intellectual cinematography. Almost unknown to any but close observers of the cinema, there exist today several groups of film thought in Europe and America, each having its own theories and following of directors and writers. Upon investigation, it is clear that the work of such groups must be considered as being quite distinct from the usual forms of commercial cinema to which we are generally accustomed. It is not as yet widely recognized that the Russian cinematographers aim at the development of the film into a new intellectual form, a vast synthesis of art and science which is 'the purpose of all intellectual activity'.

It is essential that the progressive and in some cases valuable work of such artists, for thus they may well be termed, should be put on permanent record for educational and referential purposes. Added to which, there are other supplementary objects in connection with the cinema worthy of preservation. such as the best film posters (those in circulation on the Continent are infinitely superior in artistic merit to the lurid scenes usually displayed in England); critical books on the film

[1] Since the date when this piece was written, numerous film museums and archives have been established, notably in Britain, United States, France, Denmark, the Netherlands, Sweden, Germany, Italy, etc., and exhaustive search has discovered many early films believed lost.

written by authoritative writers; designs for settings and costumes by well-known film architects; as well as a large number of 'still' photographs from various distinguished productions. In this way, with the main body of the collection composed of outstanding examples of cinematic art, could an interesting and informative museum, of great value in the future, be inaugurated.

The basis for such an institution is housed at the moment in the Science Museum at South Kensington. This is the collection of films and cinematograph equipment belonging to Mr. Will Day, which has been on loan, and which there is every reason to believe is unique. Over a period of thirty years, Mr. Day has gathered together any exhibit that is connected with the evolution of the cinema, from ancient wax figures used in Chinese shadow-shows, all manners of colour tops, kaleidoscopes, devices for optical illusions and panorama peep-shows, from Paris, London, New York and other parts of the world, to Edison's original Kinetoscope and projector, Paul's animatograph camera and a Lumière combined projector and camera used for the first public exhibition of films in France in 1896. There are also scraps of early films of historic interest: of King Edward VII's Coronation, of the Delhi Durbar, a copy of Georges Méliès's *Trip to the Moon* (1897), as well as a series of photographic plates taken in Pennsylvania by Edward Muybridge for his famous work, *Animals in Motion*. Although Mr. Day's collection is more of scientific than aesthetic interest, nevertheless it would form an admirable nucleus around which a museum of wider conception could be built. There have, I believe, already been some attempts to found an institution such as that indicated above, but so far as I know, they have failed to materialize.[1]

There are, of course, several other collections of old films in existence, such as that of Mr. Pearl Cross, who has from time to time loaned examples for exhibition at the performances of the London Film Society. Three instances of this have been

[1] The National Film Archive of the British Film Institute was not set up until 1935. Its permanent National Film Theatre was opened in October, 1957, by H.R.H. Princess Margaret before a specially chosen audience of those distinguished in the Arts—including the Cinema. The author was not an invitee.

episodes from one of the first serial films, *What Happened to Mary* (1912); *The City of Westminster from an Argyll Car*, made by Hepworth, providing some amusing views of Edwardian London; and *Athalia, Queen of Judah*, an old French Pathécolor picture. Various producing companies, also, possess rare copies of celebrated films, such as *The Cabinet of Dr. Caligari*, the famous 'expressionist' film made by Robert Wiene in 1919, which created a revolution in cinema circles; *Destiny*, made by Fritz Lang in 1921; and *The Golem*, made by Paul Wegener and Henrik Galeen about 1920. Rare versions of these and other notable pictures, several of them the only complete copies in existence, are in the guarded possession of the Ufa Company in Berlin, and are seldom to be seen. The Gaumont-British Company in England recently edited a number of old 'topical' newsreels into one picture, *Royal Remembrances*, which included scenes taken at the funeral of Queen Victoria, the Coronation of King Edward and other famous occasions of historic interest. The original film version of *Dracula* is now extremely rare. This was made in Germany by F. W. Murnau in 1922, without permission having been secured from the copyright owners of Bram Stoker's novel. In consequence, a court ruling was obtained and all copies of the picture were ordered to be destroyed. One, however, escaped the flames and when shown two years ago at the London Film Society, proved to be of remarkable artistic value. Yet another challenging aspect for the collector is the possibility of acquiring, probably for a small sum, portions of films that have been removed by the censor, owing to historical, political or even religious reasons!

Thus it will be seen from the few instances cited that not only have films as well as cinematograph equipment assumed a collectable value but that there is a definite and urgent need for the establishing of a permanent collection, to be constantly brought up-to-date by examples of each new movement, either technical or aesthetic. For only in this way will it be possible to follow the rapid evolution of the cinema both as an art and as a scientific achievement.

—The Connoisseur, *July*, 1930.

Old Film Stills (1956)

Young people mostly collect something. I collected 'stills'—photographs from films. At first I begged them from a kindly cinema manager in a small Surrey town not so far from London when he took them down in his lobby at the end of the week. Then, more boldly, letters to strange addresses in Wardour Street often, but not always, brought results. Some of the very first were of Douglas Fairbanks, Sr., in *Headin' South*[1] and *Knickerbocker-Buckaroo*, and Elsie Ferguson in *Barbary Sheep*, which about fixes the date for film historians. But I could hardly have been expected to have foreseen that so many of the several thousand I collected over the next twenty-five years would eventually find their way into the Sixty Years of Cinema Exhibition, organized by *The Observer* newspaper in London in 1956.

Stills are usually regarded as commercial publicity aids to a film itself. They may be the work of a still-photographer attached to the production company, who takes photographs as near as possible to certain selected scenes as they will appear in the completed film. Such stills all too often appear 'staged', which indeed they are. Alternatively, stills may be 'blown up'—enlarged—from the actual cine-negative of the film, a method mostly obtaining in documentary and experimental films where still-photographers are an unnecessary luxury. But despite their main purpose of publicity, stills can be of value to the film student enabling him to revive his memory of films seen in the past if the film itself is unavailable. Their worth as records in the future, when the films they illustrate may possibly have been destroyed, is suggested by the prominence given to their collection in recent years by the various film archives in Europe and America. Yet we must always remember that stills are 'frozen

[1] See Plate 5.

movement' and can only at best give a feeling of the original dynamic film. Nevertheless, their fascination is immense.

*

As my collection grew in the '20s and '30s, it became clear that either the thing would get out of hand numerically or there must be a specialization on quality and representation of only the most important and more unusual of the world's films. So the renters' offices were haunted in Soho and in Paris and Berlin, the search being concentrated on the best and most representative. Plums fell into my lap. The director of the first film on which I ever worked (in 1928) was Henrik Galeen, who earlier had made the famous *Student of Prague* with Conrad Veidt. Galeen encouraged a youthful enthusiast for 'good' cinema by giving me his personal album of stills from that memorable classic film. When the little highbrow magazine *Close-Up* was disbanded, a first picking of its files came my way. The lady-editor of a well-known 'fan' weekly unlocked the cupboard doors of what her staff called The Morgue which, after three days' dusty scavenging, brought forth some rare finds from Continental films considered too unusual for an English 'fan' paper. The Ufa Company in Germany and the Soviet film agencies in Berlin and Paris were generous in their gifts. It even happened that when all search for stills from a certain classic picture drew a blank, a few odd frames were shamelessly clipped from the film itself in the projection-box of the old Shaftesbury Avenue Pavilion (so imaginatively run by Stuart Davis, and the forerunner of today's many specialist cinemas[1]) and from these few frames were made enlargements—murky and grainy though they were.

In 1931, the always generous Mr. Adolf Zwemmer offered his gallery in the Charing Cross Road for the first International Exhibition of Film Stills certainly to be held in the United Kingdom, possibly the first in the world. Some 300 stills from my collection of several thousand were displayed and a catalogue published, from which an extract ran: 'Often beautiful in themselves—isolated from their surroundings—they always remain a fragment of a greater and sometimes more beautiful

[1] Cf. page 62.

whole. A still is but one photograph of the many which when projected comprise a film—allowing us to violate the essence of the cinema by examining a fraction of a second of movement frozen into stillness.' (Ironically, the remarks of *The Observer's* film critic at the time were caustic!) Subsequently, various film societies held similar exhibitions, notably at Edinburgh and Southampton.

Six years later, in 1937, a first-hand sight of the collection owned by the Museum of Modern Art Film Library, New York, confirmed the wisdom of my policy of going for quality and not quantity. Numerically, its collection far outstripped mine but whereas it had blank spots for many famous German, French and Russian films, there were very few films important in the history of the cinema from 1900 to 1937 which were not represented in my collection. In the previous year, the cream of my files appeared in *Movie Parade: a Pictorial Survey of the Cinema*, recently revised.

*

But by then other and more official collectors, such as the British Film Institute, were in the field and I surrendered the wide realm of the entertainment cinema to their more substantial resources. Instead, my concentration was directed on the documentary field, difficult because it meant stills 'blown up' from cine-negative, often grainy and of many odd sizes. From 1922, the year of Flaherty's *Nanook*, until the end of the war period in 1945, there were few of the world's documentaries from which stills did not reside in my collection.

The time came, however, when it was impracticable to maintain such a collection on an individual basis. Requests for the loan of stills from many quarters, from abroad as well as at home, created a strain which a side-line activity could not meet. Major film companies who earlier had given stills were now actually asking if they might 'borrow' them back, having destroyed their own copies! Up-and-coming young writers blossoming into print about films they had mostly never seen wanted stills for their books and articles. Thus, a few years back, the collection—begun humbly, albeit lovingly, in 1918—was made available to the British Film Institute through whose channels many of the stills now decorate the exhibition in Trafalgar Square. Except, that is, for a nucleus of what might be called 'collector's items' which remain securely in their original home.

—FILM, *the Magazine of the Federation of Film Societies*, 1957.

The 'Unusual' Film Movement (1940)

To see good films in London today is simple: you go to the Odeon or the Empire or the Academy; the Polytechnic, the Paris, the Everyman, the Cinephone or Studio One; maybe to the Curzon or the Embassy. Few good foreign films fail sooner or later to get to London.

Twenty years ago it was not so easy. Big American films had their premières at West End theatres, at the Scala, Drury Lane, Covent Garden, the Palace or the London Pavilion. But Continental films, except for the spectacular Ufa product, crept in sideways, lay about in Wardour Street vaults, got maybe (after 1925) a London Film Society showing.

The Davis brothers were really the first showmen to present Continental films of a 'different' kind in London. They owned the Marble Arch Pavilion, then London's premier cinema, and showed *Caligari* there in 1920 and followed it later by other famous Ufa films—*Metropolis* and *The Spy*. The Polytechnic, managed then, as now, by Mr. Leslie, ran *Destiny* in 1924. *Anne Boleyn* (*Deception*) and *The Golem* got Scala showings and that was about all. But none of these cinemas adopted a policy of regularly running 'different' Continental films.

If memory is reliable (curse the evacuation!), the first London cinema to announce a Continental policy was the Embassy near the Holborn Restaurant. It ran Grune's *The Street* and Volkoff's *Kean* before closing. That was in 1924. Like the handsomely produced monthly, *The Silver Screen*, the Embassy was before its time. No one else tried the experiment. Occasional Ufa pictures like *The Last Laugh*, *Manon Lescaut*, *Vaudeville* and *Berlin* went to the Capitol (now the Gaumont) or the New Gallery. *Siegfried* was given a spectacular setting at the Albert Hall, where Mr. Charles Cochran later presented *Faust*, complete with Sir Landon Ronald and a symphony orchestra.

London had no equivalent of the Paris 'little cinemas', no Vieux Colombier, Studio des Ursulines, or Studio 28.

Again the story switches to the Davis brothers. Their theatres were now (1927) included in the Gaumont circuit, but the brothers retained the right to book pictures and act as managers. They owned, among others, the small Shaftesbury Avenue Pavilion which showed pictures on their second London run. But it had become dwarfed by the big new theatres and second-runs were being well looked after by the new suburban houses. Now part of a chain, it was an awkward house to book for. Thus when Stuart Davis went to Reginald Bromhead, managing director of the circuit, and suggested a new policy, Bromhead agreed. The new policy was to show Continental films, new and old, an idea which Stuart had seen working the year before at the Cameo in New York.

Davis was lucky. Wardour (now A.B.P.C.) had long had a Ufa contract and the newest German picture was *The Loves of Jeanne Ney* which the censor slashed and Wardour retitled *The Lusts of the Flesh.* Davis took over the Avenue Pavilion, hung out a banner inviting the Shaftesbury Avenue passers-by to see *The Lusts of the Flesh,* but was shrewd enough to do dual publicity with Pabst's name and for his own new policy. The 'Unusual' Film Movement and 'The Home of International Film Art' had begun. Stuart did good business with two publics. The one that mattered to him was the 'intelligent' audience which was growing as a result of the London Film Society's private shows, the little highbrow paper *Close-Up,* the columns of one or two progressive film critics like C. A. Lejeune first in the *Manchester Guardian* and later *The Observer,* and Walter Mycroft in the *Evening Standard.* Iris Barry's book, *Let's Go to the Pictures,* must also have helped.

Stuart got, kept and enlarged that audience in the two years he ran the Avenue Pavilion. He revived all the old German classics (not so old then), *Caligari, The Last Laugh, The Street, Manon Lescaut, Warning Shadows, The Student of Prague, Tartuffe, Two Brothers, Vaudeville, Faust, Danton,* and the rest. He paid £200 to an ex-W and F salesman for a four weeks' run of *Waxworks* and took £1,800. He revived the famous Hollywood classics, *Woman of Paris, Greed, Foolish Wives* and *He*

Who Gets Slapped. He dug up the Swedish *Gosta Berling*, the Russian *Marriage of the Bear* and *The Postmaster*. He wrote intelligent hand-outs for the press. Above all, he made his theatre a place where many people for the first time saw The Film at its best. His tiny office became a meeting-place for the most ardent film followers. Stuart himself was always the charming host.

After a while the film supply gave out so Stuart Davis went off to Paris. Here was a new field, the films of Clair, Cavalcanti, Feyder, Epstein, and the *avant-garde* shorts of Deslav, Lacombe, Man Ray and the others. He bought the English rights of the lot, started a French season with a white-tie opening and the French ambassador. He introduced London to *Finis Terrae*, *The Italian Straw Hat*, *Les Deux Timides*, *En Rade*, *Rien que les heures*, *The Fall of the House of Usher*, and many others. But his greatest success was with Feyder's *Thérèse Raquin*. First-National had a copy sent over from Germany, where it had been made with a Franco-German cast for quota requirements. They were about to send it back unbooked but happened to mention it to Stuart Davis who promptly booked it. Unluckily his press show coincided with an M-G-M show. Only one critic turned up—Walter Mycroft of the *Evening Standard*. He gave it the review it deserved. The rest of the press bombarded Stuart to see the film but he refused. Next day they lined up in the public queue. The film did big business, got many provincial bookings and certainly helped to obtain Feyder his M-G-M contract in Hollywood.

Summer, 1929, saw Stuart Davis's contract with Gaumont expire. The latter decided not to carry on the policy and, at Stuart's suggestion, opened the theatre as London's first news-reel cinema.[1] Stuart Davis took over managing the Davis Theatre, Croydon, which he still does.

It looked as if London would no longer have a 'Home of International Film Art'. But down the street was the Windmill Theatre which Elsie Cohen was managing as best she could with second-run pictures. Miss Cohen had for a long time been interested in the Continental film and had worked in Holland and Germany on production. Now at the Windmill she started

[1] It was completely blitzed in the War and has never been rebuilt.

an 'Unusual' Film movement and was able to get several Soviet films past the censors, her biggest success being *Turksib.* She also revived some of Stuart's successes. This lasted until the autumn when the owner of the theatre discontinued showing films and Vivian Van Damm began his famous Revudeville.

Meanwhile a few of the old regulars at the Avenue Pavilion—among them Margery Locket, J. B. Holmes, and F. Gordon Roe—started the Film Group. Stuart Davis gave us his mailing list. We circularized 12,500 people in the London area to see if they would support a successor to the Avenue Pavilion. Eighty per cent. said they would. But no suitable theatre could be found except the Academy, run by Eric Hakim, who used to be a violinist at the Davis theatres. Stuart himself had tried Hakim with the idea but Hakim wanted too big a rent. A week or two later he let Elsie Cohen take over the house and announced a 'new' policy of Continental films, old and new. Hakim himself had little faith in the project and thought Miss Cohen crazy when she opened with Dovjenko's *Earth.* But what could not be foreseen was the talking film. When it did come, it was generally predicted that the French and German film would disappear from London. Yet next April, the Academy will celebrate a decade of its policy for Continental films.[1]

—DOCUMENTARY NEWS-LETTER, *June,* 1940.

[1] It is still running, of course, under the energetic guidance of George Hoellering, himself a film-maker.

3. Film Continuity (1928). *It might have made a "montage" poster fashionable at the time.*

4. TARTUFFE (1925), *directed by* F. W. Murnau, *with design by* Röhrig *and* Herlth: *perhaps the apotheosis of German*

Douglas Fairbanks *in* HEADIN' SOUTH (1918), *directed by* Arthur Rosson; *the first of my collection of film stills.* (*See page* 57)

6. A Modern Musketeer (1918), *directed by* Allan Dwan, *with* Douglas Fairbanks *and* Marjorie Daw. *The prologue only was in costume and probably inspired the later and more ambitious* Three Musketeers

History on the Screen (1953)

The representation of past characters and events on the cinema screen has been a matter of controversy since the film was first considered to have aesthetic quality. Although the earliest film subjects were of real life, or contemporary characters in actual surroundings, such as the Lumière films, fantasy quickly attracted the pioneers, such as Méliès. The re-enactment of history, to which film-makers soon turned, was almost certainly due to theatrical influence, and it had its beginnings, not illogically, in France, Italy, Denmark and England. *Napoleon and Josephine*, *Jane Shore*, *Ben Hur* and *The Fall of Troy* are typical of their period, fashioned by the theatrical wardrobe and replica-ed by the scenic artist. Hollywood only took up the 'costume' drama after Europeans, with their long stage traditions, had made it commercially attractive. But it is worth noting that Mr. Adolf Zukor's attempt in 1912 to emulate the French and to present established theatre actors in historical plays, entitled Famous Plays and Famous Players, was abortive. The public preferred Westerns and the Slapstick.

From the time of *Quo Vadis?* in 1912 to the *Quo Vadis?* of today, the entertainment cinema has exploited almost every period of history along the familiar methods of a Baroness Orczy or Rafael Sabatini; they seldom reached the level of a Stanley Weyman or Maurice Hewlett. Although exhaustive research is always publicized as being put into these films, few indeed have ever succeeded in capturing the period *atmosphere* of the past. Cloak-and-sword melodrama may well have its place in escape entertainment, as do science-fiction and the Western, but it is useless as a method for the serious teaching of history.

In Europe, however, notably in the 'twenties during the silent cinema, attempts were made with great accuracy to re-create the history of the past. The German *Anne Boleyn*,

Cesare Borgia and *Loves of Pharaoh* were a great deal more authentic than their Hollywood counterparts. The several films made of *Frederick the Great* (*circa* 1923) actually used original costumes, furniture and settings, but the result—no matter how accurate—was sadly lifeless. Dreyer, the Danish director, tried a synthesis of authentic and contemporary costume (rather like the vogue for playing Shakespeare in modern dress) in *La Passion de Jeanne d'Arc* (1928), probably coming nearer to interpreting the atmosphere of Joan's trial through stylized design than the spectacular French production *The Marvellous Life of Jeanne d'Arc* (1927). In France, the past was a very favourite subject, ranging from the elaborate staging of *Le Miracle des Loups* (1926), much of it filmed at reconstructed Carcassonne, and Abel Gance's monumental recreation of *Napoléon* (1924), with its triptych screen, to the light-hearted *La Kermesse Héroïque* (1935), memorable for its fine style and convincing atmosphere. The Russians, also, produced in the 'thirties such historical sagas as *Peter the Great* (1937) and *Ivan the Terrible* (1944), with immense care for accuracy of period which, allowing for ideological interpretation, made the past to a degree credible and acceptable on the screen.

Apart from the fact that all such attempts to recreate history in film terms depended on restaging, they all had the drawback that they were, for the most part, very expensive to produce, except where State backing was forthcoming. Accuracy in costume and setting demands time; it also demands a school of actors who have been trained to wear costume as if it belonged to them, an attribute especially possessed by Continental actors. There is hardly one American actor who can wear period costume with conviction, except in the cloak-and-dagger *genre* where accuracy is mostly sacrificed to romanticism. Most English actors, too, wear costume as if on their way to the Chelsea Arts Ball.

*

There is, however, a totally different approach to history on the screen depending on the medium's ability to record actuality and not restaging of the past. 'History on the screen,' remarked the late Otto Neurath, 'began when the first movie-camera filmed the world in front of its lens.' From the late 'nineties up till today, the term Living History makes sense.

In many countries, cameramen—often amateurs—began filming actual events, sometimes for the topical newsreels that began to be commercially made around 1910, sometimes on travel expeditions (e.g. the well-known work of Capt. Herbert Ponting), sometimes as amateur historians (e.g. Ing. Toscano, who filmed most of Mexico's events and main personalities from the revolution of 1910 up till after World War I). Fascinating use of some of this early footage was made by Nicole Védrès in *Paris* 1900, and in the post-war German film *In Those Days*, while the Pathé Documentary Unit in England has partially explored its newsreel vaults for several *Scrapbooks*, somewhat blighted by a facetious commentator. Louis de Rochement's *The Golden Years* (1950) attempted an impression of the 'twenties drawn from actuality sources; while Gilbert Seldes and Fred Ullmann contrived *This Is America* (1933), based on Frederick Lewis Allen's well-known informal social history of the United States, *Only Yesterday*.[1]

Unfortunately, the newsreels from which most of these compilation films have drawn their material have too often been regarded as casual entertainment and too seldom as an accurate mirror of contemporary events. To quote a trade-paper in 1945: 'The news obligation of the newsreel is happily trivial. If the newsreels had to cover the news, they would be full of charts on taxes and reports on crop reports. No one goes to the theatre to get the news.' Such a view, commonly held by the trade, is belied by the fact that both the American *March of Time* and the British *This Modern Age* either headed or were runners-up in the annually-held popularity polls for short films when these editorialized reels were in existence. It is also a proved fact that today (1953) the BBC-TV newsreel commands the largest viewing audience of all programmes.

Despite the casualness of the newsreel attitude, there is nevertheless a mass of footage stored in the newsreel vaults in the world's capitals which must have considerable historical

[1] The compilation film has had a new fillip in television, as seen in the work of NBC's 'Project 20' and CBS's 'Twentieth Century' series in the United States.

value if it can be selected and presented with sociological purpose. We can study at very nearly first-hand the revealing gestures and expressions of eminent men and women now dead, of crowds at public gatherings that took place over fifty years ago. And so often it is now not the main characters in these events that catch our eye—the monarchs and emperors and premiers—so much as the odd people in the crowd who at the time were of no interest to the photographer because of his familiarity with them. It is possible through such compilations of old footage to look backwards as no previous generation could on the living and animated face of yesterday. That Queen Victoria was indeed a 'very little woman' we know to be a fact: there is a shot of her riding through Dublin about 1900 to prove it.

*

An interesting and perhaps educationally important experiment in the teaching of history by film—or rather perhaps the historical approach—might be made by taking a given year in the last half-century and selecting authentic film material to express its social and economic, as well as its cultural and political characteristics. Obviously, the feasibility of preparing such a film of Living History, hitherto untried, depends wholly on the nature of what film footage is available. Before any given year in the past fifty can be selected, a survey must be made of what material exists and can be duplicated for educational use. The National Film Archive in Britain would, it is safe to foresee, cooperate willingly by loan of footage where copyright and preservation conditions permit, and a study of its catalogue should be a first step. At the same time, an inquiry as to the extent and nature of what exists in old actuality film might be circulated through the International Federation of Film Archives, of which there are now, it is understood, some eighteen member countries. For example, the Museum of Modern Art Film Library possesses *From Czar to Lenin*, compiled by Herman Axelbank in 1936 from material he procured in Russia and containing some remarkable footage of old Russia before 1914, including intimate scenes of the Royal Family. A film has recently appeared in Mexico called *Memoirs of a Mexican* which is a fascinating film record of the revolutionary period of that country's history from 1910 to 1925. There must be other such original material, if a search be made.

An attempt might also be made to find out what films exist that may have been taken by early amateurs, clearly prior to the use of 16mm. stock. The Royal Photographic Society and the Institute of Amateur Cinematographers might aid here. An approach to the newsreel companies should be made, stressing the educational and non-commercial nature of such an experiment: Pathé would reveal most fascinating early material because it is the oldest of the present newsreels. The Imperial War Museum still has the film collection of World War I, including some interesting civilian material. The three Services archives should not be overlooked. In the United States, the National Archives in Washington have an immense selection of preserved film. The Cinémathèque Française has information about private collections of old film. And so on.

—MEMORANDUM FOR THE EDUCATIONAL FOUNDATION FOR VISUAL AIDS,
London, March, 1953.

The Magnificence of Fairbanks (1930)

Remarkable as it may be, Douglas Fairbanks, an acrobat who is unable to put drama into his gestures or emotion into his expressions, is one of the few really outstanding figures in the art of the American film. But then I have always held that 'acting' in the theatre sense is unnecessary and superfluous in the cinema. Fairbanks, by reason of the rhythmic beauty of his graceful and perpetual movement, is in my estimation utterly a product of the medium of the film. True, he has no talent other than his ever-present sense of action to support my claim, save perhaps a flair for showmanship so well exemplified in the recent *Taming of the Shrew*, but surely this marvellous feeling for natural rhythm, in the curves of his leaping from place to place, in the panther-like motion of his swinging stride, even in the rippling muscles of his superb form, marks him as a pure child of the cinema.

Alternatively bandit, pirate, freebooter, *lantsknecht*, knave, outlaw, or musketeer, he is always the same invigorating, stimulating, disreputable, defiant and attractive Douglas Fairbanks—the Essence of Heroism.

Added to which, he is wise enough to know his limitations. He never attempts, like so many celebrities, things which are impossible or outside the scope of his specialized skill. I am certain that he realizes only too well that he is neither an actor nor an artist in the accepted understanding of the terms. On the contrary, he is something of far greater importance to the cinema—an acrobat of amazing accomplishment.

In all of Fairbanks's films every action, however small and insignificant, is the direct result of forethought and plan. I am convinced that he sees a foundation for rhythmical movement in almost every situation in the past and in the present. And just as Chaplin learned to walk the tight-rope for the making of *The*

Circus, so Fairbanks has learned to fence, to handle a whip, to throw a lariat, to cast a bolas, in order to meet the demands of the numerous roles he has played. This thoroughness is due partly to Fairbanks's tremendous enthusiasm for everything he does and partly because he sees in these accomplishments a basis for filmic movement, beyond mere acrobatic trickery. He realizes that such actions are superbly graceful in their natural perfection.

At heart, Fairbanks is a complete romanticist. He delights us equally in the swing of his cloak, the fall of an ostrich feather from his hat, the hang of his rapier, the slender form of his doublet, the tilt of his curving spurs, as in the single movement with which he mounts his famous white horse and in his innumerable hairbreadth escapes. I recall particularly the prologue to his early picture *A Modern Musketeer,* which he elaborated later into the famous *Three Musketeers,* the sheer delight of *The Black Pirate,* and the inimitable bravado of *Robin Hood.*

In all his costume films he extracts the utmost from the clothes and environment offered by the period he has selected. His Petruchio in the *Taming of the Shrew,* clad in rags, apple-core in hand, jackboot on head, propped against a column of the church, was to me a symbol of the romanticism of Fairbanks. It needed a brave man, a born hero, to carry off that crude costume. Nobody can deny that Fairbanks was magnificent. I can think of no other actor in the cinema who could have achieved so much bravado with so little concern.

The dominant note of all his pictures is his personality. Although none of them has been nominally directed by him, nevertheless his is the controlling mind underlying every detail. The spirit of Fairbanks is reflected in every factor of his productions; behind each movement, the construction of escapes and thrilling incidents, the design of the sets, the choice of the cast, the making of the costumes. Even the technical perfection of the camerawork and the drama of the lighting bear the mark of his discriminating judgement. The romantic mind of the man governs the architecture of the whole.

All the essential attributes of the cinema go to help the movement that envelops his pictures. The very properties of the camera, its device of slow-motion, add grace to his sweeping jumps, although he has yet to employ a smoothly moving camera to follow his actions. I would like his every swift move caught by the eagle-eye of a travelling camera, in the manner of the Germans.

In furtherance of his thoroughness, it has always been his principle to employ experts for the production of his films. He habitually surrounds himself with persons who make claim to artistry. He brought Maurice Leloir, the Frenchman, one of the greatest experts on historical costume, to Hollywood to supervise the costumes for *The Man in the Iron Mask.* He used the settings of William Cameron Menzies, one of the best art-directors in Hollywood, and took Laurence Irving, a young British designer for the theatre, to America to assist on the architecture used in *The Taming of the Shrew.*

And now, after rumours have been spread for months, we learn that Fairbanks is increasing his interest in the Russian cinema and in particular in the work of the celebrated director, Eisenstein. Some years ago he is reported to have said that *Potemkin* was the greatest film he had ever seen. Both he and his wife visited Russia in 1926.

In displaying this interest in the technique of the Russians, Fairbanks is making a move that may lead him direct to the height of his fascinating career. I have followed his development from the early days of the 'moral uplift' pictures of the *Say Young Fellow, Reaching for the Moon, Down to Earth* and *He Comes Up Smiling* type through the cowboy 'out-of-doors' series of *The Man From Painted Post, The Lamb, Knickerbocker-Buckaroo* and *Arizona,* which culminated in the ever-memorable *Mark of Zorro.* Later there came the big spectacular films, *Three Musketeers, Robin Hood, Thief of Bagdad, Don Q, The Black Pirate, The Gaucho, The Man in the Iron Mask* and the recent dialogue picture *Taming of the Shrew.*

But there are two principal movements in cinema: that of the players and objects and that of the film itself through editing. Fairbanks has supreme mastery over the former. The Russian directors have alone reached a state of perfection in the latter. A fusion between the two *must* result in a film of brilliance.

—FILM WEEKLY, *May* 10, 1930.

Korda (1) (*1933*)

London, October 31, 1933.

Alexander Korda[1] walked quickly up and down his office while I asked him several pertinent questions. He has just finished work on a second costume picture, *Catherine the Great*, in which we are to see the intelligent and attractive Elisabeth Bergner playing with Douglas Fairbanks Jr. In his mind Korda is planning yet a further costume picture, this time of the Elizabethan era, but although the Virgin Queen will appear in the film I gather that she will not be the central figure of interest. Korda promises more of a national theme than the flimsy *Henry VIII*, more of Tudor England's position in the sixteenth-century affairs of the world than we had in Henry's matrimonial experiences.[2]

The questions I posed him were admittedly difficult when we take stock of his responsible status as the head of a small and young company, London Film Productions, slowly steering its way to success. There are many demands to be met, the constant problem of entertainment values, the idiosyncrasies of distributors, before such a man as Korda can satisfy his own conscience.

He has, it transpired, little use for the social theme in movies, or indeed for any purpose other than the telling of good stories for entertainment with a high degree of craftsmanship. He has no time to spare for theory. He dislikes the academic approach to film; which is his dismissal of the modernists. For example, we discussed the social issues of *Kameradschaft*, and while he has the highest admiration for Pabst's craftsmanship, he ridiculed the social issues arising from the mining picture as being 'sentimental'.

[1] Died, London, January 23, 1956.

[2] Presumably *Fire Over England*, with Flora Robson as the Queen, which did not appear until 1937.

Korda (1) (1933)

Documentary, he agreed, was the most difficult of all approaches to cinema and one which demanded the most cautious handling. He would like to make documentary but he seemed to hesitate when I asked how he would reconcile this ambition with his previous disparagement of the social theme.

Presently we descended to technicalities and naturally found common ground where the delicacy and finesse of craftsmanship were concerned. Nothing irritates Korda so much as a camera movement which is not quite correct—perhaps too fast or too slow—or a timing of action which is not perfectly in accord with the motion of the camera. He appeared peculiarly sensitive towards the relation of his actors to the camera and the environment of both in the set. Where he differs from most views on film construction, however, is in the value he places on editing. Naturally, editing is uppermost in his mind when directing on the studio-floor and he supervises the assembly of his material by two cutting-assistants. Yet he does not seem to share the belief that all celluloid material is just so much dead stuff until it is given life and breath and meaning by the correlation of the film strips by editing.

Thus we find that he places primary importance on the writing of the script and its fulfilment on the floor; and really secondary importance on the assemblage, which when regarded in this light becomes a mere business of correcting floor mistakes as distinct from the vital function which the Russians and we documentary makers claim it to be.

As we parted, Korda let fall a few words which epitomized his feelings towards the movie position today. He spoke of the deplorable conditions which govern most film production, the constant compromising which a director must raise as a barrage against the demands of the money-barons, and the hampering restrictions of absurd censorial views. And I felt that within the space of a second his mind was making a lightning survey of his career since those early pictures in Budapest and Vienna after the War up till this moment when he is perhaps the most discussed director of story-films in England with a company of his own and several creditable pictures to his name.

—PHILADELPHIA PUBLIC LEDGER *and* NEW YORK POST.

Korda (2) (1956)

Some nine years ago several informal meetings were held among senior British film-makers out of which finally came the British Film Academy. One such meeting took place late one evening in Korda's apartment at Claridges. We broke up about one in the morning but as I was about to take my leave, Korda murmured to me to remain behind. Generous as usual, he gave me one of those little cedarwood boxes stamped with his initials and holding two cigars, put the brandy nearby and stretched himself out on the sofa in his cardigan.

'You are,' he said, in that inimitable (except by Ustinov) voice, 'as well as being a film-maker whose work I admire (although you do not give me that credit), you are also a historian of the cinema in your books. When I die one of these days, tell me, which of my films shall I be remembered by?'

Thinking I knew him a little, I let a minute pass and then said: '*The Private Life of Henry VIII*, Alex.'

'That is what you think *I* think. Tell me your own honest opinion.'

'The best film that you personally ever made was *Rembrandt*.'

'My biggest flop!' And he laughed.

A long silence. Then he said:

'Paul, I should like to be remembered by a little short film that I didn't make myself but helped to get finished—*The Private Life of the Gannets*. That was a beautiful and worthwhile picture. I used it as a curtain-raiser to *Catherine*. It is still playing in many places in the world after fourteen years. When Huxley showed me the rough material, I at once responded and found the money with which to complete the film. I am very proud of that now.'

He seemed very lonely that night, I remember thinking as I walked home.

—British Film Academy Journal, *Memorial Issue to Sir Alexander Korda, Spring*, 1956.

Eisenstein (1948)

Fifty years of Cinema, and there are scarcely a dozen names of film-makers who compel respect the world over. No one would deny this eminence to David Wark Griffith, to Chaplin and Robert Flaherty; few would argue against Eisenstein and Pudovkin. The influence of these five men's work can be found in all schools of film-making and, curiously enough, in most cases it is their early work which has had the most marked effect. With the exception of the Agincourt sequence in *Henry V* being based on the *Nevsky* Battle on the Ice, I would hesitate to say that anything contained in any of Eisenstein's films since *The General Line* has had wide influence on the films of the Western world. We cannot estimate, of course, in this country or in America what effect his teaching and later films have had on the cinema of his own country.

Whatever may come in the future, *Potemkin* will remain one of the major works of the cinema. Its simplicity of construction, its momentous piling of mass effect on mass effect, remain in your mind years afterwards. Its relation of rhythms of movement on the screen to the rhythms contrivable by the juxtaposition of shots, its sudden use of shock by giant close-ups, its insistence all through upon mass movement, especially of inanimate things such as the twirling parasols of the women on the Odessa steps and the wind under the sheet covering the sailor mutineers—these intrinsic filmic values which distinguish Eisenstein's work are something absent from so much of what passes today for the craft of film-making.

How the camera is set high or low; the dramatic clash of one shot following another; the rhythm within a shot, the rhythm of shots within a sequence, and sequences within the film as a whole; these are things which seem somehow to have been forgotten in this mechanical studio-bound era of gliding camera-cranes and panoraming gyros. Eisenstein needed no camera-crane or truck or optical printer to say his piece. He used the camera-lens like a marksman using his rifle. Behind every shot you feel the dominance and sureness of the man himself. Although often filling his screen with teeming multitudes, he somehow contrived to bend his camera to their action rather than fit them to his shot.

With Kuleshov and Pudovkin, Eisenstein was the first director after Griffith to understand fully and make use of the time-space flexibility of the film medium. The Czar statue falling apart and reassembling in *October*, the famous raising of the bridge with the white horse, the cab and the fair girl's hair across the crack in the road in the same film, and the world-known Odessa steps sequence itself from *Potemkin*—these were moments of great cinema which will never be forgotten.

I always wonder, when seeing an Eisenstein film, how much was premeditated and how much was spontaneous shooting? I suspect a great deal of the latter. How much of today's shooting, rigidly held to the script page, so many shots-per-hour, so much completed film shot in a day, has that spontaneous vitality which makes the work of Eisenstein and Flaherty alive today? For it is the vital living quality in these films that makes them so important and eternal. For all Eisenstein's brilliant understanding of the instruments of the cinema, for all his mastery of shot-arrangement, his films would be nothing but exercises in virtuosity if they were not charged with human feeling. There is no coldness about his early films, although he seldom dwelt for long on a single individual. There is a warmth of human contact, of people being together, that comes through from the screen even today when the photography may look murky and the speed seem too fast.

Said the French critic, Léon Moussinac: 'Un film d'Eisenstein ressemble à un cri; un film de Poudovkine évoque un chant.'

In the earlier films, Eisenstein seldom uses shots without there being action in them; perhaps the Gallery of the Gods in *October* and the milk-separator sequence in *The General Line* are the exceptions. And it is this movement within a shot that is the basis of his cutting technique. His use of the overlapping of movement between a number of shots has often been remarked.

Brilliant examples are the raising of the bridge in *October*, where tiny fractions of the same movement—the upward raising of the two sides of the bridge—are shot from a plethora of angles and edited so that there is a slight duplication of action in each shot. The whole series of shots blends into one sweeping continuous movement, creating an effect on the spectator which would be impossible to obtain by a single straight 'record' shot of the bridge opening. Another notable sequence that remains indelibly in my mind after twenty years is the procession and the prayer for rain in *The General Line*. Here is shooting and cutting used dynamically in a way that has not been seen since the speech-film blasted the lights out of so much genuine constructive editing.

Of his later films, *Nevsky* and *Ivan*, I am not disposed to write much because to me they lacked the wonderful fire and the impulsive creative urge of the early films. *Alexander Nevsky* I found too stylized and too prearranged. The well-known Battle on the Ice never roused me to the heights of response as did the Odessa steps or the Storming of the Winter Palace. It has always seemed to me that such a virile, impulsive mind as Eisenstein's demanded current living material to shape on to the screen, and not dressing-gown reconstruction and make-believe from another age. But I am one of those who does not like 'historical' films! Set against the insistent driving energy of *Potemkin* and *October*, I found *Ivan the Terrible* theatrical, posed and slow, although I appreciate that others think differently.

Though we have not been privileged to see much of his recent work, we shall miss deeply the feeling we've had for so many years of 'What is the Great Man now up to in Moscow?' Perhaps we have always secretly hoped that one day we should see his Mexican footage as he himself would have edited it; that one day we should have seen a new Eisenstein film that would make the other films in the world look dim. Alas, that can no longer be, but all the more reason then to look again and again at his old films. There is still much to be learned from them by us all.

—*Memorial Programme to S. M. Eisenstein, May*, 1948.

Eisenstein (1956)

POSTSCRIPT: July, 1956, when the above appreciation was reprinted in the Soviet magazine FOREIGN LITERATURE.

Today, I find nothing to change in what I wrote eight years ago. Eisenstein's name, writings and films are still with us and time has not dimmed their importance. In fact, I would say that the film-medium, in the Western world at any rate, is passing through an era of uncertainty and waywardness when it is more than ever important for all genuine film-makers to re-examine the fundamental principles of our medium. I am one—a writer and historian of the cinema as well as a modest maker of films—who does not believe that those basic principles so clearly established and demonstrated by the great masters, of whom Eisenstein was one, have changed.

Many films that are acclaimed today reveal only a weak tendency to return to the artificial theatricalism that misled the showmen in the 1900s! To my mind, the theatre-film and the photoplay have always been an abomination, a total misuse and misunderstanding of the real art of the film. The wide screens and other technological 'developments' introduced in the United States in an attempt to compete with the popularity of television have increased this misguided and ill-intentioned return to theatre-film. They have deprived the real film-maker of his proper and rightful methods of using the medium to interpret life as it is really lived and not as some people would have us imagine it. To me, the basic principles of the art of the film were discovered and demonstrated by the great masters—Méliès, Griffith, Eisenstein, Pudovkin and Flaherty—later to be developed by Dovjenko, De Sica, Vigo, Donskoy, Renoir, Kurosawa and others. To preserve but at the same time to develop our art, we need to restudy and reassess the work of the early masters. We may not improve on their aesthetic ideas but we may put them to still wider use in creating a more universal understanding among the peoples of the world.

Chaplin (1950)

Good news it is that two of Charles Chaplin's most famous films, *City Lights* and *Modern Times*, are to be available again for all to see. Reluctant to reissue his old pictures, with the exception of the classic *The Gold Rush* which reappeared with a cunningly devised sound track in 1942, he has kept to his belief that his last film was his best. It might suffer by comparison. But *Monsieur Verdoux*, most controversial of all Chaplin films, and *The Great Dictator*, the brilliant satire of Hitler, are so unlike his earlier work that Chaplin need not worry. A new generation of filmgoers has grown up since *City Lights* broke box-office records in 1931. To them the Chaplin of *The Circus, Sunnyside* and *The Kid* is just a legend. Those masterpieces of comic invention, *Easy Street* and *The Pilgrim*, are but names. Let them all be seen. I prophesy they will be received with all the acclaim they inspired years ago.

Last year Chaplin turned sixty. It is a long record between the young Cockney appearing first in the Keystone Company's *Making a Living* in 1914 and the superb all-round performance as author, director and actor in the screen's most devastating satire, *Monsieur Verdoux*. The whole thirty-three years' development of Chaplin's mind, from being a knockabout, slapstick comedian touring with Fred Karno, to becoming a great artist in his own right on the screen, is locked in that series of films. On the one side, he became without dispute the most popular and successful comedian the world has known. On the other, as he sought gradually to instil into his work something of his home-developed outlook on life, he found himself opposed, attacked and even insulted by those who feared his skill of satire. Throughout Chaplin has remained true to himself. He has not compromised.

Chaplin's politics, philosophic outlook and opinions on world

7. (a) THE GREAT DICTATOR (1940), Chaplin's *parody of Hitler*. (United Artists)

7. (b) MONSIEUR VERDOUX (1946–47), Chaplin *and* Martha Raye; *in some critical opinions his best film*. (United Artists)

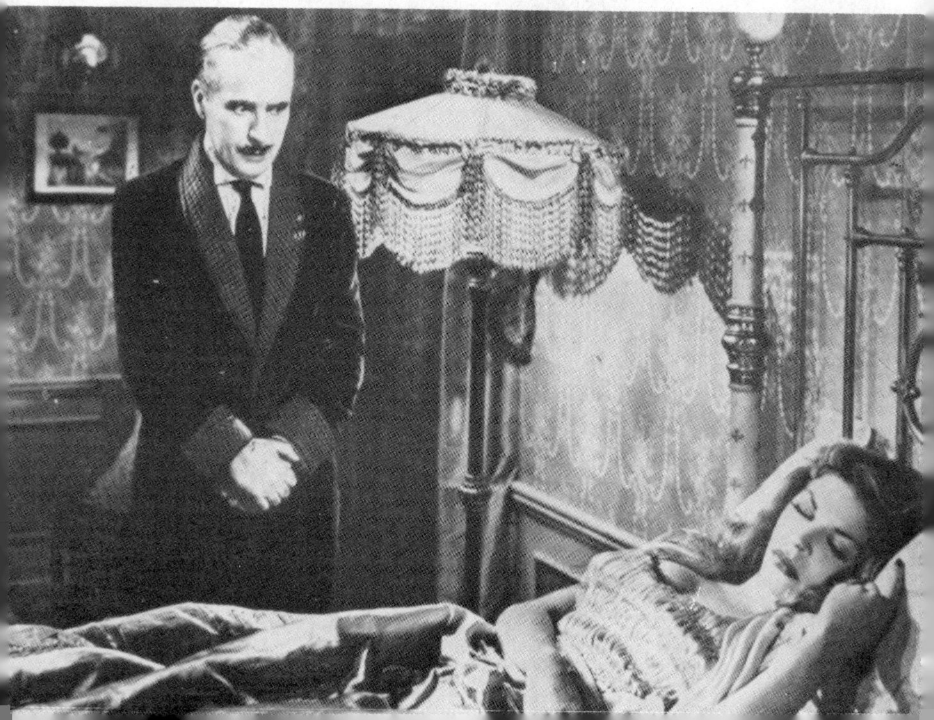

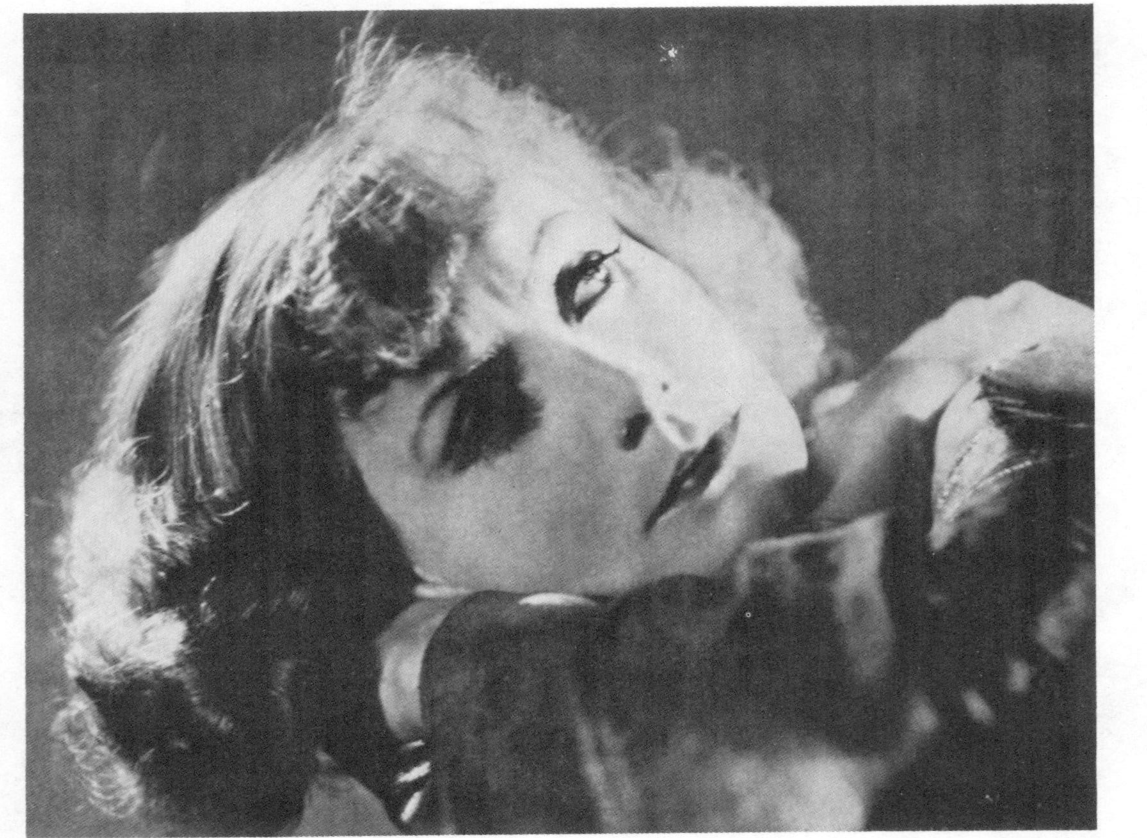

8. Garbo, *the Incomparable*, *in* SUSAN LENOX: HER FALL AND RISE (1931), *directed by* Robert Z.

9. Catherine Hessling, *of the pale blue eyes, memorable in* Renoir's NANA (1924) *and* Cavalcanti's EN RADE (1928)

10. (a) Garbo *on location for* THE SINGLE STANDARD (1929), *directed by* John S. Robertson. *Advertised as the picture that gave* Garbo *her "first* 100 *per cent American role"* (M-G-M)

10. (b) G. W. Pabst, *the distinguished Austrian director* (*right*), *and* Erich von Stroheim *in Hollywood in* 1934. (*photograph by* Hans Casparius)

affairs have, let us confess it, been of rather a homespun kind. They are charming, sincere but seldom profound. He was always for the underdog, agin' the law, ready to soak the rich, especially if it would help someone less well-off (if that were possible) than himself. These things he took in his stride so long as he remained primarily a clown. But starting with *City Lights*, which was in the making during the years of the world economic landslide, Chaplin took a more serious view of his Charlot. The side-splitting gags, the wonderful bits of inspired slapstick, the genius for using details and inanimate objects, they were all still there—but so was a Chaplin 'philosophy of life'.

Despite the criticism, Charlie stuck to his beliefs. His pictures still made a lot of money. His name was still a household word. He had clearly been an astute businessman as well as a brilliant artist. He was his own distributor as well as producer. He could afford to make films as and when he, and only he, felt inspired. In the vast, complex, monopoly-riddled industry of motion pictures, the position of Chaplin was unassailable and unique. No one else has ever approached it. That is sometimes forgotten.

All this time, it should be remembered, Chaplin's voice had not spoken on the screen. *Modern Times* in 1936 showed that he did not oppose speech for its own sake. He sought simply to maintain the silence of the figure he had created because Charlot would cease to be international and universal the moment he spoke *any* nation's language. He was up against what looked like an insuperable problem! But Chaplin's genius solved it. History presented him with a gift! He would divide his personality and play two parts in one film. He would play Hitler—the apotheosis of all the evil forces against which Chaplin fought: and he would play the international Common Man, a Jew, part dumb, bewildered, bruised, humiliated, the scapegoat. It was the most brilliant stroke of imagination in all Chaplin's career. No one else could or would have dared such a gesture. Oddly enough Chaplin was within four days the same age as Hitler. They were both born in April, 1889. There is no record that Hitler ever saw the film.

To me, *The Great Dictator* is one of the most important of all Chaplin's films. In 1940, it took a brave man to use the screen as a pulpit as Charlie did in that final speech spoken direct to the audience. Many a lesser man, with Chaplin's fortune and Chaplin's enviable reputation as the world's Funny Man No. 1, would have taken the easy way of the fleshpots. He could have said, 'I've done my share, now I'm going to sit back and rest.' But Charlie didn't. He spent his money in trying to make the world open its eyes. He was repaid by making more enemies. His private life, his public life were vilified. It was a shameful exhibition in which, I am glad to say, the British Press took little part. His films may no longer have been such good box-office in Britain, but at least no smear and smirch campaign was let loose.

Monsieur Verdoux, three years ago, was one of the most abused films of all time in America. It achieved almost no distribution. A savage boycott propaganda campaign was hurled against it and its maker by such bodies as the Catholic War Veterans and columnists like Westbrook Pegler. Chaplin was branded a 'Red', an 'Un-American', and recommended at Washington for deportation and his worldly goods to be confiscated! They made his life hell. He had made a film that said without equivocation that the mass-murder of war was good business for the capitalist. It was a savage satire, made all the more powerful by the skill with which it was produced. Its full impact didn't come clear until you had seen the picture two or three times. It is fashionable among dilettante critics to sneer at Chaplin's technique as *démodé*. Nothing could be more wrong. *Monsieur Verdoux* has brilliant cinema in much of its footage, noticeable especially when Chaplin himself was not on the screen. I maintain that it is a film which will be understood better as events change the world. It is, I suspect, appreciated for its full meaning more deeply in Europe than elsewhere.

And now? Chaplin, they say, is in New York preparing to make a film about the music-hall.[1] He ignores the insults, the calumny heaped on him. But why, Charlie, put up with it? If after all you have done for the American screen they no longer want you, come back over here to London, your home-town, and make your picture.[2] You will be understood here, at least by some people. You are still the great artist of the screen.

[1] *Limelight*, presented in late 1952.

[2] He made *The King in New York* in England in 1956–57.

Chaplin (1950)

We admire and respect you for it. Our film industry could do with a brain like yours just now. You do, at least, understand film-making. For all your sixty years you have vitality, imagination and courage, three qualities most of our British producers abysmally lack.

—PUBLIC OPINION, *May* 19, 1950.

Making Contact *(1933)*

' "In Uganda we chased elephants from the air and photographed them as they ran. That was very thrilling." "It's a beautiful thing," he exclaimed, "and I'm going to photograph it." "The exposure had been so successful that Mr. R. turned away with a smile on his face, which then changed to an expression of horror." "R. tells me that he will take as much as 50,000 feet of film." . . .'

In this way I am informed by the newsmen of my actions and my ideas, for which I cannot pretend to be responsible.

It is obviously premature to write of my intentions in the film which, variously described as depicting the 'history of civilization' and the 'conquest of the air', I have recently undertaken for British Instructional Films in cooperation with Imperial Airways, and sponsored by Shell-Mex. It is with reluctance that I allow stills to be included in this issue. I can say nothing about the present moment of editing, for anyone knows that during the period of gestation the patient prefers to be left alone.

But there are memories and experiences and swift impressions which might perhaps be of some interest.

The nature of the theme suggested that the material from which the eventual film might be shaped would fall into two parts. In England, there would be the phases of aeroplane construction, ground organization and the elaborate procedure of the airport at London. Abroad, there would be the full range of the two great Empire Routes to India and to South Africa and back.

The resultant journey was completed on ordinary service machines running according to normal schedules. No special facilities for camerawork were available. No automatic cameras were tied to the undercarriage. Opportunities had to be seized as they occurred. The twenty-two thousand miles were com-

11. *Making* CONTACT *in the desert near Assiut, Egypt,* 1932

12. *Making* WORLD WITHOUT END *in Mexico*, 1952. *The cameraman is* Carlos Carbajal.
(Unesco-International Realist)

pleted in twelve weeks and two days; one day over schedule, which in itself is a justification for the making of the film.

*

I remember:

Light rippling on the wings of the seaplane. Vistas of small islands, like spattered jewels in a dark setting. Pointed needles of cypresses stretching up in jagged rows. Every few minutes the toy towns of the Balkans: multiplications of little square, coloured houses. The ever-changing light and shade on the rounded moulded mountains. Then sheets of sparkling sea, divided into a million trickling lines of light. This from Athens to Palestine.

Before dawn, the earth surrounding Galilee dropping away in the flickering light of the paraffin flares. Above, the bursting sun revealing a new world, with its own cities, valleys and mountains—rising, towering, twisting formations of clouds. Here one is utterly remote from reality. Presently there is nothing but blinding white desert, spotted with dark bitumen pools. At the edges the sky and desert simply mix into each other. . . .

A crumbling dust-heap beneath a blistering sun. Broken-off columns of flat bricks rising up against a dark sky. A native boy stumbles and, in so doing, demolishes a portion of Babylon. The clatter of the falling mud bricks ceases in a thick cloud of dust and all is again silent. It was night, I remember, before we reached the filthy hotel in Baghdad. . . .

Dramatic white clouds piled into an indigo sky, which later burst into thunder. About dusk, there were groups of game—impala, gazelle, dikdik—in the thickets round Lake Naivasha. Too late to photograph, although the Kenya light is of crystal clarity. That day we had been to the Escarpment and looked at the massiveness of volcanic Longonot. . . .

The amazing colour of Uganda, where native women wear cloth bindings of brilliant ultramarines, scarlets and purples. They walk with a superb grace, swinging slightly from the hips, a carriage grown from the constant carrying of loads on their heads. Miles and miles of red earth roads and a profusion of fantastic foliage—cactus, hibiscus, candelabra, elephant's shiver. . . .

The tragic expression of the native miners as they come to the surface in the Rand Valley gold mines. Our car was drawn up alongside the surgery. In the compounds they sleep on cement beds and are shown old American Westerns on Saturday nights.

Johannesburg. From the roof of the highest building you can see the gold rift splitting the newly-born city in two. A veritable Cimarron city, built on gold. . . .

*

Journalists as a whole were disappointed. There were no sensations to relate. A forced landing in Tanganyika and a hasty retreat from a hungry lion in the bush near Murchison Falls. But this was nothing to palates jaded by the exploitations of a *Congorilla* outfit or a *Trader Horn* safari. Besides, we did not carry guns. A unit of three cannot be taken seriously in a continent swept by newsreel sound-vans. Yet they liked our sincerity and realized that we were looking at their country from a different point of view. Naturally, almost every town expected prominence for itself in a film that would perhaps run for an hour. They charmingly showed us every beauty spot, and quite justifiably, because it was difficult for them to grasp that I was not making a travel film.

Long before leaving England, before shooting had begun at Coventry and Croydon, I had written in collaboration with Ralph Keene a theoretical script expressive of my theme. When I arrived in an unknown village or city, it was never the question of shooting just anything of interest. On the contrary, it meant the selecting of the most significant material to express a certain sequence in the script. Had I another theme in mind, obviously the material shot would have been completely different. The wealth of material was overwhelming. Yet I returned to England with several thousand feet of unexposed negative.

Difficulties were abundant, and mostly unexpected. Mechanical camera troubles, temperaments, customs, illness—all making for an unsettled state of mind and demanding instant decisions. It was impossible to alter schedule, for tickets had been booked months ahead. But few films of this nature can be made smoothly, especially in this case when the unit had to be in a constant state of preparedness for action and at the same time travelling for weeks on end.

Occasionally news reached us. *Rome Express* had at last reached terminus. An Institute was being formed. *Rain* was not the picture one had expected. Pabst had finished turning *Quixote*. But it was all remote. It had nothing in common except the celluloid we were both using. When you are flying low over densely-packed trees, hoping that the sun will soon move round so that you can shoot; when you are damn-crazy at not having taken a shot in Arabia because you had believed the Nubian Desert was better and it proves not as good; when you are mad with the swarming onlookers in a pox-ridden bazaar while you are trying to take a close shot; when you are unpacking the camera-cases for the third time that day for still another customs examination—then you don't give a damn what they are writing or making at home. One film and only one must matter, and that is your own.

One thing was clear. Interest in good cinema is not a European monopoly. Almost everywhere I found a tremendous enthusiasm for films. In Africa particularly they are waiting for sensible, straightforward films which they are not getting. The most surprising people in the most surprising places made remarkable statements about cinema, plainly showing that they had given the matter thought.

—Cinema Quarterly, *Spring*, 1933.

Films and Other Visual Techniques in Education (1946)

(Lecture to the Museums Association, Brighton, 1946)

Only in the past fifty years, and only really noticeably since World War I, have we thrown off the tyranny of the written word. For many centuries the written and the printed word, with always, of course, the spoken word, have dominated our ways of communication and conditioned our methods of education. Since the age of Egyptian wall paintings and hieroglyphics, we have not seen a wide use of pictures as a means of communication until the coming of the photograph, with all the many technical devices for its reproduction which have been invented in recent years. I am not saying that communication by visual means has not occurred all through those centuries. It has; in the work of map-makers, heraldic designers, and draughtsmen illustrators, for example; but pictures as media to convey information have been largely overshadowed by the printed and written word.

I want to make the suggestion that we are living in a new 'Age of the Eye', that we are using today more widely than ever before visual techniques to supply facts and information.

There is no need for me to remind you of the great display of posters, pictorial journals and newspapers, cinemas and exhibitions with which we are all confronted day after day, with television on a mass-reception scale just round the corner of tomorrow. We know of the vast circulations achieved by magazines and newspapers whose appeal is based almost wholly on pictorial matter and in which the printed text is reduced to a minimum. The *Daily Mirror* has more than eight times the audience of *The Times*. I use the word 'audience' deliberately, because people *look* at the *Daily Mirror*; they read *The Times*.

Films and Other Visual Techniques in Education (1946)

Twenty-five million admission tickets are bought every week at Britain's cinemas. Millions of British people believe they know a good deal about America, not because they have been there but because for every two British films, they see eight of Hollywood origin.

Comic papers for children, cartoon strips for adolescents and often adults, the Kodak snapshot, *Life*, *Picture Post*, *Illustrated*, the Odeon and the Gaumont Palace, the poster-hoarding and subway wall—these have all become part and parcel of our social environment, as influential as the printed word, impinging on our minds at every turn with their multitude of visual techniques.

Those of you who are admirers of painting and sculpture must not think that I am overlooking the great contributions to the visual world made by the artist. But here I want to make a distinction. There is a great difference between artists who paint pictures to create an emotional and aesthetic effect on the spectator, who comprise the majority of artists, and those who seek to convey information by lines and colours. There is a great difference between pictures which create a mood when you contemplate them, create an atmosphere and an emotional response, and pictures which are specifically designed to impart clear-cut information.

Sometimes, by the way, you come across a mixture of both which is irritating and unpardonable.

On the whole, we speak of paintings as works of art, subjects of aesthetic appeal evoked by subtle craftsmanship and creative inspiration. Hardly ever do we discuss paintings as means of communication. I do not wish to dwell on this matter, save only to add that artists of the first group—those who create moods—are usually regarded as masters of the public. They present their creative work, or somebody else does for them, and the man-in-the-street comes to see it to get what reaction he can according to his receptive powers. Those who draw 'educational' pictures, however, pictures intended to convey information, are the servants of the public and a great weight of social responsibility rests on their shoulders. We are more concerned here with the latter kind of artist because we are considering visual education and not aesthetic pleasure.

Now one of the major elements in clear-cut visual communication is the use of symbols. I am not competent, nor would it be in order here, to attempt even a brief history of the use of symbols. But I must record that the more I investigate visual education, the more I come across the use of symbols, from those ancient days before we knew our present alphabet until the most recent experiments in international communication by picture language.

But there are several points I should like to make in regard to the use of symbols, whether they be employed for communication to the road-user to warn him of an approaching cross-roads or a zigzag bend, or to denote the name of your favourite pub, or merely as a trade-mark for a proprietary brand of manufacture.

The simpler the symbol in its basic design, the easier it is to recognize its meaning. If a symbol is designed to convey a meaning, which is its only reason for existence, the act of conveyance must be as near instantaneous as the relation between the eye and the mind permits. Having perfected the single symbol, easily recognizable, attractive in design and capable of multiplication without loss of visual power, next comes the combination of symbols and their arrangement into a scheme to express an argument or statement. Here again consistency of method is fundamental if the technique of creating a picture language is the aim, as it is in the case of the well-known work of the Isotype Institute.

Colour in symbolism is also of great importance, provided also that a consistency is maintained in its use and that once a colour is chosen to convey a particular meaning in a chart or a film, it must not be changed. Consistency of method and of technique of presentation is a basic necessity of symbol languages intended for visual education. The neutrality of symbols is also of significance. If facts and information are to be presented without bias, as map-makers should present their atlases, the symbols used in charts and films should have no negative or positive associations. The aim is to provide information for free discussion from any point of view and perhaps for very different arguments.

What I have just said may perhaps seem obvious, but since today it is becoming increasingly popular to use pictorial statistics and symbolic charts in newspapers and magazines and books, to say nothing of films, posters and White Papers, it needs emphasis because so many designers of these visual techniques appear abysmally ignorant of symbol principles.

In so many cases their symbols themselves, as well as the way in which they are arranged to give meaning to an argument, are spurious. Not only are they inconsistent in the design of symbols but they multiply their size and shape without understanding what they are doing. There is a great deal of phony exploitation going on today in the visual education field.

This may seem a curiously roundabout approach to the medium of the film and its place in visual education, which is the main subject of my address, but I have deliberately laid this stress on symbolism as a means of communicating information because it has, in my opinion and in my work, a most important part to play in the development of film technique for educational purposes.

In addition to which, the film is only one medium of those available for visual education and it would be unfair of me, a film-maker, if I were to discuss the film apart from its allied media—the film-strip, the pictorial chart, the exhibition and the picture textbook, and possible three-dimensional models, the diorama and the epidiascope—all these are instruments in our orchestra for visual techniques. Perhaps, however, I may say something about the film first, without implying that it is necessarily the most important medium of the group, although unfortunately it is usually the most costly to produce.

Its technical devices are well known to all of you. I needn't list them but merely remind you of its powers over actual time, most easily seen in slow-motion or fast-motion cinematography, and even the reversal of time backwards; its remarkable power of selection of detail in magnified size; its capacity for continually changing the point of view of the camera and therefore that of the observer; its actual mobility of viewpoint, approaching or retreating from an object with the smoothness and aerial characteristics of a magic carpet; its capacity for relating things one to another, not only side by side but also one after another despite their actual physical separation by perhaps thousands of miles: and so on.

As to what it can show, there are practically no limits. The techniques of paintings or modelling or pottery-making, the elementary principles of machinery in action, the principles underlying design whether static or in motion; the development of architectural styles; these are only a few random subjects which the educational film can present in visual terms with greater clarity than perhaps any other medium.

On the other hand, rich as the film may be in technical devices, it has certain limitations which I fancy its over-ardent exponents do not always admit. The speed at which a film is projected, for example, cannot easily be varied and the visual images are on the screen for the same length of time for each member of the audience no matter what the individual degrees of quickness of apperception. A cinema audience has to deal with one shot at a time when looking at the screen and the last shot leaves the strongest impression, unless great skill is employed in the real craft of the medium, in the editing, so that the impression left on the audience is the sum of a number of shots, not of just one shot itself. Again, although the film can slow down very greatly the real-life speed of movement, this is not in itself a substitute for a series of comparative still-photographs which enables us to compare stages of movement progressively and simultaneously.

While the small changes in the shape of an animal, or a drop of liquid, are visible when you compare the stages simultaneously, they may pass unnoticed when we see them in motion on the screen, however slow the movement may be.

We should not, I suggest, think of motion as an advantage in itself, just as we should not think of the use of three dimensions as being an advantage in itself.

In our subject we are, of course, especially interested in the film's capacity to animate charts and diagrams and other arrangements of symbols, cross-sections of machinery, maps of all kinds, and chemical formulae. I believe that we are only just beginning to understand the immense possibilities of animation, both in colour and in black-and-white. In some films, where the use of animated work is not continuous throughout, we are faced with the extremely interesting problem of relating two-dimensional animated drawings with photographic visuals carrying the illusion of three-dimensional representation. I say

13. OCTOBER (1927–28) *often known as* THE TEN DAYS THAT SHOOK THE WORLD, Eisenstein *and* Alexandrov's *massive reconstruction of the October Revolution of* 1917. (Sovkino)

14. Erich von Stroheim, *one of the great personalities of the cinema both as an actor and director, in* LA GRANDE ILLUSION (1937), *directed by* Jean Renoir *in France*

'problem' because, for example, the two-dimensional animated charts or diagrams ignore orthodox perspective, which is anti-symbolic, whereas the photographic visuals apparently conform to normal principles of perspective.

The whole technique of map presentation is again full of exciting experiments on the screen, although much of it so far has followed the conventional lines of the schoolroom atlas. Schematic maps, maps that are profiles, maps that combine symbols and world surfaces in motion, all these call for experiment and research.

It has become popular recently to talk of Visual Units, by which is meant that a number of visual techniques are used to comprise one Main Unit which embraces a single subject. For example, not only is a film produced on a subject suitable for visual education, but with it go several film-strips, a series of wall-charts, printed matter combining text and pictures, and a teacher's handbook. Each of these media should be used according to its particular characteristics. The film-strip, for example, is static as compared with the continuous movement of the film. It needs a special technique of its own and little genuine experiment has yet been made with it. Film-strip is the modern form of the old lantern slide, and has the advantages of mobility, lightness and cheapness. Wall-charts and display exhibits we are already familiar with, but we have much to learn from their use in connection with films and film-strips. The Ministry of Education is at present experimenting in this Visual Unit technique and many of us are anxious to see something of the results.[1]

The Visual Unit should ideally be the work of one producing group because although the techniques differ, there is much in common between them. The research needed into subject matter is valuable to all media. The Visual Unit should, therefore, be a single creative production. Its use in schools, or in adult education, has yet to be tried out effectively.

In all its media, the Visual Unit will make use of symbols and picture-languages and hence again my emphasis on the need for consistency of presentation. If the symbol language used in a film differs from that used in film-strips or wall-charts, chaos will result in the audience-mind.

[1] Needless to add, we never did!—P.R.

This mention of the Visual Unit inevitably brings up the always stimulating discussion about the attitude of the audience, or class, or individual observer or spectator, to visual techniques. Here again there is room for much study.

In making exhibitions, charts and models must be clearly understandable and therefore as simple as possible. Charts and pictorial matter in books, however, can be rather more complicated. A reader usually has more time at his disposal and can look at a visual argument at his leisure. He can easily refer back to the book later. The visitor to an exhibition or a museum, on the other hand, can only have another look later by taking the trouble of making another visit. Exhibitions and museums have peculiar characteristics distinguishing them from book illustrations or films. Visitors, for example, can stand around an exhibit and discuss it freely. If they think one picture can be explained by another, they can walk from one to the other to collect their knowledge. An exhibition gives freedom and stimulus to community life. If some people need more time than others there is nothing to prevent their viewing the exhibits again. This is difficult with a film. Posters and exhibitions are not poor substitutes for films. Each has educational characteristics of its own.

There have been many interesting new experiments in exhibition techniques as, for example, those arranged by the Ministry of Information and A.B.C.A. during the war, and others more recently on the Chemical Industry and on Housing at Dorland Hall. There is no doubt that we are evolving new techniques in this direction which may perhaps have some influence on our permanent museums and collections.

I am engaged at the moment in editing and preparing for the press a manuscript left by the late Dr. Otto Neurath, of the Isotype Institute, which will be published this year under the title of 'From Hieroglyphics to Isotype.'[1] I would like to quote you an excerpt from the MS. by Dr. Neurath which deals with a new technique in exhibition making:

'In the Hague, Rotterdam and Amsterdam we set up exhibi-

[1] This project was finally incorporated into 'From Cave Painting to Comic Strip' by Lancelot Hogben, with illustrative material by Marie Neurath (Parrish, 1949).

tions in department stores. They were visited by thousands of people who ordinarily would not have gone to a museum. One such exhibition, "Around Rembrandt", tried to present to the public a knowledge of a period in history together with some analytical information about Rembrandt's work. Isotype charts were shown demonstrating that Rembrandt worked during a period when the textile production of Leyden, the artist's birthplace, increased for a time and then decreased; at the same time, the number of students at the University increased considerably and then decreased; and it was also the time when, after a long period of relative stagnation, the population of Amsterdam increased considerably and then remained fairly stable. Other charts showed the life-lines of Rembrandt and his family, those of famous contemporaries and of certain institutions against a background of war and peace. One particular chart showed how the number of Rembrandt's pupils increased so long as he conformed to the traditional technique of painting, and how it decreased when he initiated what we may call a more modern technique.

'We intentionally avoided showing any of Rembrandt's actual paintings. Instead we showed photographs of some of his pictures for comparative purposes. We tried to give some understanding of the painter's brushwork by showing a hand painted when he was young, and one painted in his old age. To give visitors some idea of how his technique changed, we arranged a collection of photographic reproductions of all his self-portraits. We assembled these chronologically so that you could easily see at which stage each portrait had been painted. If we had not done this, we should have had to label all his etchings and paintings with their dates, thus burdening the visitor with more detail than he could absorb.

'This particular exhibition had a "question and answer" apparatus. Sets of pictures were shown and the visitor was invited to say which set he thought correct. Assuming that he had looked at the exhibits and their explanations, he would be able to decide which he had seen before. By pressing a button, he could put a machine in motion which would tell him if his choice was correct. This machine belonged to a group of such apparatus we had already used for self-teaching in Vienna, a method we found people liked very much. They like to test their knowledge and also to watch other people doing so. The illustrated guide provided at the exhibition suggested further lines of research. The exhibition as a whole showed how an interest in the arts and an understanding of a certain historical period can be combined by means of a well-arranged, language-like technique of presentation.'

Most educationists will agree, I think, that we are moving out of the era when exhibitions and museums were collections of dead pieces inadequately related to their environment, their very presence explained to the public by little illegible labels.

It is realized today that museums are living places and that methods of presentation are devised with the need for public information in mind and not merely to satisfy the personal aesthetic taste of the director.

In our era education must compete with entertainment. A museum is just as much a part of visual education as the film or wall-chart. In fact the museum may very well in time make use of these new visual techniques within its own walls. It is no idle thought that perhaps one day each museum of any reasonable size in the country, like every public library, may have its resources for visual units such as I described above. How excellent a thought it is that the forthcoming 'Britain Can Make It' exhibition is being designed to take place in the Victoria and Albert Museum.

There is one further point at which museums and the film touch, and that is in the preservation of films for record and artistic purposes. This is an elaborate subject, worthy of an address in itself. As the film gradually takes a serious place in the arts of the day, as it offers a unique medium for record, it becomes more and more worthy of preservation and study.

We are inclined to take its existence too much for granted because it has for too long been left in the hands of the profit-seekers and public exploiters. Only slowly is it being appreciated that the cinema is a powerful social influence and that it can, like other visual techniques, be used for the common good in fields other than escapist entertainment.

In editing Dr. Otto Neurath's book, I find that he makes use of a quotation from Samuel Smiles's *Self-Help*, and I would like

15. Jimmy Cagney, *King of the Corner-boys, star of so many gangster films produced by* Warner Brothers *in the early thirties*

16. Pola Negri, *the Imperious, in* FORBIDDEN PARADISE (1924), Ernst Lubitsch's *Ruritanian satire on Hollywood.*

to end my address with a passage from his manuscript. Referring to Smiles, he says: 'He wrote of those who excelled, not in killing or exploiting others, but in efforts to attain a well-balanced happiness for all mankind. The importance of common sense, cheerfulness and pertinacity was emphasized. Perhaps when I read the chapter called "Example Models" I absorbed the meaning of the following sentence without realizing it:

"All persons are more or less apt to learn through the eye rather than the ear, and whatever is seen in fact makes a far deeper impression than anything that is merely read or heard. This is especially the case in early youth, when the eye is the chief inlet of knowledge."

—*Reprinted in the Museums Association's Journal, July* 16, 1946.

Presenting the World to the World (1956)

People often ask what sparked the idea that has lain behind The World series of films and television programmes with which I have been associated on and off over the past fifteen years. They began way back in 1942 when the then Ministry of Information commissioned what it intended to be a short film for non-commercial audiences about how the British were benefiting from American food under Lease-Lend. What finally evolved was *World of Plenty*, the first film about the world-to-be after the war had been won, and which had ultimately as wide a distribution in many countries as possibly any other documentary of the war years.

That was fourteen years ago.

Today, the theme is being continued in the BBC television series *The World Is Ours*, initiated by me there in April, 1954, and ably produced by Norman Swallow. Eight have so far been shown and four more are in preparation.

Now there is a new film which I hope to make for the United Nations this year from a script that I have written on the peaceful uses of atomic energy in relation to world energy resources as a whole.[1]

In between there have been *The World is Rich*, made in 1946-47, which stirred up so much fuss in spite of its being officially sponsored by the Government, and *World Without End*, made for Unesco in 1952-53 by Basil Wright and myself, which has had probably the biggest world distribution of any documentary made since the war. Other units, too, have taken other aspects of The World story and made such excellent films as *Today and Tomorrow* by Robin Carruthers and Arthur

[1] When this script was accepted by the United Nations in 1956, it was found that adequate funds which had been set aside for its production were no longer available. The film was to have been called *The Power of Peace*!

Calder-Marshall, *The Teeth of the Wind* by James Carr and the recent brilliant *The Rival World* made by Bert Haanstra for the Shell Film Unit, while the United Nations Films Division itself has made numerous less ambitious films over the past ten years.

To my own World films many people have contributed and deserve great credit, but the real credit for the theme of the original *World of Plenty* lay with the late Eric Knight, best-known oddly enough as the author of *Lassie,* on sequels to which so many other and lesser pens have worked. Those who read the extracts from Knight's letters (written between 1932 and 1943) published three years ago under the title of *Portrait of a Flying Yorkshireman,* will recall that that tough fighter for goodwill among men was deeply perturbed way back in the 'thirties by the inequality of food distribution throughout the world. He was then farming himself, as well as writing, and came up against the crazy stupidity of farmers being compelled to restrict their output while at the same time people were dying of hunger.

In the winter of 1942 Knight was in England and offered to write a script for the Ministry of Information without fee. Together we saw the scope of *World of Plenty.* Actually, Knight was unable to complete here because, immediately after Pearl Harbour, he returned to the United States to take up service there. We continued to collaborate by air-mail and cable and he spoke one of the main voices of the film before being killed in an air-crash in January, 1943. At a later stage that noted actor and playwright, Miles Malleson, contributed some final dialogue.

The opening words of *World of Plenty*—wonderfully spoken by the American radio reporter and writer Robert St. John—were: 'This is a film about Food—the World Strategy of Food. How it is grown—how it is harvested—how it is marketed—how it is eaten. In peace or war, Food is Man's Security Number One.' The film went on to show the problems of world food 'as it was', 'as it is', and 'as it might be'. We had the inspiration of Sir John (now Lord) Boyd-Orr, the great nutrition expert, of Ritchie Calder (the science-writer who has done so much in his own medium for the World theme and collaborated later on several films), of the novelist Arthur Calder-Marshall (at that time script-editor at the Ministry of Information) and the late Carl Mayer (the script-writer of the early German films such as *The Cabinet of Dr. Caligari* and *The Last Laugh*, who was working with my unit at the time). So we proceeded to turn what was meant to be a little picture about Lease-Lend food into a film that challenged the world and astonished the three hundred delegates and Pressmen from forty-four allied and neutral countries who had assembled for the first World Food Conference at Hot Springs, Virginia, in May, 1943, by anticipating many of their conclusions.

World of Plenty was not made without many difficulties, official and otherwise, being put in our way; but with our immense faith in the basic rightness and common sense of our 'message' it finally reached a world public. Of the many, many letters and comments that reached me about the film, perhaps the one that moved me most was a postcard from a girl sergeant in the ATS on 48-hour leave in London who simply wrote: 'Your film more than anything else has shown me why I am fighting in this war.'

In 1946, a direct request came from the Prime Minister's Office to the British documentary people for three major films on international subjects, the first to be again on world food in the light of the post-war situation and the setting-up of the United Nations and its Specialized Agencies. As it was in direct continuity to *World of Plenty*, the film came to me to make and I invited Calder-Marshall to script, with Ritchie Calder again as adviser. It was finished the next year and again encountered many obstacles to its showing, both official and trade. At last, after good friends in Fleet Street and in Parliament had thrown their weight behind it, a British release was obtained and it also was shown widely overseas, with stimulating results.

It is often said that *World of Plenty* began a new technique of film argument, derived from the American stage *Living Newspapers*. This is only partially correct. The first film in which I tried this technique of using every trick and device of the movie medium—stock library footage, diagrams, cut-in interviews, an argumentative voice track, trick optical effects and so on—was in *New Worlds for Old*, written and made in 1938 on my return from New York. It was a curious combination of *Hellzapoppin*, and the *Living Newspaper* that suggested

17. Faustino *and* Gabrielito, *his son, net-making on the island of Yunuen on Lake Patzcuaro, Michoacan, Mexico. They are Tarascan Indians and played the main parts in the Mexican sequences of* WORLD WITHOUT END (1952–53). (Unesco-International Realist)

18. Mother *and* Child *in a yaws-infested village in the Thai sequences of* World Without End, *directed by* Basil Wright. (Unesco-International Realist)

to me that in film one could take this 'argument' approach even further than on the stage.

The technique of *World of Plenty* was also a matter of expediency. At the same time as making it, I had seven or eight other films to produce at my unit. As a result of Lease-Lend, it was possible to obtain a great deal of stock footage from American sources at cost or for free. Thus, compilation in the cutting-room with little fresh shooting became the only way out if it was to be a 'personal' film. The method was subsequently developed in my film about Housing—*Land of Promise*, in 1945 (assistant Francis Gysin) and *The World is Rich* (assistant Michael Orrom). The latter film, however, largely dropped the use of direct speech because of the need for a wide number of foreign versions; but it retained the 'argument-between-voices' which I have again used in my script about world energy and what atomic power can do for mankind if used for peaceful purposes.

The odd-man-out of the group was *World Without End* but only in its style, necessitated by two directors collaborating to make a single unified film from footage shot by them separately in two countries 10,000 miles apart—Siam and Mexico. This Unesco film, now seen by many, many millions in eight different language versions, carried the same basic theme of there being one world in which we are all neighbours, a theme beautifully interpreted by Rex Warner's writing of the narration from a draft by Basil Wright and myself. Perhaps because Wright, my co-director, is one of my oldest friends, this was the happiest and most harmonious picture on which I have worked in the twenty-eight years of my film career. It has been said by a shrewd critic in New York that this happiness pervades the film itself and hence audiences respond to its warmth.

In naming the many contributors to these films I must mention the big part played by music, always specially written. William Alwyn, Clifton Parker and Elizabeth Lutyens each in turn wrote magnificently and tried out many musical experiments. Credit, too, must be given to the team at the Isotype Institute for their diagram designs which helped to explain some of the complex 'economic' aspects of the two food films. Their long experience in developing an international picture language with symbols without doubt helped to secure the world audiences for these films.

None of these films has been easy to get made and, when made, to be found a release. They have carried a message of goodwill and the need for a more equal sharing out of the world's riches, neither likely to be popular subjects with the film trade. But once the films had been lifted over the hurdles to the public, that public responded fourfold. To make a film in which you believe something important to mankind is said with sincerity and passion has always been a fight, and never more so than today. From the great D. W. Griffith to De Sica—by way of Flaherty, Vigo, Stroheim and many others—the path has been grim and difficult, but it is the only path that a film-maker who believes in the basic goodness of human beings can take if he is true to his medium and to himself.

—FILMS AND FILMING, *April*, 1956.

People to People (1955)

(Extracts from a Speech to the Films Council of America, New York, April 6, 1955)

My theme is the role of the 16mm. film in international understanding. My remarks—which I make in a private capacity—will not, however, be restricted to the sub-standard film although some will specifically relate to its immense opportunities. But as things are today, what is sub-standard film? Is it 16mm. or 35mm. or 60mm. or what? Frankly, it does not matter what size the picture is, so long as it is of good classical proportions; none of your mail-box slits for me! In any case, it is what goes on to the motion picture screen that matters. Gauge of film-stock has nothing to do with content.

Now those of you who may know my work in films may have noticed my absorption with the World Theme. Indeed, if Mr. Wendell Willkie hadn't used the title, one of my films would surely have been called *One World.* But there has been *World of Plenty*, *The World is Rich*, *World Without End* and currently on British television *The World is Ours* series.

There has been a common theme, a common purpose, running through all these films from 1942 until today—a theme of the deep need for mutual understanding and mutual tolerance between peoples of all races, religions and countries. 'Homo sum,' says the voice at the opening of *World Without End*, 'humani nil a me alienum puto.' That is a quotation from Terence in 190 B.C. and being translated means, 'I am a Man myself and I think that everything which has to do with human beings has something to do with me too.'

Mr. E. M. Forster, whose work I am sure you know well over here, put this nicely the other day in a letter to the Press: 'If I say I am an atheist, the obvious retort is, "That sounds rather crude"; if I say I am an agnostic, the retort is, "That sounds rather feeble"; if I say I am a Liberal, the retort is, "You can't be; there are only Tories and Socialists"; and if I say I am a humanist, there is apt to be a bored withdrawal.' On the whole, I think that Humanist is the best word.

That remarkable philosopher, John Macmurray, of Edinburgh University, has pointed out: 'The life of human beings is constituted by their relations to one another. That is what makes us human beings. Confucius held that you cannot have one man unless you have two men in relation, which is a denial of individualism. We are not really human beings until we are in relation with one another.'

That's a pretty tough thing for me to say as a guest of a nation that prides itself on being comprised of 150 million individualists but I beg you to consider its validity in a world of neighbours such as is inevitably our world today.

Now in case you should dismiss this as starry-eyed dreaming, I want to make the point that there is a dangerous tendency in these anxiety-strewn, ulcer-giving post-war years to spend too much time on the gloomy, the despondent, the depressing and defeatist side of things. We tend, I think, to overlook and minimize the positive things that are happening to human beings all around us. Nations wanting to know about other nations is a truism we are always forgetting in this complex, over-hurrying world of ours.

The question of whether one country gets a fair and accurate picture of another country through the people and places and events shown in its motion pictures. is something that has exercised many minds in recent years. It has been said that if we foreigners formed a picture of your United States from the movies we get from Hollywood, then we should have a pretty unbalanced impression of your 150 million people and your ways of living and thinking in forty-eight great States. There is, of course, an element of truth in this but, you know, it works both ways. Alas, I should not perhaps judge American womanhood by Miss Marilyn Monroe (bless her!) any more than you should consider Mr. Alec Guinness as a typical Englishman, or that we English spend much of our time riding from London to Brighton and back in forty-year-old motor-cars called Old

Crocks. Such broad generalizations are amusing but dangerous.

They recall to me a letter which I had from a New York writer friend of mine (alas, now no longer alive) just after I had returned to England from this city in 1938. I had observed my friend at a party deep in conversation with a distinguished visiting English novelist—or rather my friend was doing the listening. His amazed expression was explained by a postscript to his letter which I received a few weeks later. It read: 'If you should happen to see Mr. So-and-So (naming the English novelist), tell him that we've now got the Red Indian problem well in hand.'

The opening reels of that wonderfully enjoyable musical, *On the Town*, will always influence me affectionately and irresistibly to this great city of New York, even if I needed influencing which I do not. But I wonder if New Yorkers themselves ever see it that way? I think that the motion picture screens would be the losers if they no longer had Miss Monroe and the versatility of Mr. Guinness, but we should remember that they are of the romantic world of entertainment. On the other hand, I cannot help but think that if Society and the Law had won instead of Marlon Brando in *On the Waterfront*, it would have been better democracy.

Allowing for some distortion and bias, there is no doubt that a nation's films do reflect a great deal of that nation's character. That is why the documentary film and the informational film are so important in international human relations. Perhaps the best kind of film to create understanding between countries is the one that tells the truth and gives the facts, unglossified and without Cellophane packaging and not masquerading as entertainment. Let us by all means select the things of which we are proud and say so; but do not cover up those things of which we are not so proud—rather let us show what we are doing to grapple with problems of that kind. Some of you may remember the great quarrel about what kind of documentary films of Britain were to be shown at the New York World's Fair in 1939. One school of thought believed that we should show an England of thatched cottages with roses round the door and rustic peasants in smocks. Others (of whom I hope I need hardly say I was one) conceived our films as showing a living democracy 'with its sleeves rolled up.' When both sets of films came to be shown in New York, there was little doubt as to which of us was right.[1]

In the years just after the war, some of us believed that the film was firmly recognized as an integral part of our information services both at home and overseas. When John Grierson addressed the New York Films Council in 1946, he said, and I quote: 'In the United Kingdom there is no public discussion nor even public thought of giving up the Government information service. One significant point in the British scene is the wide knowledge and recognition by Government Ministers of the work which the documentary film has done over the past fifteen years.'

Alas, the maestro was not to have foreseen the complete dissolution of the world-famous Crown Film Unit only a few years after he had made that speech, and the abandonment to a large extent of fresh documentary film-making under official auspices for overseas showing. Thus, after twenty-two years of continuity, a foundation stone was torn out of British documentary. Today it is slowly recovering. The nationalized industries of Coal and Railways have their own units doing steady work. The Shell Film Unit maintains its fine international reputation. The BBC documentary department is breaking new ground with television as its outlet. But the problems today are very different from those of the 'thirties or the war years. The One World picture has become of supreme importance in spite of Cold Wars and Iron Curtains.

Today, with this great and pressing need for better international human understanding of points of view and ways of living, it is of first importance that those of us concerned either with making or showing films of social integrity should have contact between us. That surely is one reason, one basic reason, for your Conference in New York this week and perhaps why you have shown such courtesy and generosity in inviting me as your main speaker. It is a basic reason for the Edinburgh Film Festival each year, which strides from success to success as both a meeting-place of people with common interests and common problems and as a forum for showing the world's most important new films that tackle seriously the world's problems.

[1] Cf. pp. 222, 224, 242, 243.

People to People (1955)

I believe that at this Conference in New York it is hoped to set up a national organization to embrace as many film societies in the United States as care to join. That is excellent news. The film society movement all over the world is of first importance to those concerned with making and using films for good international relations. Just before leaving England, I was making a brief survey of the world film society activity. Statistics and information are not to hand for all countries but at a conservative estimate it was possible to say that at least nineteen nations have some 1,500 societies whose total membership must well exceed 330,000. There are societies in nearly every country in Europe, in Japan, in Uruguay, in all the British Commonwealth countries. Since the first film society in the world held its opening performance on October 25, 1925, in London, the need has spread for developing the movement to show new, experimental and off-beat films which do not get a general distribution. Our Unesco film *World Without End*, which was first shown over BBC-Television, achieved a wider audience through film societies and non-theatrical bookings following television in the United Kingdom than if it had been booked into the commercial cinemas, even if it had been considered suitable as entertainment by the film trade, which was not its intention.

A well-organized film society movement is, then, of great cultural importance in international affairs. There is, I believe, an embryonic international federation with headquarters in Paris and if it does not function very reliably as yet, then we must stimulate it to do so or form a new one. That is an activity that should interest Unesco.

If I seem to have dwelt overlong on film societies and the showing of films, and have neglected production, it is only because I have long held the thought that one day the expanding film society movement in the world might provide an economic basis for the making of films of a special kind not suitable for commercial release. It would need much planning and organization and the avoidance of hurting commercial vanities, but I believe it could be done. The fact that you in this country may be about to form a national federation is a landmark in film society history and if it is done it will create much interest in Europe.

But it is very important to see that the great motion picture industries do not view this development as a rival—if only a small one. It is rather a field for experiment for new ideas and new imaginations, without which commercial film-making itself would dry up. The growth of the film society movement and the future prosperity of the film industry should be interrelated and interdependent, from which they could mutually benefit. That is very important to remember.

In any survey, however brief, of international relations in the film field I must not omit mention of the film museums, the institutes, the libraries, archives and *cinémathèques*. Here in New York you are fortunate in having the magnificent Film Library at the Museum of Modern Art, which with its limited resources is doing work that is much admired abroad. You are fortunate, too, in your other collections at Eastman House and out on the Coast. They have, I am told, harmonious relations with the film industry, which is excellent. As you may know, there are similar bodies in Denmark, France, Italy, Switzerland, Sweden, Czechoslovakia and the United Kingdom, as well as the Netherlands and other countries. Very recently the Netherlands Filmmuseum invited me to show some of my films to societies in Amsterdam, Utrecht, Rotterdam, The Hague and other cities, and I found audiences ranging from 750 to 1,500 people thirsting for information about good films from overseas. In this field the International Federation of Film Archives has much to achieve, not unrelated, obviously, to the film society movement and of great future significance to all film industries.

Now perhaps let me say a word or two about the 16 mm. field of operation. I am not myself a 16 mm. film-maker, although I once starred in a 16 mm. film about cowboys and Indians made one sunny Saturday afternoon some years ago on the banks of the Hudson river. But I do believe that the portability and economy of the 16 mm. camera offer increasing opportunities for the experimenter and the pioneer in motion pictures. Where the necessarily exacting needs of commercial movie-making tend to restrict experiment, the sub-standard operator can explore fresh fields of subject-matter and plot exciting new techniques. The lone-wolf film-maker voyaging to the ends of the earth, or merely discovering his own backyard, is a vital contributor to the motion picture's future—and today he's the guy with the

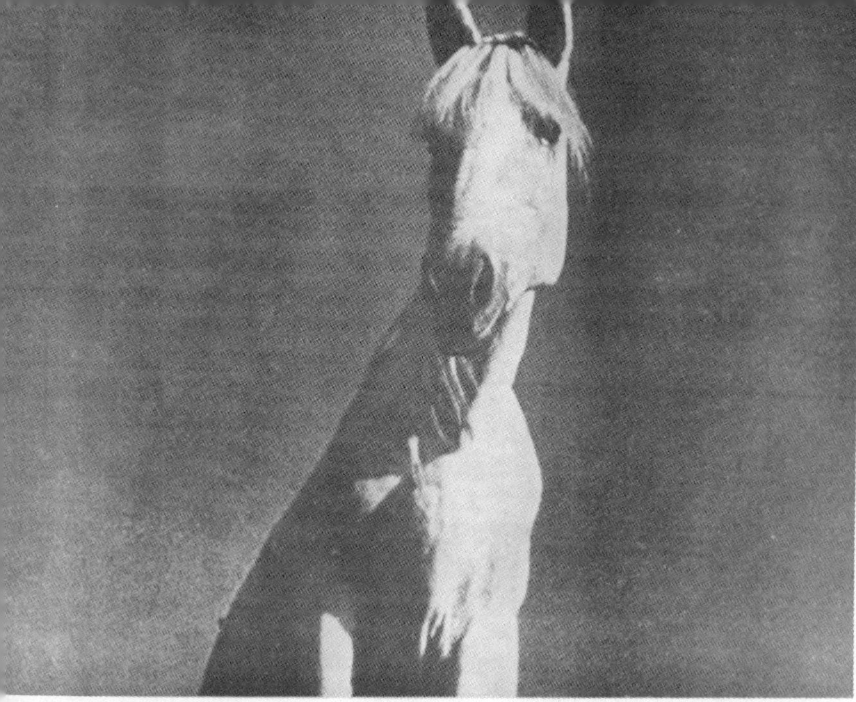

19. (a) EARTH (1930), *directed by* Alexander Dovjenko *in the Ukraine*; *one of the great silent films*. (Vufku-kino) *A frame from the film*

19. (b) DESERTER (1933), *directed by* V. I. Pudovkin, *partly in Hamburg*. (Mejrabpomfilm, U.S.S.R.)

20. (a) Intruder in the Dust (1949), *directed by* Clarence Brown *from a* William Faulkner *novel, with* Juano Fernandez *as the Negro.* (M-G-M)

20. (b) Hunted People (1932), *directed by* Friedrich Feher, *largely made on location in Marseilles*

16 mm. camera. Some of the best colour photography today is being done in the sub-standard field and this is bound to be of importance when colour comes in television.

A word now, perhaps, to the film-makers among you. Lift up your cameras; uncover your tape-recorders! A new era can begin if you go about it the courageous and adventurous way. Twenty-five years ago there were no such bodies as the Film Council of America or the Edinburgh Film Festival. The progress made is staggering and old veterans like myself almost envy the up-and-coming youngsters of today.

But the art of film-making must still be learnt the hard way. Seeing so many films these past few days makes me think that the movie today has lost much of its innate capacity for seeing and revealing—that capacity which the great Robert Flaherty so finely possessed. Movie today talks and shouts and expands itself and, in so doing, has lost something of its wonderful and unique power of revelation. The 16 mm. movie-maker can, if he wants, recapture that power. If that great man Flaherty were alive today and setting off to remake *Moana* or *Nanook*, I am sure he would most seriously consider making them on 16 mm. Tom Stobart could never have shot his *Conquest of Everest* with a 35 mm. camera at 26,000 feet. At the same time, we must remember that Stobart is a professional film-man with documentary training, not an amateur. 16 mm. production needs just as much professional skill as 35 mm. That is often overlooked. Enthusiasm, always welcome, is never a substitute for professionalism.

You will have noted that television has reared its ubiquitous antennae in my remarks. Indeed, you cannot keep it down. The problem with TV is that, unlike the movies, you can never keep up with it. I do not intend tonight to say anything about television as a medium of production in its own right, with all its exciting techniques of immediacy and spontaneity and viewer-participation. But the little screens of television as a means of distribution for motion pictures are something that should interest us all a very great deal. It offers a market of vast scope and possible remuneration, especially to the 16 mm. man. With the rapid spread of television all over the world—there are now more than twenty countries with effective services—here is another tremendously influential factor in international human relations.

Collaboration between several TV countries holds out exciting and stimulating possibilities. An example is a film programme now being jointly produced by the BBC and Unesco to show the social impact of television on the world. Eighteen countries, including the United States, have agreed to collaborate in its production and to shoot special film sequences as called for by my script. When completed, the film will be available for showing in all those countries who contributed to its making.[1] This is *real* international co-operation: a *real* window on the world. Here the specific purpose of mutual world understanding underlies the whole conception.

And so there is today a wide network of personal contacts between individuals who love film and who wish to see it used for better human purpose. It is an untidy and haphazard means of contact but it works in its strange way and will, in time, give rise to these international organizations and federations about which I have briefly spoken.

Scientists have recently given us instruments of untold power about which it is not my brief to talk tonight—but none is of more immediate practical human good than the means of communication between man and man offered to us by the motion picture, radio and television. Let us get ahead to use them to the full so that all peoples may enrich their lives. But let us be very careful that we know *what* we are saying to other people; let us soberly reflect that human relations must be based on *mutual* respect. Only in that way can we perpetuate the dignity of thought and the liberty of outlook which are man's most cherished possessions.

[1] *The Challenge of Television*, first transmitted by BBC-Television, September 3, 1956. Its international importance was ignored by the parochial outlook of British television critics. Even the BBC's hierarchy failed to understand the historic value of such wide nation-to-nation collaboration on a single programme.

II
FILMS IN REVIEW

1931-35

Earth

Dovjenko's *Earth* is presumably one of the last of Russia's contributions to the silent cinema before the Soviets turn their attention to the problems of the sound film. It is all the more interesting, moreover, because Dovjenko's method of working provides a sharp contrast to those of the more exhibitionist directors of the left wing. *Earth* affords an excellent comparison between the violent, feverish styles of Pudovkin and Eisenstein and the peaceful, slow, yet strongly dramatic style of Dovjenko.[1]

Not only this but *Earth*, as well as the earlier work of the same director, marks a different outlook in Soviet production. It attempts the philosophical rather than the sociological or political thematic content. Whilst the subject-matter deals to a certain extent with the contemporary Soviet problem of the adoption of collective farming, as did Eisenstein's *The General Line*, the real intent of *Earth* is the cinematic representation of nature and the expression of a new attitude towards birth, life and death set in an environment of extreme natural beauty. The age-old theme of the supremacy of the new over the old, the Soviet methods overthrowing the ancient privileges of the Kulaki (the rich farmers) and the superiority of the machine over the animal, these are all present, but they are subservient to Dovjenko's beautiful rendering of nature and ingenuousness of the peasant mind. A crude form of propaganda is overcome by a visionary outlook—an outlook that seeks to express the richness and materialism of life. There is nothing glorifying in the coming of the tractor in *Earth*: rather does Dovjenko evoke our sympathy and love for the graceful horses and milk-white

[1] Died, November 25, 1956, aged 62.

oxen whose tasks are now at an end. *Earth* gives us something new in cinema, something which—although slightly similar in technical methods of approach—is a thousand removes distant from the revolutions of an Eisenstein and a Pudovkin or the shuttlecock activities of a Dziga-Vertov.

The slight narrative interest which Dovjenko has written for the theme of *Earth* is remarkable for its simplicity, since any complexity of plot would have impaired the main purpose of the interpretation of nature. In a small village in the Ukraine, the peasants and Kulaki are quarrelling. The youth of the peasants seek to further the setting up of communal farms while the youth of the Kulaki seek to protect the land which is theirs by ancient privilege and right of possession. The fathers of both, rich in experience of toil, watch on, mistrusting the new inventions and at the same time jealous of each other. A tractor is sent by the Government, and Vassily, a young peasant, brings it in triumph into the village. In his joy he drives it across the lands of a Kulak, as the result of which he is shot by Thomas, a Kulak's son, as he returns to his home in the quiet of the night. At the urge of his father, Vassily is buried by his friends not with the customary ceremonies of religion but with the spirit of the new faith, with fruit and songs and joyous belief in this new philosophy; whilst Thomas, his murderer, admits his guilt but is ignored by the singing peasants. That is all.

A calm, slow, measured development distinguishes the opening sequence as Dovjenko gradually absorbs us into his mood. Great expanses of corn and wheat ripple in the wind. There is fruit on the trees, great clusters of apples and pears. We are aware of the luxuriant fertility of the soil, of the sun that ripens and the rain that softens. There are smiling faces, sunflowers and happiness. Amid banks of fruit, surrounded by his son and grandson and great-grandson, an old man lies dying. For many years he has toiled and lived on the fruits of his toil. Death does not mean much to these men of the land. Life takes its natural course. This death is but an incident in the life of something greater. The old man eats an apple and as he does so his eyes wander to a child eating an apple also. The beginning and the end, all is the same with the fruit of the soil. All his life this old man has worked and he has received no medal for it. Medals are only given by the new collective farm and he is too late for that. An interchange of words brings out the primitive beliefs of these peasants. 'Send me word, Peter, what heaven or hell is like.' The old man smiles with happiness and quietly sinks back into death. The whole sequence has been peaceful, marked out by shots held on the screen for a considerable length of time, leisurely and with little movement.

Suddenly we come to the faces of laughing women, to uproarious mirth, blatant and ugly. The cutting quickens with the rise in mood. The women are jeering at the rich Kulak. He is the laughing stock of the village. He resents the overtures of the communal farm. Then we shift to the peasant's house, where the son, Vassily, is trying to convince his father of the need for the communal farm, of which the father is both suspicious and resentful.

Down a long dusty track stretching over the fields, we await the coming of the tractor. The young men have gone out to bring it into the village. The whole landscape seems to be waiting. Grouped in positions of vantage are the peasants, waiting to see for the first time this marvellous machine of which they have heard so much. Even the horses and the cattle are assembled, curious to see their successor make its triumphal entry into the village. The grouping of these shots, each related to the next, is magnificent. A single white cow, two great oxen, a man between two horses; one man, two men, three men standing quite motionless against a sky that is almost black; photographed from below in dramatic perspective. A row of horses' heads, three Kulaks, a single white sleek-flanked mare. Shots arranged in deliberate progression, compositions of superb beauty, expressing anticipation of the sight of the tractor.

Far along the road the machine has broken down. The radiator is empty. At the headquarters of the communal farm they do not believe it. A tractor cannot break down! Backwards and forwards we flash from head to head, split up with titles, 'It's coming!', 'It's stopped!' By their own resource, the peasants refill the radiator and Vassily drives into the village, followed by a cheering crowd.[1] Men look at the tractor and exclaim with surprise, 'It's real!'

[1] In the original version Vassily and his friends fill the radiator by urinating into it, but it is said that the Soviet censors deleted the episode. *Vide*: *Soviet*

We follow with a swift sequence of harvesting. Vassily, delighted with the efficiency of his new love, waves to his father who is scything away as he has done season after season. 'Throw away that old broomstick of yours, Dad.' The cutting quickens as we watch the girls binding and stacking until the whole screen is vibrating with movement. Corn, grain, flour; moving here, there, everywhere. A frenzy of speed and achievement.

Then quietness comes again as evening draws on. Rest and peace descend after the labour of the day. Shadows grow long across the screen. It becomes difficult to see. Layers of creeping mist circle over a pool of water. Groups of men and women stand together, holding hands in the cool of the evening. Supreme in safety, a girl leans her head against her lover's breast. Fingers are entwined with fingers, rough with the touch of corn-stalks. There is perfect stillness in the dusk. Away in the distance the Kulak's son is reeling home, dancing drunkenly from side to side of the road. A neighbour follows and tells him that the tractor has been driven across his fields. Elsewhere, Vassily is returning to the village, his heart filled with joy at the success of his day. It is now almost dark and deathly silent. A horse grazes in the dew-strewn grass. Vassily stops and wonders as his mind is filled with the greatness of life. Gradually he begins to dance, gently at first and then quickly, movements of joy and happiness. Faster and faster he twirls in the dusty cloud at his feet, advancing step by step up the winding white road. The camera retreats before him as he throws his whole heart into this dance of passionate joy, until he comes near the lights in the village. Suddenly, at the height of his movements, he drops flat in the dust. The horse lifts its head, startled by a shot. Vassily lies dead.

The father is stricken with grief. He shouts to the four winds across the expanse of the fields, 'Who has killed my Vassily?' A priest comes to his house but is refused admittance. Instead, the father goes to the communal farm and asks that his son be buried in a manner befitting the new spirit, with songs and hymns to the future instead of with the mockeries of religious pomp. The funeral takes place and Vassily's friend addresses the

Cinema by Thorold Dickinson and Catherine de la Roche, page 31 (Falcon Press, 1948).

crowd. A branch of leaves sweeps across the calm face of the dead boy. Thomas can keep his secret no longer, and running across the field looks down on the people. He clutches at the ground, buries his hands in the earth—his earth by hereditary possession. He shrieks to the crowd that he killed their Vassily —in the night—but they take no notice. He is puzzled and angry and he shouts. But the peasants are too occupied with their singing to listen to him. He screams with dismay, dances the dance of a madman, buries his face in the bare soil. Until finally the film closes with a beautiful series of shots of fruit splashed with rain and the gradual breaking through of the sun. A cluster of apples, three apples, two apples, one apple filling the screen.

So moved am I by Dovjenko's film that I find it difficult to express in words the full meaning of the moving images that are at once lovely in themselves, lovely in sequence and lovely as a unified work of art. So well has Dovjenko welded his separate images into a single, vibrating, immensely powerful whole that it is almost sacrilegious to probe and dissect its construction. The images sweeping from cloud to earth, from fruit to sunflower, from graceful steeds to sturdy oxen, from small figures of men on the distant horizon to great close-ups of heads, are so beautifully arranged that they defy literary description. The gradual changing of mood from silent calm to noisy excitement, from sun to wind and rain is so skilfully effected that we are unconscious of the means employed. The touches of mysticism, the deep feeling for soil, the sensitivity to all that is lovely are so new to the art of the cinema that for the moment we are dumbfounded. We are left with our minds satiated with pleasure, with a curious wonderment as to the birth and origin of what we have just seen.

*

Alexander Dovjenko is, or was, a painter, and his arrangement of pictorial composition and extremely delicate sense of beauty is apparent not only in *Earth* but in his earlier work. Both *Zvenigora* and *Arsenal*, the former a queer mystical fantasy of the changing ideas and strong belief in folk-lore in an Ukrainian village, and the latter an account of revolution in the Ukraine, revealed Dovjenko as one of the most interesting of the Soviet directors. In these two films his technical ability was not sufficiently developed to do justice to his breadth of vision. Although fascinating by reason of their unique conception and use of contrasted static and moving images, they did not reach the high level attained by *Earth.* But despite their uneven qualities they sufficed to show that Dovjenko would very soon develop into a cinematographer of exceptional genius, an expectation that has now been fulfilled in *Earth.*

An intense interest in the life and customs of the Ukrainian people is strongly indicated in all these three films, so much so that portions of *Zvenigora* which dealt with local poetic legend and traditional customs were quite incomprehensible, not only to Western audiences but to people in other parts of Russia. In *Earth* we see this characteristic brought out in the old man listening at the grave of Peter for word of what heaven and hell are like, and in the particular stress laid on dancing—the drunken dance of Thomas, the wonderful death-dance of Vassily and the final frenzied dance of Thomas when he refuses to part with his lands. Moreover, throughout the film we can perceive Dovjenko's peculiar understanding of local types, mentalities and superstitions, a quality that is not to be found in the work of other Soviet directors but which is linked up with Réné Clair's appreciation of human weaknesses, Chaplin's sensitivity to pathos, Griffith's feeling for intimate sentiments and Sjöström's tendency towards poetical lyricism.

Projecting through the beauty of the theme, the new spirit of Russian youth is thrown into relief against the traditions of the older generation. In the Soviet Union today it is the young rising generation which is being systematically schooled into a new form of life as laid down by Lenin. The elders are being left to finish their days in comparative peace so long as they outwardly conform to Soviet doctrines, but the young men and women are being rigorously trained to their tractors and collective farms. This new attitude is expressed throughout *Earth* in the gaiety and enthusiasm of Vassily and his friends, in their delight for the tractor and in their ruthless devotion to the interests of the communal farm. Set against this, we have the older generation typified by Vassily's father at first dubious of his son's keenness for the new methods but converted to the new way of thinking by Vassily's death, and the still older generation in Vassily's grandfather who dies at the opening of the picture. Dovjenko has chosen these types as being representative of the transition that is taking place today, together with the tractor as symbol of the machine that is the god of modern rural Russia. These are the bones to carry the main drive of the film.

I have already made clear the wonderful poetic quality of Dovjenko's work, so implicit in the grassy hillside slopes of *Zvenigora* and even greater in the many magnificent shots of fruit and foliage, animals and landscape in *Earth*, and I repeat that as far as I am aware nothing quite like it has been achieved before on the screen. In my experience, there are few directors who are capable of taking such a fundamental and universal theme as *Earth*, expressing it in terms of visual images on the screen, and translating the poetry of fruit and flowers into cinematic images, as Dovjenko has done, without becoming sentimental. Such a work demands delicacy and restraint of direction, qualities that are most characteristic of Dovjenko's style. In every portion of the film, whether the mood is one of excitement or one of sadness, this admirable restraint carries the theme across with a high degree of emotion. Added to which, Dovjenko maintains a very firm hold over all his material—script, photography and editing. This is evidenced in the exactitude with which each shot and each sequence plays its part in the make-up of the whole. Had he relaxed control for one moment, the intimacy with nature that dominates the film would have been lost. Moreover, the restrained key in which so much of the picture is played greatly amplifies the more exciting moods. This is especially noticeable during the first reel when, after the long, leisured sequence in which old Peter lies dying, Dovjenko abruptly switches to the heads of the laughing women. It is such modulation of mood that goes to the making of a great film.

The artist's mind of Dovjenko, thinking in terms of lovely pictorial compositions with the material on the screen at rest, is apparent in the entire length of *Earth*. He has a strong tendency towards building up mood with a series of static shots approaching the crescendo of a sequence by increasing the grouping value of the screen material—that establishes his painter's outlook. I have referred earlier to the powerful effect of this method of editing in the scene in which the peasants and the animals are awaiting the arrival of the tractor, and we find it employed again in other parts of the picture. In the same manner, the beautiful sequence of the falling of dusk and the gradual creation of the peace and quiet of the hot evening in the village is achieved almost entirely by a slow procession of static shots, each matched perfectly with the other in grouping and intensity of light. From this description, it may perhaps seem that the artist's outlook of Dovjenko would tend to isolate the images, as in Dreyer's *La Passion de Jeanne d'Arc*. But happily Dovjenko is able to think also in terms of cinema, that is to say, in terms of constant movement of the celluloid as well as movement of the material being photographed, with the consequence that his work is doubly effective. As I think correct, his shots rely equally on their compositional value and their time-length on the screen for the full expression of their content. This matter of the artist's static outlook and its relationship to the cinematic outlook of the film director is worthy of considerable study.

By this emphasis on Dovjenko's use of the static image, I do not imply that he eliminates movement of the screen material altogether. That would be absurd. On the contrary, when desirous of employing movement other than that of the celluloid and of the camera, Dovjenko's matching up and intermixing of rhythms is admirable. No better example of screen movement could be found than that of the gradually increasing tempo of the gathering of the harvest, the binding, the stacking, the sifting, the dough-kneading and finally the baking of the bread, the movement being so speeded up that at the finale the whole screen is rocking with energy.

If fault be found with *Earth* at all, I think it lies in the funeral scenes of the last reel. To me these do not reach the beauty or the power of the preceding reels, firstly because they are not conceived in such measured terms of relationship between images and editing as the rest of the film, and secondly because their photographic value does not achieve the same standard as that of the earlier scenes. To make a comparison, I prefer the famous religious procession in *The General Line*, an episode which admittedly marks the height of Eisenstein's work to date, but which nevertheless has a certain affinity to the procession in *Earth.* Whereas in the former film, Eisenstein collected a hundred small movements of both intellectual and physiological significance into one magnificent whole for the expression of the futility of religious belief in the face of nature, Dovjenko in *Earth* conflicts a simple moving mass of people with the isolated figure of Thomas running against the horizon. Eisenstein gathered every thread of his argument and so cleverly interplaited them that, with the aid of brilliant rhythmic cutting, the emotional effect of the scene was tremendous. But Dovjenko loses the threads of his theme, as well as his photographic excellence, and were it not for the sudden compelling madness of the Kulak's son and his remarkable dance, this sequence of Vassily's funeral would be a blemish on the film.

Despite the simplicity of the story, I found the continuity and consequential development of the incidents—especially in the earlier portions—a little difficult to follow. There were certain points of narrative interest which were not clear until I had seen the picture a second and third time. I would add, also, that the priest's visit to Vassily's home seemed poor in dramatic quality and might well have been eliminated except, of course, that it served as anti-religious propaganda.

Some comment should be made on Dovjenko's selection of acting material because, like other of the Soviet naturalistic directors, he disapproves of the use of professional actors and actresses. He is consistent in his employment of actors chosen for their type from the ordinary people, and I am given to understand that he believes every person is capable of playing at least one part for the screen—that of his or her individual character. To contradict this, however, I note that the actor Nicolas Nademski plays both in *Earth* and in *Zvenigora,* his performance in the latter being distinguished by his clever make-up as an old man, an artificiality that surely opposes the creed of naturalism?

These remarks on Dovjenko as a film director would be incomplete if I neglected to stress his wonderful ability to create mood by the relationship of visual images. No words of mine can describe the amazing spirit of youth and vigour with which he contrives to invest the scenes of Vassily and the tractor. I am unable to express the gaiety with which he surrounds the girls as they bind the corn, any more than I can capture the magic of the fruit scenes with their sun and rain or the rising mists from the river. Perhaps it is because Dovjenko is seeing with an artist's mind and setting down the truth of what he sees aloof from any false ideas of entertainment value. Perhaps it is because of his passionate love for the soil, for the fertility and for the beauty of his native Ukraine. Perhaps it is because his marvellous rhythm of emotions runs through man, beast, and land alike. Perhaps because he combines the inspiration of a poet with a rare genius for cinematography. Whatever hidden quality it may be, there can be no denial that Dovjenko now takes his place beside the creative geniuses of the film. Even in such a prolific medium as the cinema it is seldom we see such an emotional and well-made film as *Earth,* especially one with such a perfect blending of creative impulse, technical accomplishment and rich pictorial value. From this point of view, *Earth* is unique.

In the Soviet cinema as we can see it from Britain, Dovjenko projects as an isolated figure quite alien to the main flow of cinematography headed by Eisenstein and Pudovkin. His poetic outlook and his love of mysticism set him apart from the formalist school, with its great interest in technical problems. The simple technique employed by Dovjenko—and it is remarkably simple when compared with the complex montage principles of Eisenstein—is merely a means to an end and not an end in itself.

To the believer in real cinema, Dovjenko's film offers an immensity of feeling, a sensitivity to the progress of life, a susceptibility to heaven and earth and nature, an expression of the building of a new country, in place of an artificial story performed within the limits of a cast-iron studio by made-up actors and actresses who by their ill-assumed sophistication merely succeed in being vulgar. *Earth* is one of the few films in the cinema up till now which means something.

—*Reprinted and abridged from*
CELLULOID: THE FILM TODAY
(*Longmans, Green,* 1931).

The Private Life of Henry VIII

The sensation caused by the first public showing of *The Private Life of Henry VIII* is the main gossip topic of the British movie-world. Generally speaking, the picture has received an unprecedented ovation from the Press here as the dual result of its undoubted excellence and a carefully-planned long-range publicity campaign. By our more responsible critics it has variously been described as a 'good film', a 'great film', a 'Rabelaisian show', and funniest of all, 'a documentary'.

It has been praised as being 'more likely to bring prestige to the British film industry, both at home and abroad, than anything we have done in the whole history of film-making'. It has been attacked as 'defying history and enshrining entertainment, libelling a great period and caricaturing a great King, and being calculated to please any alien element concerned to poke fun at British institutions and ideals'. This last from a dramatic critic.

In the midst of all these superlatives for and against, it is perhaps important to retain a cool head and investigate not the film, but precisely its achievement and what its influence is likely to be in the near future.

The real truth of the matter is this: that it is to the everlasting disgrace of our producers here that it has been left to a charming Hungarian, schooled first in Vienna and Berlin and then in Hollywood, to come to London, form a small company and with discrimination select a bouquet of talented technicians and actors to appear in a picture about British history and traditions.

Quite apart from Alexander Korda's[1] individual ability as a director (and he is no Pabst) there is little in *The Private Life of Henry VIII* which could not have been produced by any

[1] Died London, January 23, 1956

intelligent producer. After all, the skilful photographic craftsmanship of Georges Périnal, one of the outstanding features of the picture, was available to any other producer who cared to employ him. We had already seen his ability in Clair's *A Nous la Liberté*. Similarly, much comment has been made on John Armstrong's costumes. Well, Mr. Armstrong has been designing costumes for several years and would have been delighted, I am sure, to design costumes for any film during that time if any producer had had the sense to ask him. And the same goes for the sundry good-looking girls in the picture. Most of them were extra-players a year or two back. As to Laughton's Henry himself, well he has always been there for the using.

In making this film Korda has shown up the ossified sterility of British producers and has clearly demonstrated that the stumbling block in the way of progress for British films is not the lack of technical knowledge, or histrionic ability, or good-looking women, or equipment, or the British climate but simply the sheer inability of our producers to recognize and employ good talent.

Recently I was talking with a well-known Hollywood writer-producer, a man of wide movie experience and intelligence, who has been visiting the studios in and around London.[1] He remarked in particular upon the absence of young directors. He seemed puzzled that almost every picture which goes on-the-floor is assigned either to a veteran or to a stage producer. He contrasted the directors now working on a certain Hollywood lot with the directors of a British studio. Whereas the American company included several directors in their mid-twenties with only one or two pictures to their banner, the British studio boasted little save greybeards. British producers have always been frightened of youth, alibi-ing themselves on the grounds of the lack of money for experiment. This attitude is, of course, sheer idiocy and reveals all the more plainly how easy it has been for a man like Korda to sail in and produce the first significant 'British' film.

This is not suggesting that Korda's task was easy. It was far from that. He risked a great deal in making a costume picture. He risked more in being unable to secure a release for

[1] B. P. Schulberg, of Paramount, died 1957.

his picture in advance. He threw all his resources into this picture and he has pulled it off. But no matter how great its success, it would be foolish to imagine that this single film will change the attitude of our Methuselah executives. For Korda it will mean, I hope, an assured future. For British films it will mean just one picture of which we may be proud. But it offers no hope of changed attitudes in the general studio kingdom.

As an example of courage and confidence Korda's film will receive tremendous praise but this must not blind us to its real meaning as a film. For British audiences it is brilliant entertainment. It is polished, hugely amusing in a smutty way and luxurious in production value. But it is not, I suggest, the ideal of a good film and Korda would be the first to admit it. In his position it was the ideal picture to have made. But a picture in itself is not enough. It must serve a purpose beyond itself if it is to live and have meaning.

—PHILADELPHIA PUBLIC LEDGER
and NEW YORK POST, *November* 21, 1933.

I Was a Spy

When a picture evokes almost unanimous praise from the popular critics, I always feel that we should approach the gilded shrine on bended knees. True, Gaumont's new *opus* has not been likened unto a 'mountain peak dominating the surrounding landscape', but I think it might well be described as a bump impeding the traffic of the Strand. We have been asked so many times by our Sunday papers to give the Gaumont boys a big hand that it must have become a habit with us poor writers, but I must confess that Saville's new picture brought me up with a jerk in my seat. Let me describe it.

The story is taken from the adventures of Mlle Marthe Cnockaert, a Belgian, who nursed German wounded in the small market town of Roulers during 1915, for which duties she was awarded the Iron Cross. While thus engaged, she was persuaded to undertake espionage work on behalf of the British, causing cylinder dumps to be blown up and sending information which led to Allied aircraft bombing German troops at prayer. At length, her duplicity (or heroism, according to taste) was discovered by the Town Kommandant, but she contrived to avoid the extreme penalty by amazing good fortune. Such is the material from which the film is constructed, with suitable additions in the form of a love-interest and a bawdy week-end in Brussels.

Here we tread carefully. As was expected, there is no attempt to show the unvarnished truth of war nor even its stupidity. The cause of war is assiduously ignored. From this viewpoint the picture has no social value. But, acutely self-conscious of his difficult theme, Saville at least has laid the guilt for war barbarity equally on each conflicting army. The Germans employ poison-gas in the field while the British drop bombs on their enemies at prayer. So far, so good. Among the opening titles, however, is a prefatory note by no less a worthy than Winston Churchill, from which we gather that the job of a spy is gallant, courageous and heroic, enlisting at outset our sympathy for Marthe (Madeleine Carroll) and 'her side'. I wonder if that same tribute would have been included had Marthe been of English nationality? Only recently it was proclaimed from every roof-top that no Englishman, or was it Briton, could be guilty of espionage. This apart, a final note of patriotism is struck in the closing sequence when the British occupy evacuated Roulers and Miss Carroll's face lights up with ecstatic joy as the pipers lead the procession. We cry 'For England and the Right'.

Technically, there is much to offend if reckoning be made of the picture's cost. Saville's camera approach is frank and industrious, the set-ups being chosen on pictorial rather than dramatic context grounds. When his camera drops low, I failed to observe its significance. Admittedly, he has not been aided photographically. The presentation of the Roulers set built on the lot at Welwyn Garden City does not do justice to its architect. The long shots are grey and poorly exposed. The marching of troops is dull and repetitive. Of cutting for dramatic effect I noticed little, but deplored the constant use of wipe-dissolves to cover the weak continuity. The direction of players seemed uncontrolled. Conrad Veidt assumed his usual dominance. Carroll tried bravely, sometimes looked attractive, but broke down before Veidt's superiority. Nevertheless, she remains perhaps England's only intelligent female star. Herbert Marshall was not permitted to forget his canopy value, and the part might well have been given to a lesser-known player. Of the smaller roles, I have nothing but praise, except that Donald Calthrop's barnstorming methods are becoming tedious.

And so I raise my hat to Gaumont for attempting a film of serious stature, but replace it when I see the spirit in which the deed is done.

—CINEMA QUARTERLY, *Autumn*, 1933.

Hunted People

(Le Loup-Garou)

Little seems to be known as to how this picture came to be made, when or where it was produced, or even who financed it. It opens with a fancy impression of Marseilles—the docks, the narrow streets, the steel bridge, the Ministry of Justice—and then by means of the viaduct along the coast takes us to the little village of Longville. Here a stout, middle-aged and prosperous joiner has just been married for the second time. He has risen in the world and has secured as his new wife the pretty daughter of the mayor. But while the nuptial festivities are at their height the local *gendarmerie* has identified the husband in a photograph of the bridal pair published in the Press as none other than an escaped convict. According to the law of France, the husband cannot be reimprisoned if he has eluded capture for ten years. Needless to say, the ten years are up except for two days.

A *gendarme* presents himself at the house. Immediately the jolly joiner knows the game is up, but he decides to make a run for it. Accompanied by his small son, Boubou, he contrives to get away from the guarded house by hiding in a coffin (a good piece of cinema, this) while his wife and guests are still making merry. He jumps a lift on a train, escapes in a tunnel and wanders about the streets of Marseilles. At every corner he hears a broadcast description of himself and his son. He secures a change of clothes for them both from a pawnbroker (admirably played by our old friend Vladimir Sokolov), sleeps with the down-and-outs in the docks, is disturbed by the fort sentries, makes a dash for a fair-ground where the legless lady in a freak show turns out to be the sister of the woman he is supposed to have murdered and who really committed the crime herself.

In all this you will see ordinary melodrama without any

distinction. But three things lift the film above the conventional: the treatment, the acting and the music.

In these days of 'come-up-and-see-me' entertainment it is seldom we come across a film which is built on an analysis of a single mood. For that we must go right back to the tradition of the early Germans—to *The Street*, *New Year's Eve*, and *The Phantom Carriage*. The events in Feher's film are immaterial. There is one situation at the beginning; the rest is logical conclusion. The fast-moving sequences are simply a framework on which to hang a study of fear, a grim paralysis of body and soul such as only the German cinema used to express with full horror.

The fat jolly joiner, who is suddenly seized with a paroxysm of fear that his carefully-built-up life will be shattered, is played by that stage actor, Eugen Klöpfer, whom you will recall in *The Street*, *New Year's Eve*, *Martin Luther* and *The Earl of Essex*. He has the true Germanic laboured style of heavy movements, which remind you of Jannings. But it is his acting, drawn out by Feher's handling, that largely makes this picture interesting. His acting spreads beyond him, envelops the environment, bends the material to his will, just as Veidt did in *The Student of Prague* or Wegener in *The Golem*. But it has this difference, that unlike the early German films it is played largely against an authentic background. The streets and alleys of Marseilles play as great a part in the building of the fear mood as the bogey man of Boubou's imagination. That is where Feher has been clever.

Although no credit is given for the music, it is obviously specially written for the film. Its phrasing is admirably in sympathy with the changes of mood. It swells to a climax, cuts sharp to silence, builds slowly again and so on. It is essentially an accompaniment emphasizing the action. I found it singularly successful.

—CINEMA QUARTERLY, *Winter*, 1933.

La Maternelle

This surely is the child-picture to end child-pictures for the time being; and no better picture could be found to mark a semi-colon in this vogue for child actors. But let me say outright that this is in many ways an admirable film, most intelligently made, and played on all sides with a tenderness and sensibility that compel respect. It is a story of Rose who, disappointed in love and deserted by her fiancé, takes work as a nursemaid in a children's school. Among the kids is Marie, whose mother is a tart, and thus the child is left much alone. She is known to the staff as being 'difficult', in that her mentality is curiously complex. Her particular liking for animals plays an important part in events. When the old cook is about to throw a live mouse into the fire, it is Marie who struggles and bites to prevent the creature from being harmed. And as you expect, Marie's queer aloofness attracts to her the suppressed Rose. When, once again, little Marie sees a man taking away her beloved one, just as she had seen her mother depart, the child throws herself into the river. A rescue is effected.

Not particularly well-edited or photographed, the picture is notable for its brilliant treatment of the child-mind. The two directors, Jean Benoit-Lévy and Marie Epstein, are to be congratulated on their knowledge of child-psychology. Throughout there are frequent incidents which reveal a deep understanding of children's mind-behaviour, from the little boy who cannot smile to the odd, twisted attitude adopted by Marie when she is unhappy. The naturalness of the characterization on the part of the adults and of their attitude towards the children—one of the most difficult things to obtain on the screen—demands particular praise. Comedy is plentiful but is never forced. Sympathy is forthcoming for even the headmistress. Her moronic mind is presented so naturally that her narrowness of outlook is to be pitied rather than condemned. Such sympathetic handling is all the more remarkable when we consider that no single player could be described as being physically likeable. Even little Marie, with her crooked teeth, sticking-out plaits and wan, thin face, is hardly attractive, and yet our sympathy is wholly with her. There are many emotionally disturbing moments; the final scene, when the doctor and Marie shake hands and become friends, is among the high spots of the year's cinema.

The production as a whole is unpretentious, singularly free from novelty technique and obviously inexpensive. In no other country but France would such a theme be considered movie, and yet it teaches every producer in Britain and America the value of psychology and treatment in movie-approach. Apart from its general appeal, which should be wide, it is a film which I should like to see shown to every school-teacher and worker in child-welfare organizations. They would find much to learn.

—CINEMA QUARTERLY, *Winter*, 1933.

Deserter

We owe a debt of gratitude to the London Film Society for importing this new Pudovkin film, for although it may not take us with fire, as did *Storm Over Asia* and *Mother*, it is nevertheless a sizeable attempt which demands serious consideration.

In *Deserter* Pudovkin[1] tries to cover a greater social canvas than perhaps any director before him, selecting a theme more complex and wide-meaning than any yet tackled by the Soviet film industry. I confess to being unable to describe the material in detail. In its giant stride the narrative embraces most of the vital social problems of a harassed world today—the struggle between the classes, unemployment and poverty, the tragedy brought about by economic crises, the suffering of the working-class, new hope in new leaderships, new ideals and new generations. There is tragedy, deep-down and stark. There is comedy, transient but catching. There is satire, penetrating and unanswerable. Whatever its faults, and it has many, its director was inspired, and that is a sign of greatness. By its very stature the picture is awe-inspiring. Perhaps only a Pudovkin could have attempted the task and only a Pudovkin could have fallen short of success by so small a margin of failure.

In brief, the central figure is a dock-worker in the Hamburg shipyards, involved in endless strikes and wage disputes. He is chosen as a delegate to the Soviet Union, where he decides to remain and join in the work of the Five-Year Plan. But he realizes that he is a deserter to his comrades in Germany and returns to take up the struggle on his native soil.

The relation of the German worker to the mass is maintained by dialectic argument. Long and frequent passages of dialogue, treated in the crudest newsreel method, serve to put across the

[1] Died Moscow, July 1, 1953.

Marxist ideology. To an audience with no knowledge of the Russian language these are naturally the dullest moments, relieved only by the sudden crises of strike and conflict. The first part of the film is probably the better. Pudovkin has always excelled at setting the stage and the initial statement of his argument. You will recall *St. Petersburg* and *Storm Over Asia* in this respect. The sequences in the shipbuilding yards at Hamburg, the weakening of the strikers and the final breaking of the strike by blacklegs and machine-guns are the finest descriptive passages. Yet even in these I felt that Pudovkin failed to get below the surface of the incidents. His proletarian meetings did not get my sympathy. There was no sense in the shouting mouths of workers. They behaved like bawling agitators and not like workmen fighting for their rights. By now, also, I had imagined that Pudovkin had realized the futility of exaggeration, but still here is the capitalist presented as a worthless, half-witted maniac, too lazy to speak, too tired to yawn. The generalization is so grossly distorted, the effigy so patently childish, that the social purpose fails to score. Pudovkin cannot afford to lie, no matter what propaganda is served. It weakens his case and destroys our attention.

Technically, the film is as uneven as the presentation of its theme. Moments of inspired direction and brilliant cutting are alternated with long passages of mediocre cinematics which do not seem the work of the same man. Here and there flashes of technical skill stab us in the dark—falling chains, riveters at work, a riot with the police, a suicide in the street. But they are all too rare amid the monotonous treatment of the dialogue scenes. The sound is handled carefully and is based on a theory of conflicts. Unlike most opinions, I found some of it effective. Shaporin's music was well edited with actual sounds. At times it was used to create audience emotion in direct contradiction to the visual images. Gay music accompanies a suicide, busy traffic is cut to the rhythm of a waltz to express the lazy luxury of the capitalist world, with the policeman at point-duty performing the dual tasks of conductor of traffic and music. But against all this we must bear with long, ugly silences and black-outs, disjointed and irritating.

Two years of toil have gone into the making of this strange

mixture. With *A Simple Case* Pudovkin entered a side-track, seeking to impose formal method on theme. With *Deserter* he has penetrated further into the wilderness. I cannot help but admire his courage and inspiration, his integrity and knowledge; who are we to say whether he is right or wrong when the cinematic ground he is treading is still unexplored?

—CINEMA QUARTERLY, *Winter*, 1933.

Queen Christina

I do not find it in me to write about this picture; it would be too cruel. I must write instead of Garbo, who contrives, though Heaven knows how, to surpass all the badness they thrust upon her. Of her many Hollywood pictures, all without exception have been trash; yet this astonishing woman surmounts the very crudity with which they choose to surround her. Here, a lithe figure sheathed in men's breeches and with stamping boots, she strides into our presence and again reveals her dynamic personal magnetism. She is a woman, it seems, destined to continue in a world that spells misunderstanding. No director who has tried to harness these grave features to his will has yet been able to create a film which brings us the woman as she is. *Queen Christina* perhaps comes nearest; with its great close-ups and sublime fading shot. But the showman tricks of Mamoulian and the base falseness of the environment conspire against her. Before it is too late, before the synthetic background against which she moves takes final reckoning, may she, like this old-time Queen of Sweden, set her back to the call of glamour and give herself just once into the hands of a mind which may try to understand her, so that such a film above all others may be preserved for posterity. That this imagined picture can only find its shape in Europe I have no doubt.

—CINEMA QUARTERLY, *Spring*, 1934.

Jew Süss

Nine years ago Feuchtwanger ushered in a new era of historical fiction by writing what is to some minds the greatest historical novel of the century. *Jew Süss*, the film, might have ended an era of costume pictures by in turn being the best effort of its kind. Instead it continues the vogue which Korda must be given the credit of starting.[1] But because of what *Süss* might have meant for cinema in general and British films in particular, because of the widespread discussion it must provoke, and because in some ways it is a very ambitious endeavour, it deserves greater space than the other historical pictures of the year.

With his magnificent opening chapter, Feuchtwanger set the scale for his whole story of the Jew. We were conscious at once of the wide horizons of eighteenth century Europe, of the bustle and life and intrigue within these limits of Württemberg. Everything that followed, the craft, the guile, the whoring, the praying, the intriguing, the private struggles and public issues fell into place on this vast canvas. Everything had significance within the boundaries of the epoch. Therein lay the greatness of the author's approach. It is precisely this vision, this magnitude of mind, that the film does not possess.

The book has been well pilfered. All the plums are here, all the bombastic moments, all the bloody minutes, all the natty spectacle and all the shining pomp. On the surface it spreads a grand array. Men talk of doing this and doing that, but never do we see them doing it. Süss declares his lust for power, becomes the Duke's prop, is the indispensable and hated Jew, but why and how he contrives these things is a mystery. Never are we taken beneath the gilded scene, never are the real issues behind Süss's behaviour or the economic motives underlying

[1] With *The Private Life of Henry VIII*.

the political intrigue revealed. Here is no cross-section of the eighteenth century which might have been such grand material for cinema. The film is founded on the superficial appearance of men and things.

This is no destructive broadside. The film is too big for that, big enough to stand criticism. Big in money. So big that all the furniture, the costumes, the jewels, the nick-nacks and baubles might well have been ticketed with their hire-price. I remember some publicity about the countless dozen tulips for Süss's garden, real tulips. But, alas, they mean little on the screen. They are overdone. It is all overdone. Except taste, which is absent. There is nothing of the finer qualities of observation and selection, of the instinctive feeling for what is right and what is wrong. There is no modulation or balance. That is a director's job and that, I think, is where Mendes fails to qualify for the task. Why, I wonder, was Lothar Mendes chosen to make this film? His previous record shows *The Four Feathers*, *Love Makes Us Blind* and *Dangerous Curves*—all probably estimable pictures of their kind, but that kind was not *Jew Süss*. Small wonder, then, at the opportunities missed. The climax, for example. Why ignore Feuchtwanger's special emphasis on the iron cage and its history, when it offered such dynamic reference to the hanging?

Veidt we have watched since Cesare in *Caligari*. A parade of Borgia, Nelson, Ivan, Baldwin, Orlac, Louis XI, Gwynplaine, Rasputin, and Jew. They are all here. The demoniacal laugh, the furrowed brows, the straying locks of hair. He shares with Garbo a physique rich in photogenic meaning. But since he has lost touch with significant direction, he has given way more and more to mannerisms. Some call this 'great acting'. It is powerful but it is not great. With the exception of Cedric Hardwicke, most of the others over-act, with Frank Vosper's Karl Alexander the worst offence. Scarcely any 'wear' their clothes save the dignified Gerald du Maurier, who alone of the company appears to know how to manage his sword when he sits down. But the part of Weissensee, important in the book, is so clipped that, from the anxious expression on his face, Sir Gerald must have been bewildered at his own presence. The sets are lavish; but then Jünge can do this sort of thing standing on his head. Did he not design hunting-lodges for Franz Joseph?

What, then, is the result? I do not believe that anyone will ever make better, if as good, historical films than did the Germans in their heyday—*Federicus Rex*, *Dubarry* and *Manon Lescaut*. They gave everything (save fantasy) that cinema has to give in their attempt to bring alive the past. And they achieved nothing better than museum value. When shall we realize that the camera belongs to the present, that its concern is with actuality not artificiality?[1] The newsreel of the Marseilles assassination shown in this same programme proves this better than my theory.[2] Its chance rendering of a living (and dying) moment transfixed the audience. What chance had the mere several hundred thousand odd pounds of *Jew Süss* against reality?

—Cinema Quarterly, *Autumn*, 1934.

[1] Cf. *History on the Screen*, p. 65.

[2] One of the most famous newsreel scoops in history—Gaumont-British's coverage of the assassination of King Alexander of Yugoslavia, Marseilles, October 9, 1934.

Sanders of the River

Zoltan Korda's *Sanders* follows the movie pattern set by *Trader Horn*. Here are the same old Murchison Falls as a background to palaver and war-dance (those Murchison Falls to which conducted tours from nearby Kampala and En Tebbe are weekly affairs), the same eagerly snatched chances for black nudity, almost the same friendly faces of the local natives. What else did you expect?

A unit in Uganda with, I suspect, no script that mattered. A bright idea: Paul Robeson. Corollary: Nina Mae McKinney. Weeks and weeks of Africa—built at Shepperton and Elstree (they forgot the clouds are different)—and Negroes dug from agents' files and café bars. Later, much later, some hints thrown out by *Bengal Lancer*. It's Jubilee Year as well. So this is Africa, ladies and gentlemen, wild, untamed Africa before your very eyes, where the White Man rules by kindness and the Union Jack means peace!

You may, like me, feel embarrassed for Robeson. To portray on the public screen one of your own people as a smiling but cunning rogue, as clay in a woman's hands (especially when she is of the sophisticated American brand), as toady to the White Man, is no small feat. With Wimperis's lyrics of stabbing and killing, with a little son to hoist around, with a hearth-rug round his loins, a medallion on his navel, and a plaster forest through which to stalk, what more could Robeson do, save not appear at all?[1] For the others, they do not matter. Just one moment in this film lives. Those aeroplane scenes of galloping herds across the Attic Plains.

It is important to remember that the multitudes of *this*

[1] I am told on good authority that on the night of the première in London, Robeson—having just seen the complete film for the first time—locked himself in a dressing-room and refused to make a personal appearance on the stage.—P.R.

country who see Africa in this film are being encouraged to believe this fudge is real. It is a disturbing thought. To exploit the past is the historian's loss. To exploit the present means, in this case, the disgrace of a Continent. What reception will it get in Africa? Similar, perhaps, to that of *Bengal Lancer* in India, *The Scarlet Pimpernel* in France, *Red Ensign* on the Clyde. Who cares? It is only entertainment, after all! Sursum Korda!

—CINEMA QUARTERLY, *Spring*, 1935.

Man of Aran

Hope has been built upon hope around this picture of Flaherty's, for at last here was the father of documentary with an honest break to do something big in a manner after his own heart. Two long years in the making, month after month of waiting by us poor folk who knock out a humble living at backdoor documentary, and the film is here to give us more or less what we expected and something else beyond. In all respects it is the best work that Flaherty has done in cinema and in its particular sphere represents the furthest lengths to which documentary of this sort has been taken. But I would lay emphasis on category, for *Man of Aran* pursues only one of the several paths of documentary and must be considered only within those limits.

There are moments in the film when the instinctive caressing of the camera over the movements of a boy fishing or of men against the horizon brings a flutter to your senses; so beautiful in feeling and so perfect in realization that their image is indelible. And again there are softer passages where you have to collect your thoughts and wonder if the sequence construction is built up quite so firmly as documentary of any kind demands; and whether dawdling over a woman carrying wet seaweed across the shore, beautiful in itself to behold, does not tend to weaken the main shape of the picture. It might be that two minds have disagreed, each seeking the major issue of the theme and each finding a different answer. Either the dramatic grandeur of the sea or the thrill of the sharks must take precedence, but they disturbingly share the peak between them. So great is Flaherty's shooting of the sea (nothing like it has ever before been seen on the screen) and so overwhelming the sweep of the Atlantic that the sharks, I feel, are commonplace.

It is true that they spell box-office to the commercial mind, but in such a film as this these considerations should be superfluous.

Beyond this small point, raised only because of the film's stature, *Man of Aran* is unique for its quality of visual loveliness. Seldom have such superb scenes lightened the movie-screen. Only in previous Flaherty pictures have we seen that anticipation and awareness of natural movement which is Flaherty's particular genius. Here and there were scenes which I could watch a dozen times, lingering over the selection of camera set-ups and admiring the smooth grace of the camera's action. Flaherty can give us a boy casting a line, a man repairing his boat or a stone being split into fragments more superbly than any other director, but his relation of these to the wider theme of the whole is a matter open to discussion.

The absence of any artificial narrative is a final justification of the documentary approach to cinema. Here is the living scene as it appeared to Flaherty recreated in terms of living cinema. Its complete success serves to show up the humbug of those epics of the Frozen North and Hot Africa to which we have so often been subjected. In the control of his human material, Flaherty has shown us the value of restraint. His approach is wholly impersonal. What really happens on Innishmore is not his or our concern in this conception. At no moment is there 'acting' in the sense that the word is customarily used. His characters are normal persons doing things which are normal to them. But because of Flaherty's approach this normality has been transmuted into an idyllic work.

Descending to technical details, Goldman has made a solid job of the editing under Flaherty's supervision and Greenwood has written some quite good music which is not well recorded. The dialogue, some of which is in Gaelic, I found unnecessary, but not disturbing. Special mention should be made of John Taylor, a recruit from the Empire Market Board Film Unit, who assisted Flaherty throughout the production.

As this appears, *Man of Aran* will be in the cinemas. It remains to be seen what people will make of it. So far all concerned in its birth and growth, from producing firm to laboratory worker, deserve congratulation; and this does not exclude the publicity which has accompanied the production and exhibition of the film. Its fate, and incidentally that of much unborn documentary, will lie in the purses of the public.

—SIGHT AND SOUND, *Summer*, 1934.

1950–51

Neo-Realism

We start with New Year luck. A brilliant film is on view in London; in my opinion the most brilliant film for many years. It reaffirms all one's faith in the cinema. It fulfils hopes long held. It proves conclusively (if anyone doubted it) that a man with ideas and skill, with a simple story and a movie-camera can still make a film which outshines all the gaudy expensive products of the film factories. This is the real art of cinematography.

Vittoria De Sica's *Bicycle Thieves* arrives here garlanded with international prizes and praise unstinted from critics both American and European. It deserves them all. His *Shoeshine* will be remembered. Here is a story of an out-of-work, gaunt-faced man in an industrial suburb of Rome—the sort of Rome you do not usually see on the screen. Here is his wife, patient yet desperate in her struggle to keep things going. And here is their young son, eager, puzzled, wanting to help and understand. Then comes the chance of a job, bill-posting, but only if the man has a bicycle. He has, in pawn. So in its place goes the bed-linen. The wonderful next day dawns with work to be done. But within the hour, the bicycle is stolen. With it goes all, save the faint hope that the thief can be found. The search begins and goes on all Sunday. The bicycle is not found, the thief is; but there are no witnesses. In utter despair, finally, the man himself steals a bicycle—one among the hundreds he sees around him. He is chased, caught but generously released. He walks home with his son through the crowds.

All my life I shall wonder what happened to Antonio, to his son and wife—and then I realize it was all a story. No bicycle; no sheets. It only happened for the camera. Antonio is really

21. Bicycle Thieves (1948–49), Vittorio De Sica's *masterpiece from* Cesare Zavattini's *script*. (P.D.S.)

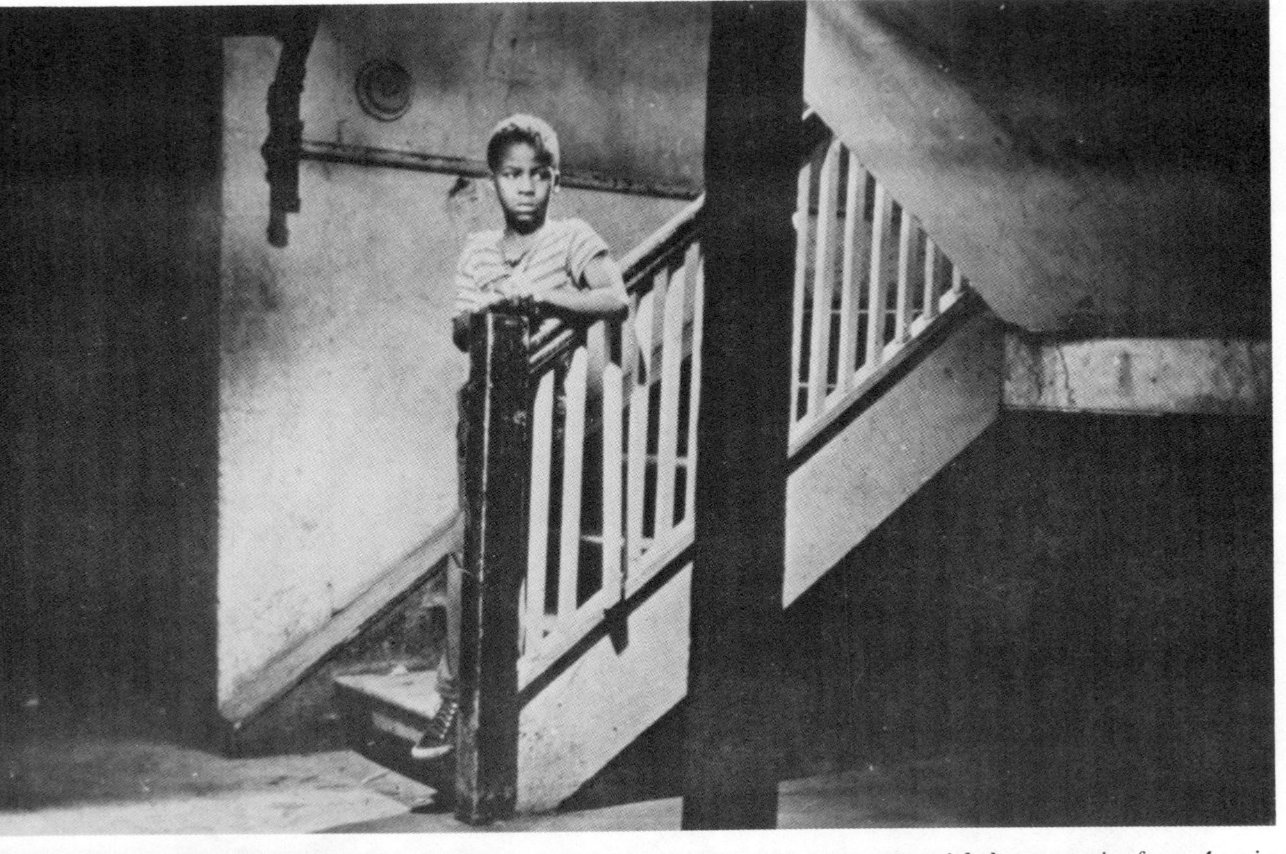

[illegible] social documentaries from America

Lamberto Maggiorani, a metal-worker from Breda. Says De Sica, 'He left his own work for two months to lend his face to me.' The boy, Bruno, is Enzo Staiola, 'the most lovable child in the world . . . son of refugees whom I met by accident.' The rest of the characters, with only one exception, are also real people. The surroundings are not sets in the studio; they are the streets, the markets, the passages, the little rooms, the stark concrete blocks of flats, the very reality of workaday Rome.

They say this is a simple film because the basic story is simple. To me it is not a simple film; underneath the few events and the handful of characters is the profundity of a wealth of human experience and a wide range of cinematic skill. It is not easy to film real life except as raw newsreel record. It is fantastically difficult to film a drama of events taking place in real surroundings where the director seems to have control over the very crowds and traffic of Rome. To make things even harder, De Sica deliberately chose to set one of his incidents in a torrential downpour of rain, which meant that in the remaining sequences the streets and pavements had to be wet to preserve visual continuity. Throughout, the photography is magnificent. The American *Naked City* had a naïve crime story superimposed on some real filming of New York. *Bicycle Thieves* has a deeply emotional, intensely human story arising from, and an inseparable part of, post-war Rome. I know of no other film that catches and dramatizes everyday existence and shapes it to tell a story with such subtlety, observation and penetration. Comparisons are a waste of time. This is not a pioneer picture but a deeply-rooted milestone that will be looked back on for many years. It is a complete vindication of the man with the camera and a conscience.

From the opening scene on the steps of the Labour Exchange to the closing shot of the camera moving with Antonio and his weeping son along the thronged pavements at dusk, one wonderfully subtle sequence follows another to create the pattern of the whole. The covey of young priests sheltering from the rain, the cabaret rehearsal taking place alongside the political meeting, the piles of bed-linen reaching high up to the pawnshop ceiling, the chase among the outraged girls in the brothel out-of-hours, the epileptic fit of the thief in the sun-drenched back street and the crowd ganging in to protect him, the dumb little gathering of believers in the fortune-teller's bedroom, the meal in the restaurant when Antonio tries to restore his son's confidence in him, these are only a few of the thousand images which pursue me from this film. And the little moments within a scene: the expression on the fortune-teller's face when the boy tries to give the fee to her instead of to the maid, the police-superintendent more concerned with the armed jeeps getting to the labour meeting than with a workman's stolen bicycle, Maria venting her bitter anger on the zinc wash-tub—these moments reveal De Sica as a director to be placed on the level of Stroheim and Pudovkin at their very best.

Satire is there, deliberate barbed shafts that hurt where they are intended to hurt. I have no sympathy for the wounded in this battle against poverty and humiliation. I have no use for the hypocrisies of the well-off. I side with De Sica in his stinging comments on the care handed out to the poor herded into the soup-kitchen church.

The search for the stolen bicycle could easily have been just another search, but it is paralleled with an expression of the relationship between father and son that is moving in the extreme. Universal in its appeal, it cannot adequately be described. Frustrated and angry in their abortive search, Antonio abruptly and without cause strikes his son. The moments that follow leading up to the father's sudden thought that the boy has thrown himself into the river are handled with a psychological understanding and a skill of cinema that are unique in many years of films. It is no use talking of this child's 'acting'; it is behaviour, not acting. The look in this boy's eyes, his movements and reactions, are not acted. Between him and De Sica, between the others in this film and De Sica, lies a secret something to which only a great film director knows the answer. We cannot probe it; we can only admire it.

Nothing is irrelevant in this film. What speech there is relates only to essentials. The music of Allessandro Cicognini is beautifully unobtrusive, there when needed and then sparingly. Fundamentally it is a visual film. De Sica and his cameraman, Carlo Montuori, tell it all through the eye. 'To see,' says De Sica, 'is very useful to an artist. Most men do not want to see because often the pain of others troubles them. We, on the contrary, want to see.' And he sees not only tragedy, pain and pathos but humour, joy and laughter. The film, although tragic, is full of comedy. Some will call its ending inconclusive. How, in truth, could it be otherwise?

Let Mr. Rank, balance sheet in hand, observe this film. Let Sir Alex stroke his leonine head in envy, for here is something that will live longer and give more pleasure than all the reconstructions of Tolstoi and Wilde. Let Mr. James Lawrie (of the Film Finance Corporation) forget for a moment to be photographed with film stars and mark how a film can be made on a shoestring if the genius, the ideas and the purpose are there. Let the producers, directors and other makers of films in our academies and unions look humbly at a work which burns with sincerity and technical brilliance. *Bicycle Thieves* is a true work of cinema which, if exhibitors everywhere have an eye to good business, will satisfy audiences of every kind. But it is useless to play it between the Huggetts last week and Betty Grable next week. It offers a challenge to exhibitors, not to their audiences. It must be presented with a new kind of showmanship that must be learnt for other films as well as this if the industry is to survive.

—PUBLIC OPINION, *January* 6, 1950.

Dark Victory

Perhaps the most intriguing thing about the American cinema is its trick of delivering, without warning, an outstanding film. For weeks on end, reel after reel of the same old candy-floss oozes on to the screens. Tipsters signal us from the other side to look out for this or that. Suddenly, with no advance build-up, up pops a picture for which we can forgive Hollywood some of its habitual disregard for the adult-going cinema audience. Such a film is M-G-M's *Intruder in the Dust*.

It is a pity that this should be the fourth American film recently to reach British screens dealing with the Negro dilemma. *Home of the Brave*, *Pinky* and *Lost Boundaries* (although not made in that order) may to some extent have tired British audiences of this very important social subject. *Intruder in the Dust* is head-and-shoulders above these three. I hope, indeed, that it will outlive them and secure the widest bookings. It deserves our warm support.

Clarence Brown, the director, must now be a man over sixty and has been making pictures for many years. *The Goose Woman* with Louise Dresser as far back as 1925 brought him to notice. Since then he has directed many M-G-M successes—*Flesh and the Devil*, *Anna Christie* and *Anna Karenina* (all with Garbo) and in later years *The White Cliffs of Dover* and *National Velvet*. I should never have suspected that he had it in him to make such a sincere film as this adaptation of William Faulkner's novel.

Although the end-title bears the legend 'Made in Hollywood, U.S.A.', *Intruder in the Dust* was largely shot in real surroundings in Oxford, Mississippi, Faulkner's home-town. Faulkner himself is said to have had quite a hand in the shooting. It is the story of an old, proud and dignified Negro who has been left a plot of land, and his sojourn in the town gaol under the threat of being lynched while four Whites, a lawyer, the Sheriff, a young boy and a little old lady, make it their business—albeit somewhat reluctantly at first—to prove his innocence of murdering a White farmer. That they are finally successful brings no real satisfaction because all four realize that the White intolerance, born out of ignorance and fear, will persist. Even the Negro whose life is saved gives no thanks but with pride settles his debt to the lawyer whose conscience, prompted by the boy and the little old lady, finally caused him to act.

The film gains immeasurably from its understatement. Here is none of the hysteria and frenzy that whipped up the mob in Fritz Lang's *Fury*. Instead, here is a Saturday in a dry, dusty Mississippi small town turned into a holiday because of the prospect of a lynching. The horror of this situation becomes intense because of its apparent casual inevitability. A Negro, respected and liked in his locality, has been found by a White man's shot body. He has a pistol in his pocket. Nobody questions his guilt. Nobody troubles to see if the bullet which killed came from the Negro's pistol. A Negro has shot a White man. The unwritten custom is to lynch. So they come into town with their children as if for a holiday outing. The loudspeakers blare music, the children play yo-yo, a girl waves a rattle, a woman makes-up, and the ignorant dumb bastards of men just stand around and watch the doors of the gaol, waiting for 'the fun' to start. Only the Negroes stay home; the side-walks are all-White this day. But the little old lady, scared stiff and fortified only by her conscience, takes up a position of strategy. She sits and does her mending in a rocking-chair just inside the gaol doors. Even the threat of being set on fire with petrol fails to shift her. While she staves off 'the fun', the Sheriff, the lawyer and the boy are finding the evidence to release the Negro.

My praise for this film is high. Its calm, unhurried style is dead right. Some sequences are not so well directed as others; for example, the opening-up of the grave at night is poorly done. But in all it is a wonderful achievement aided not a little by some superb acting. The Negro, Lucas, is played by Juano Hernandez with a strength, a dignity and a restraint that are deeply impressive. His final scene in the lawyer's office when he pays his debt and his massive, black frock-coated figure as it strides slowly across Main Street to be lost in the crowd is something long to be remembered. Elizabeth Patterson's little old lady, David Brian's lawyer and Claude Jarman Jr.'s young boy are all beautifully handled. Above all, the atmosphere of the town itself is so amazingly well caught. The loitering crowds, the automobile-choked street, the little front gardens, the well-lined village store, the Negro's overcrowded cabin, these are utterly convincing because they are real. In presenting them the camerawork of Robert Surtees is admirable.

Intruder in the Dust is the first film to portray honestly the dilemma of Negro-White relations in the United States. It offers no easy solutions. It states a case. But it is not negative. By demonstrating that the courage and belief in rightness of a small handful of persons can defeat, if only temporarily, the brute, ignorant sadism of the mob, it has done a fine thing. You cannot reason with ignorance; you can only fight it with courage. Few have the courage to stand up against the mob. When they do, they win.

M-G-M deserve great credit for having made this film; I do not understand how and why they did, but they did. Perhaps Doré Schary is the answer?

—PUBLIC OPINION, *February* 10, 1950.

Test Case

Coming to British cinemas soon is a film which is a test case. It is made by an independent producer who took the speculative chance of completing his picture without knowing in advance that he would get distribution. When it was ready, a distributor agreed to take the film but the booking-managers of the three big cinema circuits turned it down.

Now failure to get a circuit-booking for a film in Britain virtually means financial death to a producer. True, there are more independent cinemas than the aggregate of the circuits, but they are in the main the smaller ones and many are competitive houses. Faced with this refusal, the producer showed his film to the Cripps Selection Committee, set up in 1946 by Sir Stafford Cripps for this very purpose of helping independent producers secure circuit distribution.[1] To date this machinery has been little used for the obvious reason that since it only passes judgement on a completed film, finance is almost impossible to obtain for a film that might be rejected by this Committee *after* the money has been spent. The Committee saw the film in question, liked it and unanimously agreed that one of the three circuits *must* legally accept and show it, in addition to the independent bookings that it may achieve.

Thus a unique position is established. One of the three big circuits is compelled to exhibit a film which it has rejected in the normal way. All kinds of queries arise. What kind of presentation will the circuit give it, presentational publicity meaning so much to a film's success? Will it be issued as a first feature, or passed off as a second feature so that its share of takings will be proportionately less? If the film is a success with the public, will the circuit exploit that success for the benefit of the producer, or deliberately 'play down' the picture as has been

[1] *Vide* pp. 282, 292, 293, 296.

done before? It is worth remembering that Mr. Rank entered the distribution and exhibition sides of the British film industry because he could not get a fair distribution for his own first feature film, *Turn of the Tide.* It happens that one of Mr. Rank's two circuits, Odeon Theatres, is the one chosen by drawing straws to accept this film unwillingly. I hope Mr. Rank now remembers his own experience with *Turn of the Tide.*

What of the film? It is called *Chance of a Lifetime* and is produced and directed by Bernard Miles, well-known as a character actor, from a story he wrote in collaboration with Walter Greenwood. Its main actor, in addition to Miles, is Basil Radford. It is a first-rate piece of entertainment, well-made technically, well acted and in places very amusing. Why, then, did the circuits refuse the film? For 'political' reasons, it is said. What nonsense!

Here is the story in brief. A small factory makes tractors. It is very much a one-man company. A trifling incident causes a strike. The owner, in a moment of temper while addressing the employees, challenges them to take over the responsibilities and worries of running the firm. To his surprise, they accept. He walks out and takes an enforced holiday. The workers appoint representatives and to begin with all goes with a swing. But trouble arises; a big order is cancelled; the bank refuses facilities, and so on. The owner, unable to keep away from his work, returns and helps the workers' management out of its mess. Owner and operatives shake hands. Labour and Capital settle down together. Highly dangerous political dynamite? It is really a little essay in labour relations, fair to both sides and most unprovocative, with a happy compromise ending.

From a production point of view, of course, the film is revolutionary. Is that why the circuits, who are part and parcel of the studios, don't like it? *Chance of a Lifetime* is made in the documentary manner. No studios were rented for it. Instead, Bernard Miles and his unit shot most of the film in the disused half of a woollen mill in the Cotswolds, and all the other locations are real. This was probably not much cheaper than shooting in a studio but it is a great deal more convincing. The whole film to me was authentic. That is more than can be said of most Denham and Pinewood pictures.

As the factory owner, Basil Radford gives an admirable performance. What a calm, polished actor he is! Bernard Miles has learned to restrain his sometimes too-folksy characters and his portrayal of one of the opposition is one of the best things he has done. Well-rounded pieces of characterization come from many in the cast, too numerous to mention. On the technical side, Bernard Miles shrewdly used Alan Osbiston as his co-director. Osbiston has learned his job the hard way, has graduated from the cutting-room, and if given chances in the future has all the signs of becoming a first-rate director. Eric Cross, the cameraman, has a fine record and in this film he adds to his achievements. Photography in these conditions must have raised some hard problems but Cross has turned in a highly creditable job. And the many others in the unit, from production-manager to clapper-boy, deserve praise.

If given a fair distribution deal, with the Board of Trade keeping a watchful eye on the proceedings, I cannot but estimate that this test case will be a full success. If it is, Bernard Miles and his merry men will have created a precedent and given new hope to other independent producers and directors who are really interested in making worthwhile pictures. It is out of projects such as this that a genuine British cinema can be developed.

—PUBLIC OPINION, *March* 10, 1950.

Too Hot to Handle

Lovers of real American jazz—not the commercial swing put out on millions of discs and over the radio stations *ad nauseam*—have waited for many years for Hollywood to get around to Miss Dorothy Baker's book, *Young Man with a Horn*. We thought that here was a subject, alive, vibrant and contemporary, that just could not be mussed up. The story of Rick Martin, as everybody knows, was based loosely but in essentials accurately on the story of the legendary Bix Beiderbecke, the first hot cornet-player of the 'twenties who was also the first White musician to adopt the Negro style of hot jazz. He learnt from those ace trumpet-players Louis Armstrong and Joe Smith but he developed an emotional tone which drew from him through his instrument his whole personality. His vibrato, that no one ever equalled for subtlety, his strong and pure tone, his amazing skill for improvization—these caused him to be almost worshipped until his early death from pneumonia at twenty-six in 1931. Miss Baker's novel fictionalizes but never loses the basic honesty to music which was the lifeblood of that group of musicians.

Warner Brothers have not filmed Dorothy Baker's book. They have taken some of its characters, changed their names and colour around a bit, adapted some of the situations, used snatches of the original dialogue and produced a hybrid called *Young Man of Music*. Here are some of the 'adaptations' surgically performed by screenwriters Carl Foreman and Edmund H. North. In the novel, Rick Martin's introduction to jazz comes through his beautiful friendship with Smoke Jordan, a Negro who works alongside him at Gandy's Pool Hall. That friendship lasts through Rick's life. In the film, Smoke Jordan becomes Smoke Willoughby, a White pianist played by Hoagy Carmichael, who doesn't appear until Rick has learnt his music from Art Hazzard, a Negro trumpeter. Smoke has a sister called Josephine, a singer who is unimportant in the book. In the film, Josephine becomes a White girl crooner played by Doris Day who loves Rick all along and eventually marries him. And so on.

Why *do* they do it? Why take Dorothy Baker's book about Bix Beiderbecke alias Rick Martin and castrate it? It is impossible, it seems, for a Hollywood studio to adapt a book without losing the essence of it. They must 'dress it up'. I think back to Charles Jackson's *The Lost Week-end*, Eric Knight's *This Above All*, Raymond Chandler's *The Big Sleep* and *The High Window*. They were all mussed up. It is elementary that any work of fiction needs adaptation to the screen, but there is a wide difference between adapting for the film's special technique and distorting characters and events to suit some mythical commercial aim. To some extent I can comprehend Hollywood producers doing this with books about subjects and places of which they know nothing. But with jazz, the real jazz that came from the Mississippi Delta and moved north to Chicago (where Bix was at his best), there is no excuse. Even the music in this Warner picture is wrong style. Where are the famous tunes such as *Chinaboy*, which the Wolverines and Bix improvised for one long hour to cover up a gang fight on New Year's Eve, 1923, at a roadhouse called the Stockton Club near Cincinnati?

So in *Young Man of Music* Kirk Douglas acts much as he did in *The Champion*, though now he's a trumpet-player. He looks like a boxer all through. Doris Day sings herself along as Josephine, all white and soft instead of being Lena Horne. I felt sorry for Lauren Bacall as Amy North, the 'intellectual' Rick married. Maybe she should have been a boxer too! Hoagy Carmichael opens and ends the picture with a soulful reminiscence, cigarette, forelock and all. I wonder if he remembers playing the piano with the Wolverines at a dance at a University of Indiana fraternity house, of which he later wrote in *Metronome* these words: 'I saw Bix get out his cornet and Jimmy told him to take the break in the middle of the chorus. He did. Bix just played four notes and that wound up the afternoon party. The notes were beautiful and perfectly timed. The notes weren't blown—they were hit, like a mallet hits a chime, and his tone had a richness that can only come from the heart. I rose violently from the piano bench and fell, exhausted, on to a davenport.'

To lovers of good musicals, I recommend M-G-M's *On the Town* (at the Empire), directed by Gene Kelly and Stanley Donen. It has an opening sequence fusing the speed, singing and dancing of a musical with the real-life background of New York that is breath-taking. There is a sequence soon after that set in the Museum of Natural History that for timing, rhythm and humour is better than anything for years. The pace of the first twenty minutes is too hot to hold, but it is the best musical since *Cover Girl.*

—PUBLIC OPINION, *March* 31, 1950.

Made with Modesty (1)

I make no apology for telling you about a film you may never see—unless you ask for it. It is being publicly shown in America, but here it has only been screened at the Edinburgh Festival (in 1948) and by the enterprising New London Film Society the other Sunday. In New York by those who know it is considered the most important social documentary film since before the war. Called *The Quiet One*, it was made without any fuss on miniature film, but it has now been enlarged up to normal cinema size.

It is the story of a little Negro boy in Harlem, a boy whose mother has no time for him. He is farmed out to his grandmother, who in turn has her own troubles of trying to exist. Completely alone, desperate with fear, finding no place in life at all, Donald eventually commits the terrible crime of hurling a brick through a plate-glass window. He finds himself in the Wiltwyck School for Boys, who produced the film in conjunction with Miss Janice Loeb. Under the special care and observation of the principal, the boy's problems are gradually revealed and to a great extent solved. This is the bare bones of the story. On the screen, it is told partly at first hand and partly by the most intelligent use of flashback. We start in the school and the child's background comes into focus in relation to his present behaviour by the most skilful telling of past events. The present and the past are brilliantly juxtaposed.

The Quiet One was directed by Sidney Meyers, but Janice Loeb and Helen Leavitt, who worked on the story, photography and editing, contributed much. Meyers came into films as far back as 1934 and as 'Robert Stebbins' worked on several early American documentaries—*China Strikes Back, People of the Cumberland* and *White Flood.* During the war he served as a film editor to both British Information Services in New York and the Office of War Information, but his natural modesty let others take credit for the fine work he did. After the war, when documentary workers were no longer wanted, he formed a small unit, Film Documents Inc., and *The Quiet One* was its first film. It cost 20,000 dollars and it is satisfying to know that it has more than paid for itself.

It is a film of which any Hollywood or British director might be very proud. The use of significant detail, the building up of atmosphere, the essentially visual way in which we understand the working of the boy's mind, the really brilliant way in which the people (there are no professional actors) are handled or observed unconsciously—these reveal cinematic skill of the highest order. There are no elaborate technicalities, no tricks or devices, but every shot is subtly planned without your being conscious of it. Composition and use of camera deserve to rank with the best of cinema. The film was shot silent but has had a remarkably intelligent sound-track added to it. There is narration, beautifully written and spoken, and there is dialogue used not in direct relation with the speaker. The boy says only one word all through the film—'Mamam'. The overall result is extraordinary: a most moving, important and memorable film.

In many ways, just at this present moment, *The Quiet One* is an object lesson to directors who have surrounded themselves with all the expensive technical refinements of the studio. How much they could learn from it! The fact is that the more elaborate and mechanically perfect film-making has become, the less directors have had to say and the less effectively they have used their medium. Everything about the cinema has overgrown itself. Films cost far too much, are over-publicized, are over-analysed and over-perfected technologically. Now that so much of film-making has become industrialized, rationalized and monopolized, there is little room for the individual with something to say and a love for his medium. He merely gets in the way of the machine filling thousands of screens for a twice-weekly change. So we look for the real examples of the medium way outside and find, on this occasion, a little-heralded picture made on sub-standard stock for a few thousand dollars, but made with an imagination, sensitivity, understanding and knowledge of what film can do.

—Public Opinion, *June* 1, 1950.

Made with Modesty (2)

Along with *Bicycle Thieves*, which has had a six-month run in London, *Jour de Fête* proves yet again that really good film-making depends not on the resources of large studios, or on huge bank loans, or on armies of technicians and pantechnicons of equipment but on the use of imagination and ideas and a simple approach to the medium. At a time when still more public money is being directed into British film-making, it is very important for us to learn the lesson of these Italian and French pictures. Good films can be made reasonably cheaply by small independent film units and can be profitable if the renting and exhibiting interests realize that not the whole of the British public wants to be fed on factory-made, glamorized pap. A wide audience awaits the provincial showing of *Bicycle Thieves* and *Jour de Fête* if exhibitors will book and publicize these films, wide enough anyway to ensure a successful return.

The day is coming in the cinema when the costly, glossy, constipated, studio-produced picture on stereotyped subjects, and with typed stars built up by publicity, will no longer attract the mass-audience. Film-making will become again an intensely individual process, less costly, less organized, less glamorized and less pre-calculated than Hollywood has made it with the British organizations foolishly trying to copy. A wonderful opportunity lies in front of British film-financiers if they understand that a new approach to production is needed, and if those in control of public money legislated to help British films also perform their duties with full responsibility.

Jour de Fête is a richly humorous, delightfully simple piece made by a brilliantly clever comedian called Jacques Tati. Almost the whole film was made in a little village in the Indre-et-Loire where the small unit of actors and technicians lived for six months. The story hardly exists but a series of wonderfully spontaneous incidents keeps alive the action, most of which is centred round the village postman. (The device of having the highlights and gossip of the village pointed out by a bent old crone seemed to me an unhappy mistake.) What matters is the apparent freshness and naturalness of everyone and everything, and, of course, the essential mime acting of the central character.

Jacques Tati, it appears, was a rugger-player who made a hobby of mimicking other sportsmen and athletes. He became a professional music-hall turn, made some not very good 'quickie' films and then with Henri Marquet decided to gamble on *Jour de Fête* in the manner described. That is exactly the way good films can and should be made. It is perfectly obvious that Tati has studied cinema, has realized the sensitive interpretive powers of the camera-lens and has controlled all his sense of timing and mimic gesture to that end. To that extent, he can be compared with Chaplin but there the comparison ends. Chaplin has devoted his life to building up one character. Tati's *Le Facteur* will not, I think, appear in the next Tati film. A new character will, I hope, be invented. The ancient Peugeot bicycle, which becomes a machine with a mind and purpose of its own, will surely be replaced by another instrument with which Tati can display his genius for improvization. The same village will not again, I hope, become a location for a film. The world is surely large enough for cinema to explore it for many years without duplication.

Although the telling of *Jour de Fête* is mainly visual, great care has also been paid to the sound-track, not only to its sparing use of speech but to the natural sounds of the countryside. The bee (or hornet) that pursues Tati so viciously, the hens and the cows—they all come alive in the sound-track with success. The music of the village band and of the roundabout are contributory factors. In fact, and this is an essential point to grasp, the film is conceived as a whole. Comic and clever as Tati may be, he is also a contributory factor. *Jour de Fête* is not, as some critics suggest, a one-man piece although it may be a one-man conception.

—PUBLIC OPINION, *July* 13, 1950.

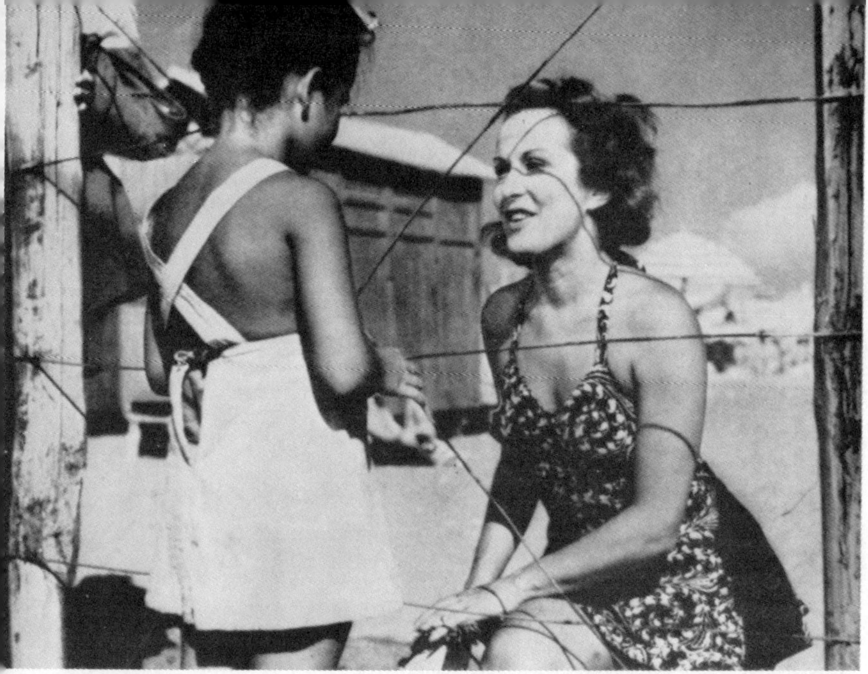

23. (a) SUNDAY IN AUGUST (1950), Luciano Emmer's *social comedy of a Roman week-end.* (Colonna Films)

23. (b) BORN YESTERDAY (1951), *directed by* George Cukor *from* Garson Kanin's *satire on the Washington merry-go-round, with* Judy Holliday *and* William Holden. (Columbia Pictures)

24. (a) Ace In The Hole (1950), *directed by* Billy Wilder, *with* Kirk Douglas. (Paramount)

24. (b) Il Bidone (The Swindlers), (1955), *directed by* Federico Fellini, *with* (*left to right*) Richard Basehart, Broderick Crawford *and* Franco Fabrizi. (Italian-French co-production, Titanus-S.G.C.)

Living History

The career of Louis de Rochement in cinema has been distinguished. Associated for many years with the monthly issue of *March of Time*, he did fine work in the war years by supervizing and editing such memorable combat pictures as *Memphis Belle* and *The Fighting Lady*. More recently, he took the hard, journalistic, factual approach into commercial production. *The House on 92nd Street*, *Boomerang* and *Lost Boundaries*, all produced by him, were box-office successes as well as examples of the wedding between the documentary approach and commercial feature production. A man of great energy, strength of purpose and versatility, de Rochement has long been fascinated by the possibilities of compiling actual newsreel recorded events into a coherent, meaningful whole. In 1932 he made *The Cry of the World* from stock material, and followed nearly ten years later at March of Time with the feature-length mixture of compilation and re-enaction, *The Ramparts We Watch*. The editing of the authentic material was more successful than the staged events which strung the thing together.

Last year, de Rochement completed another mammoth task, a compilation called *The Golden Twenties*, the story of the Jazz Age, based roughly on Frederick Lewis Allen's famous informal history of the 'twenties *Only Yesterday*. The film was shown privately a few days ago and it is unfortunately not the intention of 20th-Century Fox to release it publicly in Britain. It is, I suppose they feel, too American in interest. While agreeing that its appeal might be restricted, at the same time it is a pity that such a fascinating collection of historic moving pictures is denied to the specialist cinemas and the film societies. Perhaps 20th-Century will think again?

Allen's book has, in point of fact, been used before as a film basis although I do not recall if acknowledgement was paid to

L

him at the time. Gilbert Seldes and Frederic Ullmann's *This is America* in 1933 was certainly inspired by *Only Yesterday.* Ullmann later continued the title for the monthly series he produced for RKO-Radio when *March of Time's* distribution was switched to 20th-Century Fox. De Rochement's new version is a brave attempt to weld hundreds of disconnected persons and events into a coherent picture of the American 'way of life' in those golden days that succeeded World War I.

Obviously the major problem of a compilation film is to find the theme; secondly, to find a method of telling it that avoids the collection of vault material becoming merely a catalogue. The socio-politico-economic line of argument that held Allen's book together so well (and that made later attempts at the same thing appear pale imitations), does not transcribe into film terms. It is not sufficient to tie pictures together in rough chronological sequence using a different narrator for politics, sport, entertainment and so on. An overall framework is needed into which the many events can be fitted. The device invented by de Rochement of a young student going to the public library to read up material for an essay on a chunk of American history is too corny and too thin to engage us. It lacks edge and comment. What was needed, perhaps, is the kind of approach developed towards social history by the late Dr. Otto Neurath, used in 1945 in an M.O.I. short called *Total War in Britain.* Photographs, even when moving and with words added, cannot explain structural trends, still less make clear the motives that inspire events. Realizing this, no doubt, de Rochement relies on his mixture of voices to explain his film, forgetting that when the eye is held by the very authenticity of the screen's pictures, the ear pays little retentive heed to the soundtrack. This, I feel, is the reason for the failure of *The Golden Twenties* as a social document. It resolves itself into a catalogue evoking only comment from the politician that there is too much sport and from the sportsman that there is too much sociology.

The material itself is inevitably fascinating and of great historical interest. Here, in the age of marathon dancing, pole-sitting and human flies, are Woodrow Wilson, Warren Harding, Calvin Coolidge and Herbert Hoover (raising his hat three times for the benefit of the photographers). Here is J. P. Morgan snooping out of his Wall Street window but he was abroad when a bomb explosion rocked the stronghold of American finance. Here are Sacco and Vanzetti, victims of the 'Red' scare, reminding us that political hysteria is no new thing in the American 'way of life'. Here are the K.K.K., the strike-breakers, the bootleggers, the gangsters to exhibit the fierce sadism that runs so near to the surface of the American 'way of life'. Here are clips from the memorable movies of the period with Doug. Fairbanks, Garbo, Chaplin, Will Rogers, Valentino, Gloria Swanson and that breaker-of-the-silence Al Jolson. Here is the wild scramble for real estate, the Florida boom, the Florida hurricane. In front of our eyes is the 'long count' on Gene Tunney, the tall strip of Big Bill Tilden, the wrinkled face of Babe Ruth, the wizardry of Houdini. Pavlova and Chaliapin feed the swans. Harry Lauder leads a pipe-band up the boat-deck. Coolidge is initiated as a Red Indian. Lindbergh sets out in 'The Spirit of St. Louis'. Visitor after visitor arrives from Europe 'to see for themselves'—Wells, Galsworthy, Conrad, Caruso. 'Ticker-tape welcomes' down Broadway punctuate the period. And then—the Great Crash—the avalanches of October 24 and 29, 1929. The era ends.

Said President Wilson when he was shown Griffith's *Birth of a Nation*, 'This is history written with lightning'. Here is history revealed with a vengeance!

—PUBLIC OPINION, *July* 20, 1950.

The Writing on the Wall

The Americans have a term—'think-film'. Mme Nicole Védrès's *La Vie Commence Demain* is a definite 'think-film', so much so that it has the doubtful honour of being the first British 'X' certificate film; that is to say, children under 16 cannot see it with or without an adult. Considering that the world's children are the most likely audience to be affected by Mme Védrès's message to mankind, this seems a pity.

On a French country road, Jean-Pierre Aumont tries in vain to thumb a ride. An obliging helicopter descends and a journalist, André Labarthe, offers him a lift to Paris. Jean-Pierre is out to see the conventional sights of the capital—the Conciergerie, the Mint, the Waxworks, but M. Labarthe soon persuades him that today and tomorrow are more exciting than yesterday. After a brisk little visit to an existentialist night-spot (where a number named Dominique appears), Labarthe dispatches Jean-Pierre to see Jean-Paul Sartre, who rather rudely accuses Jean-Pierre (and all of us) of being responsible for the appalling state of world affairs today. Jean-Pierre then moves on through a series of meetings with those personalities whose thinking and work can affect the future. After an uneventful interview with Daniel Lagache, the psychologist, he has a frightening time with a charming old gentleman called Jean Rostand, an eminent biologist, who tells (and shows) him all about sex-transformations, artificial insemination, fatherless babies and such delights. Next he visits Le Corbusier at the top of his part-completed monster block of flats at Marseilles, where the architect makes some sensible points about building for the future. Then for a quick drop-in on Picasso, in patterned shirt and abbreviated trunks, moulding some very lovely pottery, and a ten-minute look-see with André Gide who is preoccupied with the wonders of a tape-recorder. Finally,

Labarthe whisks him off to a Unesco session, at which a terrifying vision is presented of the horrors of atomic energy. A vista is put before us of all the powers of science for constructive good or destructive decline. It is according to the will of governments and politicians. This is presumably where the meeting with Communist Professor Joliot-Curie took place which has been discreetly deleted from this version of the film. We all end up at Versailles, where for the first time in history Labarthe's helicopter alights to transport a mystified but mentally superior Jean-Pierre back to the provinces from which he came, accompanied by Dominique who has reappeared.

La Vie Commence Demain is a striking, sincere, provoking and challenging film, certainly to be seen. It makes a direct appeal to our intelligence to awake from our apathy and prevent civilization from going down the slippery slope to oblivion. It should be shown daily at the United Nations. Every Foreign Minister should be compelled to see it every Sunday morning. It should be widely translated and distributed free to the cinemas of the world.

It could, however, have been a better film. The editing is scrappy and petulant. The various interviews are wooden and amateur. A highly-complex argument like this needs extreme simplicity of technique and a mastery of presentation. There are times when all is an utter confusion of words, titles, pictures and music. One's mind is stunned by the film's impact and one's reason, to which Mme Védrès is appealing, is incapable of reaction because of the muddle of ideas and messages. The music by Darius Milhaud does something to smooth out the corrugations. Mme Védrès is a brave trier but next time she must content herself with being producer and engage a really skilled director and editor to carry out the work. The message would then go deeper and wider. A call to action needs words of one syllable; this film throws the dictionary at you.

—Public Opinion, *January* 19, 1951.

Beside the Seaside

The Italian cinema is rich in writers. Notable among them is Sergio Amidei, an influential but unpublicized figure behind some of the best Italian films, including Rossellini's *Open City* and *Paisan.* A native of Trieste, Amidei has been 'in films' a long time. He has now become a producer with his own company, Colonna Films. His first picture, for which he also wrote the story, is *Sunday in August.* His director is Luciana Emmer, known up till now for his remarkable films about classical paintings, especially the ones on Giotto, Bosch and della Francesca. This is his first story picture, after a distinguished career in documentary.

Like the best of the Italian films, *Sunday in August* goes to real everyday life for its material. It is the story of how on a blazing hot Sunday, all the Romans who can stream out to the beach at Ostia, where they disport themselves according to taste and means. Emmer selects five such groups and only in two cases do the characters intermix. From a deserted and baking city, the rich and the not-so-rich pour out to the sea in every form of transport; the shiny automobiles, the packed smelling trains, the bicycles and scooters—all head for the beach. A boundless family arrives by decrepit taxicab; quarrelling, shouting, gesticulating as only Italians can. A bunch of youths, complete with a cheeky urchin, race there on bicycles. A pretty girl from a block of tenements quarrels with her boyfriend from childhood and streaks to the sea with a play-boy. And so on. Once on the hot sandy beach, the groups sort themselves out and are segregated, again according to means. Small incidents arise logically—some humorous, some sentimental, some tragic. Behind in half-empty, blistering Rome, a traffic policeman and his girl untangle their domestic troubles. The pretty girl's boy gets involved in an attempted robbery. Beautifully the separate stories are interwoven until the day ends and the return to the city is made. Tangled ends are unravelled and new relationships are born.

Using a few professionals and many amateurs, Emmer has used his camera simply but with what enchanting visual effect! Dialogue is there (clumsily translated in English sub-titles) and carries undoubtedly much wit and humour, but it is primarily a visual film. Emmer is a sensitive observer of the unrehearsed, which he blends magically with his directed sequences. He has what is lacking in most directors, a gentle sense of flow through the camera. Each new shot takes his film forward. What singles out this film from the casual run of pictures is its interest in people—just ordinary believable people. Some critics have likened *Sunday in August* to Carol Reed's early film *Bank Holiday*. The comparison is unhappy. Emmer's film breathes with natural, instinctive warmth and realism. Reed's picture was a completely theatrical, studio-minded approach. Untainted and uninhibited by studio complexes, Emmer goes straight to reality and reshapes it, moulds it, interprets it into his individual conception. The freshness and vitality of this approach would be hard to capture by a director brought up in studio conventions. *Sunday in August* is not a masterpiece. It is a gentle, highly observant, sincere example of film-making which promised much for its director's future work.

By coincidence, the London Film Club showed this week that delightful and witty short piece, *Muscle Beach*, which has attracted attention wherever it has been presented. Joseph Strick and Irving Lerner shot this picture on a beach near Los Angeles where athletes and sportsmen, acrobats, vaudeville artistes and a few ordinary folk go to relax and keep fit. The beautifully shot visuals are cut to match some amusing, satirical lyrics written by Edwin Rolfe and sung by Earl Robinson, who composed the music. Its opening is rhythmic and quite serious, but gradually as the film develops a devastating satirical approach creeps in. It is a highly original and refreshing piece of filmcraft and deserves a wide showing; a pity it did not accompany *Sunday in August*. The two together would have made an ironic social comment on our times.

—Public Opinion, *January* 26, 1951.

Into Battle

When the war's end was in sight, several feature films about war subjects were either withdrawn from release, or not issued at all. Producers expect to take that risk when dealing with topical themes. John Ford's remarkable *They Were Expendable* had a small showing in Britain, William Wellman's sincere *The Story of G.I. Joe* had little recognition, while Lewis Milestone's *A Walk in the Sun* was not even presented here. Now, with commendable imagination—and perhaps good business acumen, judging by the success they are having with a reissue of the same director's *All Quiet on the Western Front*—Eros Films have secured the British rights of *A Walk in the Sun.*

Made in 1945, Milestone's film was one of the few that tried honestly to express what the soldier in the field was really thinking and feeling. It tried to show the effect of war on men's minds. Based very closely, almost word for word, on Harry Brown's short novel of the previous year, I cannot remember such an accurate and successful transcription of book into film. Mr. Brown knew what he was writing about and Robert Rossen's screen-play has lost nothing. The dialogue is almost unchanged. The story is simplicity itself. An American platoon of the Texas Division lands on the beaches at Salerno in 1943. Its lieutenant is killed. The senior sergeant goes to find the captain but does not come back. Strafed by low-flying planes, another sergeant takes over. The platoon make for their objective, a farmhouse six miles inland. In the war and yet not feeling part of it, they meet an American despatch-rider who knows less than they do. He goes off to reconnoitre but fails to return. Two Italian deserters appear, are questioned without result and left behind. A German armoured car is met, bombed and destroyed. At length the farmhouse is sighted. It is occupied by the enemy. A bloody battle ensues, a vital bridge is blown up, and the story ends. Nothing more elaborate than that.

Despite its subject, this is not a war film in the sense that the recent *Battleground*, *Task Force* and *Korea Patrol* are war films. It has no mock heroics. It is a film about a group of men who hate what they are doing; who are courageous, frightened, brave, hysterical, funny, profane, as happens to men in such conditions. None of them is a born soldier. They are civilians, wanting to get on with the job and get back home. With a full-scale battle going on all round them, their nerves and heroism would make out fine. But alone on this little strip of Italian coast, with no officer in charge, a sergeant who cracks up simply because he can take no more, they are confused and fed up until they rally finally against the unknown and unseen and achieve their objective.

Of the group of a dozen or so men on which the film concentrates, the individual characters and personalities are made to stand out by the art of sheer observation. You know all about them; their attitudes and ambitions, their likes and dislikes, where they come from and what they want to get back to—unless, as says one, they'll be fighting the Battle of Tibet in 1958. Well acted, with crisp, witty dialogue that smells of the real thing, the film is immensely human, warm and understanding. Milestone has directed with a skill of camerawork and editing seldom seen today. The authenticity and naturalism are utterly convincing, although the film itself was made in California. The moments of sudden action—the low-flying bombing attack, the assault on the farmhouse, the destruction of the armoured car—are brilliantly and excitingly done. Most of the actors were practically unknown outside of America at the time the picture was made. They include Dana Andrews, Richard Conte, Sterling Holloway, George Tyne, John Ireland, Lloyd Bridges, Herbert Rudley, Richard Benedict. Several have become 'names' since then. The camerawork by Russell Harlen is outstanding, with fluid movement and fine compositions.

The film has faults. The opening sequence as the barge heads for the beaches is slow and static; it could have been one-third the length. The suspense passages between action points are perhaps a little too long. There is possibly over-much wisecrack dialogue. I am not sure about the use of the Earl Robinson ballad, nor did I like the boy's letter to his sister. But to this critic, these flaws are secondary in a film that is deeply moving and leaves a lasting impression. I urge you to see it: I shall, several more times.

—PUBLIC OPINION, *February* 23, 1951.

Love in Transit

The introduction by the British Board of Film Censors of an 'X' certificate is making itself felt. The new French picture by Max Ophüls, *La Ronde*, would certainly have been denuded of some of its wittiest and most human moments if it had been submitted under the old classifications. I do not know if the version now showing in London differs in any way (except for the English sub-titles) from the French original, but it is a highly adult and highly amusing piece of entertainment.

Max Ophüls[1] first gained critical attention here with his *Liebelei* made in 1932, adapted from Arthur Schnitzler's play. After the inevitable struggle experienced by all intelligent and uncompromising film directors, he again attracted considerable notice a year or so ago with *Letter from an Unknown Woman*, which he made in Hollywood after a spell of unemployment. It was released in the provinces without even a London Press show, and it was to the honourable credit of a few alert critics that it was rescued, brought to London and accorded its deserved acclaim.

In *La Ronde*, Ophüls has again returned to Schnitzler and Vienna and gives us a charming, witty and penetrating essay on the unchanging ways of love. With Destiny to guide us, in the sophisticated and faintly cynical presence of Anton Walbrook, a chain of ephemeral relationships is unfolded, linked together by overlapping characters and by the gay merry-go-round which Mr. Walbrook operates with affection. As it turns to the haunting Strauss waltz 'La Ronde de l'Amour', Lescadie (Simone Signoret), the pretty prostitute, entertains a young soldier (Serge Reggiani) who is ungrateful for her generously given delights. At the Prater on the following Sunday, he charms a parlour-maid (Simone Simon) into submission and, gratified,

[1] Died, Hamburg, March 26, 1957.

drops her for other attractions. The parlour-maid on duty one afternoon in her employer's house is naïvely seduced by the young son (Daniel Gelin) who, intoxicated by his easy success, sets out to make love to Emma (Danielle Darrieux), a young but neglected wife. Despite his nervous adolescence, he gains response but Emma, scared of the consequences if her husband finds out, discontinues the liaison. In bed that night, the husband (Fernand Gravey) delivers a discourse to Emma on the need for moral respectability, but under her questioning he becomes uneasy. In turn, we discover that he has been having a hole-in-the-corner affair with a shop-girl (Odette Joyeux) who leaves him for the more exciting and romantic experience of a poet (Jean-Louis Barrault). The poet soon tires of her unsophistication and lays siege to a famous actress (Isa Miranda), but she, while amused by his temperaments, is after more worldly securities in the shape of an aristocratic young officer (Gerard Philipe). But he, after a debauch with his brother officers, meets Lescadie, the street-girl. After a night spent with her, he leaves, and on his way home passes Franz, the soldier of the first episode, who is searching again for Lescadie. And so, Destiny cynically tells us, the circle is complete.

For all the cast of star-names, Ophüls never lets one of them upset the delicate structure that he weaves out of these ten encounters. They fit into a pattern which is a unity. Some incidents obviously emerge more forcibly than others but the overall balance is kept. Sharing the credit for adaptation with Ophüls is Jacques Natanson, and his dialogue is admirable. Each of us who sees the film will have our special preferences among the encounters. My own liking was for the bedroom scene between Daniel Gelin and Danielle Darrieux with its enchanting play with Stendhal, for the youthful seduction of Simone Simon by Gelin before the Professor arrives, and for the cross-talk between beds by Danielle Darrieux and Fernand Gravey. So much experience and observation lie behind Ophül's handling of these relationships. Not one character is superficial. The whole thing is done with exquisite good taste (that rare occurrence in the cinema). The costumes of the 1900s designed by Annenkov and the settings by D'Eaubonne are everything they should be; graceful, romantic and enchanting—irresistible as a fondant. The photography of Christian Matras bathes the film from start to finish with a play of light and shade that contributes to the unity of its conception.

La Ronde is a film which is screen entertainment at its best. Utterly different from the neo-realism of the Italians, or the social-awareness of some advanced Hollywood work, it has a welcome place in the art of the cinema. Its sparkle, vivacity, wit, style and warmth of emotion should captivate audiences for a long time. I doubt if it could have been made anywhere but in Paris or Vienna.

—PUBLIC OPINION, *May* 4, 1951.

Junk and Jefferson

Many of us were amused a year or two ago by the American stage play *Born Yesterday*, which Sir Laurence Olivier produced in London and which gave us the pleasure of seeing Miss Yolande Donlan. Inevitably Garson Kanin's comedy has gone through the Hollywood mill like all Broadway successes. As a piece of photographed theatre, *Born Yesterday* is as well done as it could be. George Cukor, who specializes in turning stage plays into celluloid, uses no tricks in his handling except to leave the luxury hotel apartment every now and again to remind us that we are supposed to be in Washington, D.C.

To remind you, Harry Brock is a junk-dealer who literally knows not the millions he has made. His methods are as uncouth and rough as his character. He buys what he likes, including the law. Every man has his price. He has, on the way to success, bought Billie Dawn out of the chorus. Billie is a curved, devastatingly dumb, brittle blonde. They arrive in Washington where Harry expects to pull off a vast crooked international deal with the help of a shady Congressman. Scared that Billie's *naïveté* and lack of etiquette will upset his social activities, Harry hires Paul Verrall, a young journalist of liberal views, to take her in hand and give her the know-how expected of a Washington socialite. Billie is a trying if dumb pupil as she visits the familiar historical show-places, inspects the Bill of Rights, has the newspaper editorials explained to her, and struggles with political philosophy. But before long some hard common-sense comes out from the iridium hair-do and Harry no longer finds her the ex-chorus girl whom he can shout at and strike down as he feels inclined. 'Fascist beast' is her newly-learned epithet for him. Harry's Congressman lets him down, Billie walks out on him with her educator and the scrap-iron millionaire is left threatened by exposure and ruin because much of his business wealth is secured in Billie's name. Thus 'democracy' triumphs over 'big business' and the honour of the Constitution is saved.

It is a sign of the times that this uproarious comedy, with its edgy wisecracks and tough characterization, was actually attacked in America as 'Communist' propaganda by a widely-syndicated columnist. Wisely, U.S. cinema-exhibitors thought better and played it to tremendous business. True, some of Mr. Kanin's barbs must pierce uncomfortably the skins of sundry politicians and business tycoons, but they're tough enough to take it.

A piece in this *genre* depends wholly, after plot and dialogue, on its acting. Miss Judy Holliday's playing of Billie Dawn won her the Hollywood actress award of 1950, much to many persons' surprise in view of Gloria Swanson's performance as Norma in *Sunset Boulevard* and Bette Davis's brilliant acting of Margo in *All About Eve.* Miss Holliday makes a good job of Billie with a high, rasping, scarcely understandable accent that has the characteristics of a human juke-box. Her moronic expression of utter idiocy occasionally softens into a glimmering understanding as that under-developed mind grasps a point or two. Her high-heeled, peahen strut is effected to that degree of incredibility that makes it only too real. She gets almost everything out of the part that is possible, but I still have a sneaking feeling that I preferred Miss Yolande Donlan's version of Billie on the stage. Broderick Crawford shouts and storms Harry Brock as he did Willie Stark in *All the King's Men,* which is as it should be. Americans like this exist: I've met them; I've met them in other nationalities, too. William Holden, on the other hand, does not bring the underlying firmness of purpose to the educator, Paul Verrall, as could have been done by a stronger actor. This is puzzling because I found him good in *Sunset Boulevard.* Howard St. John makes an excellent, cynical, liquor-drinking Jim Devery, a kind of public relations-counsellor-cum-legal adviser to the junk dealer, while a small study of a worldly-wise maid (only to be found attending luxury apartments in cosmopolitan hotels) is given by Claire Carleton. Is Larry Olivier's Congressman too like Mr. Truman to be accidental?

—Public Opinion, *May* 11, 1951.

Murder, My Sweet!

Cinema is so lacking in bold experiment that it would be churlish not to pay respect to Orson Welles for his long-awaited version of *Macbeth*. The young man who made *Citizen Kane* could hardly make a boring film, mistakenly though he may sometimes use his talents. Unlike the sumptuous Olivier productions of *Henry V* and *Hamlet*, Welles shot his *Macbeth* on a modest budget in a smallish studio in the whirlwind time of twenty-three days. It was, of course, carefully pre-planned. Presented at the Venice Festival in 1948, it was then withdrawn for re-voicing. Recently it has had a controversial reception in Paris, is apparently liked in Germany, and now reaches London.

Having complimented Mr. Welles on his unorthodox approach to film-making, I feel free to say that his *Macbeth* leaves me unmoved; at the same time, I confess, Shakespeare has never been cinema to this critic. There will be those who will deplore the shortenings and transitions and additions in the text. I can forgive these, even applaud them, if by so doing the play makes a good film. But what has happened is that the poetry which alone makes this brutal play acceptable has vanished. Nothing worthwhile is put in its place.

A mud-pack and plaster castle, wraithed in steam and dripping with sweat, with Gordon Craigish flights of narrow steps and rocky precipices, is a 'Gothick' nightmare of which the eye soon tires. Reminiscent of the late Gregg Toland's wonderful photography in *Citizen Kane*, the camera here is made to perform the acrobatics of a mountain goat. The worm's-eye view, the bird's-eye view, elaborate travelling shots perambulating up and down hill, studied deep-focus compositions, fuzzy optical devices—the whole bag of camera tricks is used to put the actors on the screen but not to much effect. More than once I thought back to *Alexander Nevsky*, to *Ivan the Terrible*. Square crowns and spiked circlets, hearth-rugs and battered tartans, hirsute make-ups and matted hair-do's—they smack, alas, of the costumier's wardrobe and the art student's drawing-block. Only the stealthy march of Macduff and Malcolm's tree-clad army on Dunsinane has for a brief moment a dramatic eeriness, which unhappily becomes De Mille as soon as battle is joined.

It is, perhaps, something of a feat to have produced this monstrous Mappin Terrace of crags, this grisly landscape of gibbets and bogs, in the atmosphere of one of the smaller Hollywood studios. That one must grant, if nothing else. The trick optical effects by Consolidated Film Industries put the aurora borealis to shame. Moreover, it is all peopled with actors from the Mercury Theatre group, from radio and from even Dublin who give of their best to small avail. The magic and poetry simply are not there. Nor is the verse helped by a curious Scottish burr that comes and goes as if wafted by the swirling mists. Welles's own Macbeth, naturally, dominates all. He is like an old gangster cornered on the last run. The final death-fight with Macduff calls for sub-machine guns and the F.B.I., not claymores and clanging shields.

I write this with some reluctance. Courage and original approach in cinema need all our support. The uncouth arrogance of this film does not invite critical tolerance. Undeniably it has a certain savage strength, but it is the strength of a butcher's axe, not the sure strength that comes from artistry.

—PUBLIC OPINION, *June* 1, 1951.

Full House

The tough, amoral, ruthless American newspaperman has been screened before, but never with so much savage cynicism as in Billy Wilder's new film *Ace in the Hole*.[1] Hardly one sympathetic character inhabits this bitter story of Chuck Tatum (Kirk Douglas), a top reporter fired from America's big city papers for his drinking and immorality. Knowing his only way out of the doghouse lies in finding an exclusive headline story, he hires himself for peanuts to a small-town paper in Albuquerque, New Mexico. He waits for a year. Then, while covering a routine story, he stumbles on what his nose tells him will be the story-of-the-year. Near a remote wayside store-cum-gas station, Leo Minosa (Richard Benedict) has been trapped by a cave-in while searching for Indian relics in the mountain cliff-dwellings. His bleached-blonde wife, Lorraine (Jan Sterling) couldn't care less; she's bored and sick of this kind of life. Chuck and his boy photographer crawl into the mountain, photograph the half-buried man, and send back to the Albuquerque *Sun-Bulletin* the first dispatch on the story-of-the-year. Chuck takes over command, gets a corrupt Sheriff and the rescue men on the scene, and plans the story as he wants it. Leo can be rescued in twenty-four hours by one method, or perhaps a week by another. With the connivance of the Sheriff, Chuck fixes the second way so that he can have an exclusive story long enough to hit the nation's headlines and only he can visit the entombed man.

It works. Overnight thousands of morbid sightseers arrive by coach and rail. Tents, marquees, hot-dog stands go up. The store makes a fortune with its food and curios. A carnival sets up with its amplified music. TV and radio men start operating. Newspapermen blow in from all over the country but by now Chuck

[1] Shown in the United States as *The Big Carnival*.

has it sewn up on his own terms with his ex-boss in New York. The wife falls for Chuck's ruthless power, but he'll let nothing interfere with his story. Then, within a few hours of rescue, Leo dies. From this moment, the story goes to pieces. By a sudden, out-of-character change of conscience, Chuck throws in his hand and lets his rivals have the story. Lorraine stabs him with a pair of scissors and he dies at the feet of the honest editor of the Albuquerque *Sun-Bulletin*. To be consistent, he should have scooped the final story and been reinstated in New York, taking the blonde with him, but the Breen Office would doubtless have objected. As it is, the girl gets away with murder. Chuck does not.

Full of improbabilities as the film is, you are swept along by Wilder's professional direction. His handling of crowds as they gather under the huge cliff-face or disperse silently after the circus is over, his superb use of great vista shots as well as finely-balanced close-ups, his sense of detail and small-type characterization—all reveal that in this picture Wilder technically becomes a top-rank director. Earlier films—*Double Indemnity* and *Sunset Boulevard*—with Charles Brackett as producer suggested this but now, producing himself, Wilder makes his best film. There is savage social comment here. Apart from the main exposure of the hot-news rat-race, his caustic comment on the sensation-seeking crowd is his triumph. The insurance man and his family who were first on the spot; the arrival of the 'Leo Minosa Special'; the 'Leo Minosa' theme song selling in thousands; the gawping, ice-cream sucking faces as they stare up in the glaring sun at the impassave slab of rock behind which a man lies trapped; the tragic shot when the crowds have gone of Papa Minosa wandering across the now-deserted sand among the litter—these are images chosen and filmed with genuine observation.

One point is missed: Wilder fails to link directly the scoop stories filed by Chuck with the thrill-thirsty readers that await them in the forty-eight States. Their avid hunger for sensationalism is the only justification for his amorality.

Kirk Douglas plays an over-magnified character with all the rough resources of Cagney and Bogart, at times taking it too easily for conviction. Jan Sterling's hard, hurt, frustrated, bleached Lorraine is a brilliant performance of an utterly unsympathetic part. Porter Hall's small-town editor, Bob Arthur's photographer-aid to Chuck and John Berkes as Papa Minosa are absolutely right, as indeed are all the small-part players who people the scene in this extraordinary but very unpleasant social comment on a section of the American public. Charles Lang's photography, especially the early dawn scenes, is magnificent.

—PUBLIC OPINION, *June* 22, 1951.

Quartet in Vienna

An unhappy choice of title hides a stimulating new film from Switzerland, *Four in a Jeep.* The Swiss produce few feature films but the record of the Zurich firm of Praesens-Films stands high. *Marie-Louise, The Last Chance* and *The Search* (in collaboration with M-G-M) were memorable works not only technically but in their attempt to solve the language problem for internationally-designed films. This new picture goes even further. Richard Schweizer, the writer, and Leopold Lindtberg, the director, have constructed a story so that it is spoken in four languages but is wholly understandable to English-speaking audiences (at least) without the use of sub-titles. They are to be congratulated, also, on choosing a subject that could be thought controversial: police administration under four-power rule in Vienna. Behind this idea lies a very genuine attempt to portray impartially the human relations between East and West in Europe, including the unfortunate Viennese whose city is still occupied.

The story revolves round the military-police crew of a patrol-car, one of those that supervize military personnel in the city's centre. The jeep being American, it is driven by an American, but the sergeant-in-charge is a Russian; the other two sergeants being British and French. An incident involving an Austrian girl, whose husband has escaped from a P.O.W. camp only a few days before he was to have been released, starts the spark that leads to tense relations between the three sergeants from the West and the Russian, as well as between the authorities they represent.

The Russian puts his sense of duty and his strict regard for orders beyond all other considerations, which makes him appear incapable of human feelings though he himself is human enough under an immobile exterior. The American seems to accept authority as something to be disregarded when gallantry demands, although the film happily avoids any sex entanglements which Hollywood could not have resisted. The Englishman has a tolerant, happy-go-lucky, carefree approach to the situation, wanting to do what is right without becoming involved. The Frenchman is concerned, sympathetic, but also anxious to keep clear of trouble. Added point is given to the story when it is revealed that the American and the Russian are not strangers. They met as man-to-man on the Elbe in 1945, got drunk and fraternized. Later, during the Berlin blockade, they re-met at a railway junction but this time the Russian was aloof. But this was in the past.

The American secretly moves the Viennese girl to the safety of the French sergeant's apartment, where she waits for radio news of her husband's release. His name is not given out and in desperation she goes to the railway station to meet the returning P.O.W.s in hope of news. In a brilliantly handled and deeply moving scene, she faints and is taken back to the Frenchman's house by—the Russian. Eventually the escaped husband arrives in Vienna and the couple are chased by the police. In a final, most exciting incident set in a half-constructed building, the Russian and American sergeants actually start to fight, the husband is hurt by falling debris and the French and English sergeants manage to get him and the girl to the safety of an American hospital. There is then a wonderful moment when, breaking apart from their fight, the Russian and the American realize the utter stupidity of the situation. They pull out cigarettes. They remember their first meeting on the Elbe. The American lights the Russian's cigarette. A vast meaning lies in the look exchanged between them.

The great quality of this film is its lack of prejudice or propaganda. All the characters are portrayed with sympathy and understanding. The Russian tries hard not to be put in the position of disobeying orders. Only when the American, mistakenly trying to thwart what he expects the Russian to do, puts him in a situation when he must do his duty does he do so. It is a profoundly human and moving film that can do more good for international understanding than all the fiery films from East and West. Beautifully acted and very well directed, it is an important contribution to settlement by peaceful methods.

Miss Viveca Lindfors, a Swedish actress, plays the Viennese girl with feeling and beauty; the four sergeants are excellent—Ralph Meeker (American), Michael Medwin (British), Dinan (French) and Yoseph Yadin (Russian). The latter's performance is outstanding. All the smaller parts are admirable, memorable being Paulette Dubost's exasperated French housewife and Harry Hess's restrained American captain. Much of the film was shot in Vienna, which adds to the authenticity that distinguishes the whole piece. Without question, this is one of the films of the year. It should be a hot favourite for the British Film Academy's U.N. Award and Mr. Selznick's Golden Laurels.

—Public Opinion, *June* 15, 1951.

1955-57

Umberto D

To interpret the reality of living on the cinema screen has been a constant challenge to many directors and writers since the early days. On the one hand, the newsreel reporting what its cameras see and its editors select; on the other, the fictional story played by acted characters basing its events and situations on real life; in the middle, the documentary in all its many forms, drawing from reality like Flaherty and the early Eisenstein, or intermixing actors and non-actors as in the films of the Crown Film Unit. In the post-war years, due perhaps to documentary influence, many Hollywood and British films attempted stories set against real 'backgrounds' but few, if any, achieved an honest interpretation of reality. Occasionally the French succeeded, as in Renoir's often overlooked *Toni* and in Clément's *Les Jeux Interdits.*

The growth of what is called neo-realism in Italian cinema stems from Visconti's astonishing film *Ossessione* in 1942. Those who missed the single performance of this rare and forbidden film at the New London Film Society were unfortunate. Although Rossellini's *Rome—Open City* and *Paisan* hogged most of the limelight in the immediate post-war years, it soon became clear that Vittorio De Sica and the screen-writer Cesare Zavattini were the two most significant figures. De Sica had been busy as a charming, polished actor in cinema and theatre for many years, had directed his first film *Rose Scarlatte* in 1940, and had collaborated with Zavattini as far back as 1941. In *Sciuscia* (1947), *Ladri di Biciclette* (1948) and *Miraclo a Milano* (1950), the team of De Sica-Zavattini proved to be the most formidable in the dynamic Italian cinema that was too soon to fall under Hollywood influence and consequent glamorization and decadence.

Zavattini has himself described how in each of these films he tried to get nearer to the unvarnished, unadulterated presentation of life, and seemed in 1952 to be thinking along lines that were reminiscent of Dziga-Vertov's Kino-Eye theories of the early twenties.[1] If he still holds this view, then he must quickly transfer his talents to the television outside-broadcast cameras with their capacity for immediacy and eavesdropping but with their very limited powers of selection. De Sica, perhaps because of his actor's training, has still maintained a use of characters to interpret the reality of living although he has used in the main real people or little-known actors for his purpose and has eschewed the artificialities of the studio wherever possible. So we come to the film *Umberto D* by these two distinguished film-makers, which has only recently had a public screening in London although made in 1951. And it is in England, oddly enough, that this picture has first had wide critical acclaim, a fact that has delighted De Sica and for which he has expressed his heartfelt gratitude.

It was ironic that while De Sica was being promoted by the Unitalia people as its most handsome, seductive actor during the Italian Film Festival in London, *Umberto D* was screened to the critics ex-Festival at the National Film Theatre (with De Sica present) and scooped the reviews of the week from all the critics who matter. It had languished two years in British Lion's vaults. They could not, it was said, find an exhibitor to book it, though no reason was ever offered why they did not themselves show it at their Rialto. However, we must be grateful to the Curzon for taking the icy plunge.

Umberto D, as is now well known, is a moving study of the loneliness of old age as experienced by a retired civil servant eking out an existence on a pension too meagre for the humblest living in post-war Rome. It is dedicated by De Sica to his father and is his own best-loved film. From its exciting opening sequence of the dispersal of a demonstration of old-age pensioners by the police to its almost unbearably moving ending when the old man is prevented from suicide by his beloved

[1] *Sight and Sound*, Vol. XXIII, No. 2, pp. 64-69.

dog's fear, it is a masterpiece of human observation, of detail and of mood. It has warmth, satire, humour and pathos but is never sentimental as the wonderfully handled scenes between the old man and his terrier could so easily have been. The understanding shown by De Sica and Zavattini for the feelings of the unwanted, the aged who have served life faithfully, the penniless through no fault of their own, pitifully trying to keep up the semblance of respectability, makes this film into, in my opinion, one of the great films of all time worthy to rank with the best of Chaplin, Stroheim, Griffith or the Russians.

The actors, to us unknown names and maybe some not actors, are as real people in actual surroundings, with all the suffering and pathos and delight in small things that are true of our own lives if we have experienced life fully. How much they owe in their performances to De Sica's direction, how much to their own interpretation of a 'part', is and should remain a director's secret. The scene in which Maria, the little servant-girl, pregnant by one of two soldiers in the barracks opposite but she doesn't know or much care which, gets up from her mattress on the floor to clear up the kitchen in the morning, opening a cupboard door with her toes—this is a moment when collaboration between director and actor is sacred. In its sharp satire on the Roman Catholic Church, the hospital-ward scene with its handing out of the rosaries, its brusque medicos and smirking nuns is reminiscent of the church charity sequence in *Bicycle Thieves*. These are only two of dozens of scenes that each interpret the minor daily events in the lives of this small group of people—old Umberto himself, a figure of dignity and grandeur and tenderness beautifully expressed by Carlo Battisti (said to be a University professor), his tarty, calculating, cold-hearted landlady (Lina Gennari), Maria the servant-girl, wonderfully played by young Maria Pia Casilio, the unbelievably intelligent dog itself and dozens of small portraits each of which remains in the mind long after the picture has been seen. It is photographed in the casual, almost newsreel manner of the Italian neo-realists by G. R. Aldo, who also shot Visconti's *La Terra Trema*.[1]

I can understand some people actively disliking this film, as at

[1] Aldo was killed in 1955 during the making of Visconti's film *Senso*.

its time Stroheim's *Greed* was disliked, because it is too close to reality to be pleasant to those who refuse to face up to reality. It is a social protest made with tenderness and affection. And unlike so many such protests, it has no bitterness in it. It has a purity, an unswerving integrity of purpose, and an awareness of simple people that mark De Sica, once again, as a great artist of our time. Zavattini, too, must share the credit.

Gavin Lambert has given some of the reasons why *Umberto D*, and other examples of the neo-realist group, are disliked by the authorities in Italy. He quotes from an open letter by the Under-Secretary to the Prime Minister's office to De Sica, published in the Italian Press after the première of *Umberto D*. 'We ask the man of culture,' wrote the Under-Secretary, 'to feel his social responsibility, which should not be limited to description of the abuses and miseries of a system and a generation. . . . If it is true that evil can be fought by harshly spotlighting its most miserable aspects, it is also true that De Sica has rendered bad service to his country if people throughout the world start thinking that Italy in the middle of the twentieth century is the same as in *Umberto D*. . . . We beg him never to forget this small duty of healthy and constructive optimism, which really encourages humanity to move forward and hope.'[1]

Umberto D is, of course, a film of hope, of belief in people's inherent goodness, and any tourist who wouldn't visit Italy because of it had best stay at home. Driven to attempted suicide, Umberto nevertheless draws back when he sees that belief in him, even if held only by an animal, is to be broken. We do not know how he will continue his struggle but we do know he has restored a faith placed in him.

It is quoted by Zavattini as being said that 'Neo-realism does not offer solutions. The end of a neo-realist film is particularly inconclusive.'[2] This he cannot accept. He counters: 'With regard to my own work, the characters and situations in films for which I have written the scenario, they remain unsolved from a practical point of view simply because "this is reality". But every moment of the film is, in itself, a continuous answer to some question. It is not the concern of an artist to propound

[1] *Sight and Sound*, Vol. 24, No. 3, pp. 147-166.
[2] Ibid. Vol. 23, No. 2, pp. 64-69.

solutions. It is enough, and quite a lot, I should say, to make an audience feel the need, the urgency, for them. In any case, what films *do* offer solutions? "Solutions" in this sense, if they are offered, are sentimental ones, resulting from the superficial way in which problems have been faced. At least, in my work I leave the solution to the audience.' These last are familiar words to those who understood the documentary movement in Britain twenty years ago or more.

But the present days are dark for the neo-realists in Italy, as indeed they are for many other film-makers who would interpret reality in terms of human respect and understanding. With a prosperous, glossified Italian film industry, its eyes set on the gold of foreign markets, with official pressures exercised against them, the neo-realists are hard put to it to realize their aims, relatively cheap though their films may be to make. Like Von Stroheim before him, De Sica has recently spent much of his time exploiting his popularity as an actor; only in this way can he build up reserves which will allow him to direct again as he wishes. He and Zavattini have plans for another picture; that is the best news for a long time.

—BRITISH FILM ACADEMY JOURNAL, *Spring*, 1955.

Moby Dick

Of *Moby Dick,* the book, it is said, it is like a great wave out of the sea. If Huston's film is no great wave, it is at least much more than a ripple. It has passages of physical excitement that will be talked about for months to come. More important, it carries an imprint of sincerity, so rare in today's commercial cinema. And it has production qualities that are immense.

Whatever interpretations—philosophical or theological—may be put on Melville's massive book—and they are many and conflicting—it remains at heart an epic story of the sea—of the terror-inspiring voyage which is Captain Ahab's relentless hunt for the White Whale. Its meandering, often boring, narrative has been cleverly adapted and subtly condensed by Huston and science-fiction writer Ray Bradbury. If many incidents are dropped and others created, the substance of the original has been kept. Like the book, the film suffers from a wearisome beginning. The genteel atmosphere of the 'Spouter Inn' reeks of Elstree and Father Mapple's celebrated sermon—pontifically delivered by Orson Welles—is unmoving. Ishmael's strange meeting with Queequeg is cast away with small heed to Melville's superb detail. Only when we are at last aboard the *Pequod,* and she is under way, does the film really come to life. It is as if Huston were bored with the opening sequences on shore.

Again as in the book, Ahab's first appearance on the bridge is long-delayed but, unlike the book, it is oddly sterile when come it does. It is, in fact, an entry relying more on voice-description by Ishmael than on cinematic visual. The impact of this puritanical figure of a monomaniac at war with God falls curiously flat. Gregory Peck no doubt gives the performance of his career but the handicap of being too young for Ahab undermines our belief. This Ahab never sailed the seas for forty years; this analogy with Adam rings false: this is not the 'terrible old man' of Mr. Starbuck's thoughts!

Among the crew, inevitably, are many familiar characters who even by their lusty and bravado playing cannot be turned into the common humanity—from Ahab down to Pip—which makes Melville's *Pequod* a microcosm of all ships. Melville's sailor in the fo'c'sle is all sailors, 'now and for ever'; but alas, here he is Bernard Miles or Noel Purcell or some other friendly soul with even white teeth. But Leo Genn's Starbuck has substance and authority; Friedrich Ledebur's Queequeg has dignity and strength, and I applaud drama-critic Seamus Kelly's vigorous handling of Flask—a real Melville man is this!

It has been said that 'Melville *is* the sea, *is* the *Pequod, is* Moby Dick—waves break in his vitals.' But only at rare moments did I feel that Huston—for all his costly adventure—*was* Melville, *was* the sea, *was* the . . . Perhaps it is that the film, more than any other quality, lacks poetry. The breathtaking shots of the first whirring-winged seabirds have it—for a moment: and the becalmed *Pequod* sequence has a tension that can be caught. But mostly the camera is used without penetration beneath the skin. In overall, the 'static splendour of the watery-world' is too subtle for this, may I suggest, sophisticated approach.

Yet Huston has much to show for his two years' labour; so, too, has his technical team. The typhoon night sequence, the sundry encounters with the whales and the final mighty battle with the White Whale itself are a brilliant amalgam of trick-work and actuality. Of the new 'colour style' credited to Huston and Oswald Morris, the cameraman, I was mostly unaware! Maybe that is a tribute to the film's power to grip. On the other hand, I wondered, as I have before, why Huston pays so little heed to the music of his films? This score is pedestrian: someone like Rawsthorne or Alwyn could have brought a new dimension to the picture and added poetic strength to its weakness.

Production management must have been a prodigious operation. Many back-room boys—especially Cecil Ford and Ralph Brinton—deserve the warmest praise for their imagination, resourcefulness and sheer hard labour. As a piece of production, *Moby Dick* is a great credit to British technicians. As a compromise between the commercialism of the major studios and a big picture undertaken with sincerity of purpose by a courageous producer-director, everyone will benefit if *Moby Dick* has the success—commercial as well as critical—that is safely predicted for it.

—Films and Filming, *November*, 1956.

Lust for Life

'Never let the good be killed by the best,' once said Franklin Roosevelt. Such is my final reaction to the film that John Houseman has produced and Vincente Minnelli directed about Vincent van Gogh, or van Goff as they have it. In truth, it is remarkable at all that M-G-M backed this picture with its lack of conventional box-office ingredients. Even more remarkable is that its script stays accurate in main essentials to the actual life of this tragic painter, except that it opens in 1878 thus omitting the English visits, Dortrecht and other formative periods prior to the terrible Borinage phase. Clearly much sincerity has gone into its making. Meticulous care is taken in the treatment of the paintings—so many of them well-known to us—and in the detailed reconstruction of the rooms and cafés in which van Gogh lived and worked. The cast is chosen and made-up with extraordinary resemblance to the original characters so far as we know them today from portraits and photographs. Why, then, is this film not in the 'best' class, which I should so like it to be? Having paid my respects, this I shall try to analyse.

The initial mistake was, I suggest, to have gone to a lurid and uncouth novel for a source. Van Gogh's life is probably better documented than that of any other great artist; several thousand illustrated letters to Theo, his brother, and to his friends, plus contemporary accounts, provide a rich material source, together with some reliable biographies. Yet, inexplicably, just as John Huston went to Pierre La Mure's flamboyant novel *Moulin Rouge* for Toulouse-Lautrec, so Minnelli asked Norman Corwin (the distinguished radio writer-producer) to adapt Irving Stone's meretricious book. Only one reason can explain this imbecility: M-G-M wanted the title! Unhappily, they took the trite dialogue as well.

25. (a) A WALK IN THE SUN (1945), Lewis Milestone's *futility of war film from the novel by* Harry Brown, *with* Dana Andrews. (Paramount)

25. (b) LA RONDE (1950), Max Ophüls's *enchanting satirical comedy, with* Anton Walbrook *and* Simone Signoret. (Sacha Gordine)

Secondly, the vital problem of language. Kirk Douglas has an uncanny resemblance to van Gogh and he plays this most difficult role with a talent which, to me, was unexpected. But not once in a scene in which he speaks does he convince. The reason is twofold. The atrocious dialogue itself, except when it is an occasional direct quotation from the letters, and the American accent. We accept the convention that he and all the cast must, though portraying Dutch and Frenchmen, speak in English. But for once here was a justification for post-voicing. If a European actor, say Peter Lorre or Yves Montand, had been used to voice Kirk Douglas *in broken English* (assuming the dialogue well-written), then one might have come very near to accepting this van Gogh as a recreation of the original.

Thirdly, if ever a film called for colour perfection and control, this is it. Familiar as one is with many of the originals and countless nearly-accurate reproductions, it was disappointing to find such colour discrepancies. This, however, is a small point beside the complete failure by Minnelli to use colour as a dramatic and integral part of van Gogh's life. Colour stimulated in van Gogh an intoxication. From the sombre browns and greens and monochromes of the Dutch and Belgian periods, through the awakening to colour inspired by the Impressionists and Japanese colour-prints in Paris, to the blinding impact of Provençal sun and colour and finally to the last frenzied exaltation at Auvers—this was a unique drama-progression of colour which the film's makers totally ignore. The dynamic colour impact of Arles on Vincent is conveyed by a few tatty shots of fruit-blossom against an anaemic sky, unworthy of the cheapest picture-postcards! What a major dramatic chance was here obliterated!

Of the man's personality itself, of the utter integrity of his life, of his passion for love of and between all mankind, of his primitive impulses and inevitable solitude, only an iota comes through. The flame never burns to scorch. It was perhaps too much to ask! The incident of self-mutilation at Arles is shown but not its conclusion, presumably for censor reasons. His relationship to the four women in his life is not deeply treated. His fervent desire to establish a cooperative guild of artists is skated over at Arles and ignored in Paris where it began. Van

Gogh painted from his guts. There was more understanding of this in Alain Resnais's modest little film in 1947 than in all this costly two hours of Metroscope. Metroscope, forsooth!

In isolation, a few well-composed scenes are memorable, despite the wide-screen deformity: Vincent struggling in the wind to paint Christine on the beach at Scheveningen, Gauguin declaiming at a picnic party, the attack by crows as Vincent painted the frenzied 'Cornfield with Rooks' so near the tragic end, and one or two others.

Of the cast besides Douglas, James Donald's Theo, Anthony Quinn's Gauguin, Pamela Brown's Christine, Everett Sloane's Dr. Gachet, all have a remarkable verisimilitude but the monstrous dialogue destroys our belief in them as people and the direction does nothing to help them.

Houseman and Minnelli, Corwin and Douglas, they and everyone else (especially the production-designer) have tried very hard and in the circumstances come nearer to success than ever could have been imagined. It is a far better film than *Moulin Rouge* (Lautrec) or *Moon and Sixpence* (Gauguin); perhaps Max Ophüls will pull it off with his projected picture about Modigliani?[1]

—FILMS AND FILMING, *December*, 1956.

[1] Now that Max is dead, one hears that Jacques Becker is directing. He is a gifted and fine director. I wish him well.

Il Bidone (The Swindlers)

'Fellini,' writes a critic in one of our most reputable dailies,[1] '. . . is to the Italian cinema today what Rossellini was in the immediate post-war years.' This is either a misjudgement of Fellini, or a misinterpretation of Rossellini's relationship to Italian neo-realism in its early years; probably an irresponsible both. It also fails to recognize Fellini's contribution to the neo-realist movement before he became a director. As a writer he gave much to Rossellini and Lattuada's earlier work. I remember Sergei Amidei (whose own contribution to Italian neo-realism is overlooked) saying of Fellini one fine day at Amalfi in 1948 (when Rossellini was intermittently shooting the abortive *La Macchina Amazzacattivi*), 'Behold that young man! He has far to go.'

Well, he has gone from *Il Secicco Bianco* (not shown here) through *I Vitelloni* and *La Strada* to *Il Bidone*—an extraordinary continuity. If production sources permit, he should go still further. In each of the last three films he has created somewhere an intangible half-world between realism and fantasy, which some call poetry and others surrealism. It is reminiscent of, perhaps (or derivative from?) the work of Jean Vigo, and equally repellent to the routine filmgoer and critic because it is elusive in meaning, not crystal-clear to grasp. In *La Strada* it was the least successfully created because it was most self-consciously contrived; and not helped by an artificial and shallow performance by Giulietta Massina, an opinion I know shared by few. *I Vitelloni* was for me a far more adult work. It is strange that it preceded *La Strada*. This study of a clique of wasters in a small provincial town posed a social problem, if only of a restricted kind, which *La Strada* did not. It was handled with wit, irony and insight, although some characterization was more

[1] *The Times*, London, November 12, 1956.

subtle than others, and its direction left many loose ends. *Il Bidone*, said to be disliked by the Italian critics, is the most mature and best directed film of the three.

It is the tragic story of Augusto, a middle-aged swindler who has never quite made the big-time grade, and his two 'amateur' companions—Picasso, a would-be painter, and Roberto, a would-be crooner who finds robbery less work. The trio perpetrate mean and cruel frauds on the most ignorant and poorest of their fellow-countrymen. They pose as priests to rob two old peasant women of their life-savings by 'discovering' buried treasure on their land which the women may keep if they pay over cash for masses to be said for the soul of the murderer who 'hid' the treasure. They collect 'advances' on non-existent apartments from gullible slum-families who have been on the housing-list for years. All this despicable petty thievery is performed with a gaiety and utter lack of conscience. But at a hilarious New Year's Eve party given by an old friend, now in the big-time crook class, Augusto realizes that he is too old ever to reach that envied goal himself. Celebrating after another fraud, Picasso quits his friends in a fit of drunken remorse to return to his loving wife and presumably an honest life.

A chance meeting with his daughter further emphasizes to Augusto his empty and wasted life. He promises to find her the money she needs to continue her training as a teacher. But unluckily he is arrested in her presence and gaoled on the evidence of a man he once swindled. Out of prison, he takes up with a new gang, going off again on the never-failing buried treasure trick. This time, posing as a bishop, he cannot refuse 'comfort' to the semi-paralysed young daughter of the robbed farmer. Her simple bravery and pitiful faith in him as a 'bishop' finally bring him to his decision. Taking only the money he has promised to his daughter, Augusto rejoins the gang. When they discover his weak 'betrayal', they pitch him down the rocky mountainside, filch the money and leave him, with a broken spine, to his fate.

Thus synopsized, it seems a straightforward script makeable by any competent director. But Fellini lifts it to a different level, telling it with spontaneity and unpredictability. Although laced with humour and satire, it is a strictly moral story of loneliness, of a middle-aged man longing to 'belong' somewhere, to someone, but whose chosen career makes solitude inevitable.

Augusto, confidentally played by Broderick Crawford (in a part which might have been tailored for Edward G. Robinson), and Picasso by Richard Basehart (both, oddly enough, American actors speaking dubbed Italian) are deeply-felt, intensely human characters, sensitively understood from within. Indeed, Fellini is wonderfully served by all his cast. Franco Fabrizi's Roberto and Giulietta Massina's Iris (Picasso's wife) are smaller parts but equally well done. An outstanding performance, brief as it is, is given by Irene Cefaro as the paralysed farm-girl who seeks spiritual aid from the bogus bishop. This vital and tender scene, played in the wind against a rough stone wall, is something long to be remembered. Those searching for Signor Fellini's 'half-world', by the way, will find a subtle example in the night scene when Picasso relinquishes his career of crime. The crazy, orgiastic New Year's Eve party is worthy of the Marx Brothers at their best. With excellent, hard photography by Otello Martelli (note how unobtrusively Fellini's camera moves), and admirable music from Nino Rota, this is the best Italian film to reach us this year. Fellini may still at times be unsure of himself but that he is an important and individualistic director there is now no doubt. This is a co-production, which, when we recall that most bi-national films do not favour subjects inspiring 'social attention', is in itself auspicious.

—FILMS AND FILMING, *January*, 1957.

On the Bowery

Much that is remarkable about this extraordinary film is explained when it is known that at least one of its makers —the cameraman—was associated with that other remarkable New York film—*The Quiet One.* (Why, by the way, has not that most worthwhile film had a public release in Britain?) Here is the same, but even more so, intimate observation of real people that is a miracle of ingenuity and patience. But it is also a great deal more than mere technical achievement. It is an intensely moving, warm, human but also frightening document of people—two in particular—who have reached the final depravity and hopelessness of despair and to whom alcohol and more alcohol appear the only reason for a continued existence.

Lionel Rogosin, Mark Sufrin, Richard Bagley and Darwin Deen spent months mixing among and becoming accepted by the derelict inhabitants of the Bowery, working in conditions that can only have been near to intolerable during the hottest summer New York had known in many years. Snatching a shot here and another there, trying to direct unpredictable 'actors' in various stages of intoxication, concealing a camera in a clothes bundle, coping with official hindrance and even with demolition part way through production of an essential landmark in their location—the 'L'—they could understandably have brought out only a series of disjointed shots. That they have created a coherent, sixty-minute picture, with continuity of event and time over three days and a depth of characterization in their main parts is to their lasting credit, in which the editor, Carl Lerner, must also share. Ray, born in Kentucky, ex-army because his brother joined up, not yet the complete Skid Row victim; Gorman, who 'befriends' him, ageing and utterly and irretrievably the prisoner of the gin-mill and the flop-house. These are the two men we get to know so well, and indeed to understand and feel with in their desperate fight against loneliness and being unwanted. And around them is a gallery of others, besotted, argumentative, sentimental, friendly, aggressive, bonded together by their sole reliance on liquor—licit or illicit. We hear their stories, their hopes, their smashed illusions in their own unscripted words. It is neither pleasant nor inspiring. It appals and it shocks. But it is reality as naked as it has ever been put on the screen.

They are not a pretty company—these distorted, twisted, seamed, drooling faces, but they are still human. Faces you can never forget—in the apathetic congregation of a mission-hall unresponsive to the grim warnings of the speaker, slobbering across dirty tables in the bars, twitching or flat-out down an alleyway or in a doorway, spreading newspapers to sleep on in a doss-house, wheedling with the doorman for a bed, selling worn-out rags to kerb-buyers for that badly needed quarter to buy another beer.

Mark Sufrin has said that they tried 'to make an honest, compassionate record of some human beings in a state of prolonged crisis. If we have caught something of the loneliness, the ignorance, the waste and futility of such lives, and communicated it to others, that will suffice.' They have done all that and by so doing have made one of the most socially significant films that documentary has yet known.

Said a Cockney lady-cleaner, interrupted in her morning's work by the private screening of the film when I saw it: 'They acted just as if they were *real* people.' No greater tribute could have been made to the little team who made this memorable picture. American official opinion, I understand, takes exception to the film having been shown at Venice and Edinburgh. That comes as no surprise; there are always those who dislike facing the truth. No good is done by hiding the running sores of life. The task is how to cure and prevent them. But first they must be exposed to the public gaze, which is exactly what this shocking but brave film does and why its makers merit our acclaim. What is a surprise, and I am shocked by it, is that *On the Bowery* received no diploma of acknowledgment at Edinburgh; an oversight that needs an explanation.[1]

—THE LIVING CINEMA, *Spring*, 1957.

[1] Subsequently, the British Film Academy gave the film its 1957 Documentary Award, but even this important recognition does not explain the Edinburgh Film Festival Committee's extraordinary omission.

Postscript: A Letter to The Times *(1953)*

February 13, 1953.

To the Editor of The Times.
Sir,

The analogy made in your columns on February 10 between the adoption of sound by the motion picture screen and the present scramble to use three-dimensional processes is, we suggest, mistaken. The addition of recorded dialogue, sound and music gave to the silent film a virtue not possessed by the sub-title and the live orchestra. The illusion of reality given by the 3-D process is not a comparable substitute. Cinematography as it exists is non-realistic, creating its illusions and its own special poetry and drama by spatial depth (camera mobility and deep-focus) and the selection and juxtaposition of visual and aural images. The unlimited range through time and space, from detail to distance, is the unique virtue which, in our opinion, the 3-D processes cannot emulate.

'Cinerama', as recently seen by one of us in New York, is an exciting, novel and emotional experience, and if all films are to be widened into travelogues this is the magic carpet. In their desperate search to combat television's mass-appeal the major Hollywood producers are, characteristically, turning to any new 'gimmick'. Instead of trying to make better-quality films, they are merely making the old ones wider and noisier. Visits to old films at the National Film Theatre, London, and to current programmes at West End cinemas reveal that in twenty-five years we have not progressed far, if at all, in exploring the endless powers of cinematography, in spite of all the technological devices made available by the engineers and inventors. Indeed, the short history of the film shows that technical processes are always far in advance of the creative uses made of them.

That films will be made in all the various three-dimensional processes we do not doubt, but let us at this early stage realize that there is only a handful of directors today who have mastery over the existing virtues of the film as a medium. Before the stampede begins of converting plant and cinemas (however desirable to the equipment manufacturers that may be), let us pause to consider how we can respond to the obvious public discontent with factory-made films and a widening world market by exploring fully the untold uses of the so-called flat film.

Yours &c.,

Paul Rotha
Richard Winnington

III

SOME PROBLEMS OF DOCUMENTARY

Films of Fact and Fiction (1938)

It took a world depression to shake our belief that public affairs jog along smoothly enough without much worry by the ordinary citizen. It was the depression, with its personal as well as national tragedies, that brought a ripening of social conscience in country and city. Since that memorable year of 1929 there has been a growing public thirst for information about current affairs. The constant repetition of labour strife, of political corruption, of exposures of brigandage by industrialists, of undeclared but bloody wars all over the outside world, of the darkening menace of the dictator states, all these things have urged the citizen to ask what's happening beneath the surface, and why? Public affairs have at last become of public interest.

To meet this demand, new techniques have been developed in all modern mediums for communication of fact. From the straightforward presentation of news to the dramatized expression of an editorial opinion, there have been experiments which might not have been made if aesthetic purpose had been the sole urge. The success of pictorial journalism in such American papers as *Life* and *Photo-History*, of dramatic rendition of current events over the air by the *March of Time*, and of such sociologically important productions in the American theatre as *The Living Newspapers*, *Pins and Needles* and *The Cradle Will Rock* is proof of the existence of an alert public interest in public affairs. The film industry, usually slow to catch on to new movements, has played a leading and influential part in this dramatization of fact. The camerawork of newsreel and documentary films has been mainly responsible for the great strides made in photo-journalism. Today, the movie as a medium for presenting fact, as a reflection of reality, offers more stimulating chances for creative experiment than the socially-constricted fiction film.

Films of Fact and Fiction (1938)

Regular moviegoers know what is being done to bring reality to the screen. The *March of Time* swings along with its pendulum beat. The newsreel, still shy of public reaction to screen controversy, scores an occasional success by a cameraman who has the luck and toughness to be on the spot, as at the Chicago steel riots and the *Hindenburg* airship disaster. The documentary film grows out of its infant stage of romantic impressionism and gets down to using human beings as well as machines. But at each step forward the makers of factual films are met by the same problem—the representation of the individual and the relating of that individual to his social and economic background.

The closer the movie gets to a dramatized expression of reality, and I mean current reality, the more acute becomes this problem of the portrayal of the individual. In the newsreel, facts are represented simply in terms of their physical appearance in time. While current they are news, but they soon become history. The drama lies in the vitality and authenticity of the material and not in the method of presentation. The *March of Time* monthly film issue made its appearance in America in 1935. The reel adapts from the newspaper a reporting purpose which claims to give the inside story behind current events and borrows from the fiction film a dramatic method of presentation. Using partly the same naturally-shot material which is the stuff of newsreel and partly staged dramatic scenes with both real people and actors, it tries to present a selective picture of an event which implies a comment, often ironic, upon the event itself. Like the newsreel, it uses also the method of the personal interview but bends the individual to fit its editorial purpose, as with the junk-merchant in the Scrap-Iron item recently issued. Its narration is written in a highly descriptive, provocative style and delivered with a breathless emotion which does not always coincide with the subject of its visuals. But its journalistic insistence on speed leaves little time for treating individuals; the reel lacks human quality almost as much as the newsreel from which it stems.

In the Soviet Union the dramatization of fact has been a first aim since the cinema was nationalized in 1919. Many of the earlier Soviet films dealt with what was to their sponsors and creators the greatest event of modern history—The Workers'

Revolution of 1917 and the historic events that led up to its success. Pudovkin's *Mother* was based on Gorki's novel of the 1905 revolution; Eisenstein's *Potemkin* on the Black Sea mutiny of the same year. It is worth noting that both films, along with others, departed freely from actual fact.

The physical effects made possible by rhythmic arrangements of shots, as had been first used by D. W. Griffith in *Birth of a Nation* and *Intolerance*, were exploited to put across in a semi-sensational, semi-hysterical manner this blood-and-fire material. Analysis of their editing methods showed Eisenstein and Pudovkin a way in which the film medium could conform to the fundamental principles of Marxist dialectic reasoning. Their films of mutiny and uprising were largely based on the clash of class against class, or the mob versus the military. Their drama was conflict. And so long as their subject material was the stuff of revolution, their methods were successful.

In many of the early films, natural actors were used. While they were running around in the mass, they ran as well as any trained actors could have run. But when individual characterization was required, new and serious problems arose. People as individuals in relation to their social and economic background demand psychological understanding and screen interpretation which cannot always be achieved by tricks of editing. Thus the Russians found themselves up against both a technical problem in film direction and a sociological problem of the place of the human being in society. In interpreting human beings in films, the Russians had also to interpret the individual's attitude towards the State and his economic and social relationships, a problem that had not before been seriously met in movies. In most American and European fiction films the subjects did not reflect the social conditions of the period, except in such rare cases as the modern story in Griffith's *Intolerance* and in Von Stroheim's *Greed*. But once the Soviet directors, like the British documentary film-makers later, decided that their films should deal with real life, they were inevitably involved in the bigger sociological issue.

Recent events have shown that the solution to this problem depends largely upon the development of social and economic problems in the Soviet State itself. The enthusiastic self-criticism so popular in the Russian arts has continually expressed dissatisfaction with these efforts, and at the Moscow Film Festival in 1935 it was stated that the films of Pudovkin and Eisenstein were 'undramatic' and coldly 'intellectual'. The crowd must no longer be the hero; it must be represented through the character development of its leader. The theory and practice of montage which had worked so well with non-actors and mass-movement must be reconsidered in the light of the emotional powers of the professional actor. 'We need actors with great passions,' proclaimed Dinamov; and *Chapaev,* with its actor-hero Boris Babotchkin, was the film of the year, although technically it was inferior to the work of the better-known directors. The subsequent development of this trend produced films like *The Youth of Maxim* in which story and acting illustrated the developing intellectual and emotional experiences of the chief protagonists as they reacted to changing social occurrences.

Pudovkin attempted to meet the difficulty by going straight to the individual himself, studying his behaviour, trying to understand his reactions and then building the character filmically by editing methods. He got his actors to externalize their feelings before the camera by using various trick stimuli. Eisenstein, on his return from Mexico and the U.S., did not resume production but assumed the role of professor and developed a series of methods (the 'internal monologue', the creation of a class character who will act as *pars pro toto* for the mass) by which he hoped to emotionalize and humanize the ideological film. Thus actors and acting returned in full force to the Soviet film studio. Stories and plots were invented. With this sudden swing from one use of the medium to another there has inevitably resulted a technical and aesthetic setback. The recent Russian films have had more human qualities than those of ten years ago but they have not equalled the technical brilliance that made *Potemkin* and *Storm Over Asia* world-famous.

In Britain, the documentary film-makers are at present faced with this same problem of the individual. Technically and aesthetically, the documentary film includes most of the innovations of the past ten years but it is important to remember that, as in the Soviet cinema, aesthetic purpose has come second to

27. ON THE BOWERY (1955–56), *a documentary made about the alcoholics of New York's skid-row, directed by* Lionel Rogosin *and* Mark Sufrin, *with photography by* Richard Bagley

28. (a) NORTH SEA (1938), Harry Watt *and* Cavalcanti's *documentary of the ship-to-shore radio service in Scotland.* (GPO Film Unit)

28. (b) CHILDREN OF THE CITY (1944), Budge Cooper's *social study of juvenile delinquency in Scotland.* (Ministry of Information *and* Paul Rotha Productions)

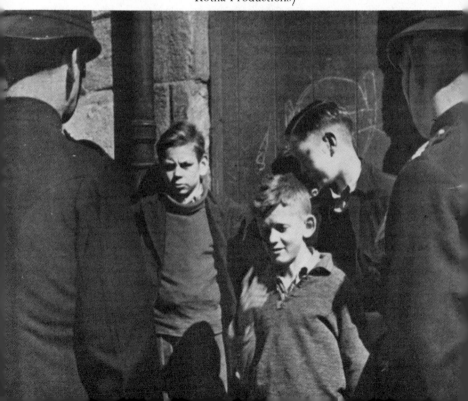

sociological aim. Through historical research, social reference and economic understanding, they try to bring the ordinary citizen closer to the world which is intimately his own. Like the Russians, they aim to interpret the modern scene but their basis of production is different.

Although subsidized, these documentary films should not be confused with commercial advertising pictures such as are produced in Britain and America.[1] The documentary film is an outcome of a public relations movement and results from a conscious desire on the part of government departments, industrial firms and various public bodies to create a deeper understanding between their activities and public awareness. Their makers take subjects which are only of acknowledged public interest and pursue the line that their films provide a basis for discussion on some of the more vital social issues of current living. By creating on the screen a dramatic picture of how people live and how public services work and what status the ordinary citizen can have in everyday life, these films have achieved a certain civic value. During the last six years films have been made on such divergent subjects as airways, shipping, unemployment, slum-clearance, radio and postal-communication, electricity, gas, education, book-publishing, railroads, nutrition, and city administration. Thus while such social problems as unemployment and slum-clearance had been discussed in Parliament and the Press, the living fact of each as it affects the people has been brought to the screen, making audiences conscious of their vital concern in current public affairs.

Most of the early British documentary films, like *Industrial Britain* and *Contact*, treated the individual simply as an uncharacterized type. He may have been given a name and a place by the commentator but he was invested with no human feelings and related to no background beyond his immediate job. In many cases, the interest of the film director lay in the job and not

[1] Some thirteen films representative of the British documentary film movement are now (1937) deposited in the Film Library at the Museum of Modern Art, New York, from which they may be hired for non-commercial performances.

Addendum: (August, 1957). The circulation later given to these films and the prestige they accumulated did much to build the foundation for the subsequent nation-wide distribution of British documentary films in the United States by British Information Services. Cf. p. 246 *et seq.*

o

in the man who was doing it, unless it was to make him the romantic figure of a craftsman as did Flaherty with his glass-blowers and pottery-makers in the Black Country. Most often the documentary film-makers were embarrassed at the thought of handling their people *as people* and took the easiest way out by treating them as symbols ('the man behind the machine'). In addition, most of the directors were young and lacked familiarity with the materials of the medium. When Grierson made *Drifters* in 1928, he confesses that he did it 'without knowing one lens from another'. Again, the romantic style most nearly approached the 'interest' pictures and travelogues to which audiences were accustomed and thus the films made in this style, like *Contact* and *O'er Hill and Dale*, were at first the most popular. It was not long, however, before simple lyric films like *The Country Comes to Town* were developed into such an aesthetically satisfying film as Basil Wright's *The Song of Ceylon*, and the striving after social analysis made something more of *Shipyard* than just a descriptive film of shipbuilding. This trend continues to be developed, using new techniques of sound and speech, and has resulted in such emotionally exciting and sometimes romantic films as *Night Mail* and *The Future's in the Air*, although the place of the individual is still largely ignored.

The personal interview with camera and microphone, first used in Elton's *Workers and Jobs* and Anstey's *Housing Problems* in 1935, cut right across this impressionist style. Here were real human beings spontaneously speaking and gesturing right into the lens and microphone. This was not acting but normal behaviour far as the presence of the camera would permit. Sociologically, this was important; but the method deprived the documentary film of much of its cinematic quality. It became an illustrated lecture studded with personal interviews which provided 'documentary' evidence that the unseen commentator was speaking the truth. To set up camera and microphone and to record what is placed before them, occasionally cutting away from the portrait of the speaker to visuals of what he is talking about, is nobody's creative fun except that of the newsreel cameraman. *The Nutrition Film* (*Enough to Eat?*), *Smoke Menace* and *Children at School* followed the same method although the latter staged small scenes in which professional actors were used. Valuable as sociological documents, and it is important that they are being made, these films contribute little to the fundamental problem of the dramatic presentation of human beings. Aesthetically, they mark a conscious effort to break with the romantic approach of *Coal Face* and *Night Mail.*

This danger of journalistic reporting and the snapshot influence of the *March of Time* were recognized by Cavalcanti. In *We Live in Two Worlds* he tried to combine both the interview and the impressionistic style in an intimate globe-side chat with Mr. J. B. Priestley. But even this was not using the individual as actor. The Swiss peasants were as uncharacterized as the glass-blowers in *Industrial Britain.* The attempt to humanize the postal-workers, especially the nervous trainee in *Night Mail,* was more successful. So far only two British documentaries have got down to the real problem.

The Saving of Bill Blewitt, a story of fisher-people in a small Cornish village, is perhaps the best example of the handling of natural actors in documentary. But the plugged publicity angle of the Savings Bank was so incongruous beside the honesty of the people themselves that despite its subtle introduction, the audience was resentful at being fooled. For all the natural quality of the acting and the technical skill of Cavalcanti and Harry Watt's production, the film never got beyond being a publicity film as did *Night Mail* and *The Song of Ceylon. Today We Live,* a film of social service activities, carried a slight story based on fact and alternated between two locations—a town in a depressed mining area in South Wales and a country village in the Cotswolds. The characters were played by unemployed miners and country villagers. None of them was required to do anything which he or she did not do in ordinary life, with the result that, although sincere, their 'acting' was without emotional appeal. By nature of its dual location, moreover, the film lacked the space to develop human characterization in each sequence and would have succeeded better, I believe, had its sponsors agreed to tell one story instead of two. Despite this, *Today We Live* gave an authentic picture of life as it is lived in two widely differing parts of Britain and, for almost the first time in documentary, had intentional humour. The characters grew out of their surroundings and their economic circumstances determined their actions. It is doubtful if professional actors would have done the job better.

The few available American documentary films do not contribute much to this discussion. The Mexican-made *The Wave* used non-professional actors but either lack of direction or the superimposition of a philosophical argument on persons who did not fully understand its implications resulted in a picture of embarrassing awkwardness. Neither of Pare Lorentz's well-known films, *The Plow that Broke the Plains* or *The River*, had any attempt at characterization. Despite its difficult production circumstances, Joris Ivens' *The Spanish Earth* had considerable human feeling which arose, I suspect, from the very nature of the material and Ernest Hemingway's narration.

In retrospect, we must not overlook the films of Robert Flaherty. It is true that he is mainly interested in the re-enactment of fading customs and crafts among semi-primitive peoples, but Flaherty, more than any other documentary film-maker, has known how to handle his people in front of the camera. He is helped, of course, by the fact that most of us are unfamiliar with his people and it is only when he treads on the home-front, as in *Industrial Britain* and *Man of Aran*, that we realize his shortcomings. But his habit of digging himself in, absorbing the background and letting the theme emerge gradually is, without doubt, a sensible method if the production budget permits.

As far as the individual in the studio-made fiction film is concerned, we shall find that few fiction films deal with subjects which have their roots in reality. While subjects have little in common with real life, this discrepancy does not matter. But when the movie touches social reality in the gangster film, Cagney cannot be just Cagney. No more can Muni be just Muni when the social background becomes real, or pretends to be real, in *Zola*. Here was a character who must needs be deep-rooted in his background. Relation of character to background is a familiar matter to the stage actor but it is more difficult on the screen. More difficult because the illusion of background on the stage is known and accepted as an illusion, whereas the screen can present a background that, for all its studio artifice and back-projection, is very close to the real thing, in fact, often is. A wide difference exists between Muni playing Zola with the aid of an elaborate make-up and weeks of historical research, and Cagney playing Tom Powers in *The Public Enemy.* The first was a deliberate fake; the second was real. I am not suggesting that Mr. Cagney is, or was, a gangster but I am saying that he, like so many other born New-Yorkers, knew what he was acting about. He knew the smell of the thing because it was contemporary and real. As a result, he was able to create a closer relationship between character and background than did Mr. Muni, whose performance was nearer to that of a filmed photoplay than a film. I doubt if it is the screen's function to show dressed-up history. The medium is perhaps too real.[1]

I have raised, I hope, a whole series of questions that go right to the heart of the movie. Can the studio-made fiction film with actors and sets come as close to presenting reality as the realist film? No matter how faithful the sets, how convincing the acting and how accurate the research, can a studio reconstruction achieve the dramatic intensity which is inherent in the real thing? Could the trick department restage the burning of the *Hindenburg* so as to give us that same sense of horror which we got from the newsreel? Shall we not always be aware of the fake? Then is it possible to bring about a blending of the two methods; or should the fact film and the fiction film pursue their divergent courses? Only on such rare occasions as Pabst's *Kameradschaft* have the two approaches been married with success. Pabst's mixing of actors with real people, or real exterior backgrounds with studio-built interiors, was so perfectly done that the audience was not aware that it was not seeing reality. It is surprizing that so little has been done to develop Pabst's theories, theories which he himself has been unable to develop owing to the unsuitable subjects of his later films. But *Kameradschaft* does suggest a logical development of the realist film which takes the best from both the fiction and the fact film.[2]

—THEATER ARTS MAGAZINE, *New York, March*, 1938.

[1] Cf. p. 66.

[2] The Italian neo-realist approach dating from Visconti's *Ossessione* (1942) developed this intermixing of reality with fiction, culminating in De Sica's masterpiece, *Umberto D* (1951). Recent examples are Dassin's *Celui Qui Doit Mourir* and Bresson's *Un Condamné à Mort s'est Echappé*.

Films of Fact and the Human Element (1938)

A frequent criticism of the British film industry is that the majority of its films do not describe life as lived by British people. Of the many reasons given for this failure to express the national spirit and the national character on the screen, two are most probable. Our producers and directors, it is said, do not mix with ordinary people and hence their films are untrue to everyday life. Our films should, it is claimed, in supposed likeness to the American product, aim at an international market and therefore the subjects and their treatment must be without national characteristics. The fact is overlooked that American films are usually Hollywood first and international second. Despite the cosmopolitan citizenship of Hollywood, many American films deal with stories and people that are typically American, whereas the British only succeed in being British when they are dealing with a historical subject, which leaves no doubts as to its locale.

In the days of the silent film, our producers often made films of stories true to real life that had a characteristically British strain about them. Films like the original version of *Owd Bob*, *Fox Farm* and *Hindle Wakes* were unmistakably British and they were well liked at home and abroad. Since the coming of the talking film, however, fewer subjects of this kind have been made. We have had a new *Owd Bob*, *The Turn of the Tide*, *The Edge of the World* and *Bank Holiday*, but they have amounted to a small proportion of the total output. It is generally acknowledged that the only films which have consistently expressed real life as it exists in Britain have been documentary films, which the cinema-going public sees only by chance. They have been short in length, without a story or actors, and occupied a minor place without advertisement in the cinema programme.

For some time it has been apparent that a new trend in British films might result if the creative and technical skill of the documentary film were blended with the stories and acting appeal of the feature film.

Indicative of this development were documentary films like *The Saving of Bill Blewitt* and *John Atkins*, by the G.P.O. Film Unit, and the two social service films *Today We Live* and *Eastern Valley*. In them the characters, acted by ordinary people, played a more important part as beings of flesh and blood, with sentiments and emotions, than did the lay-figures of the earlier documentary films like *Face of Britain* and *Aero-Engine*. The structure of these new films, moreover, although centred round a theme, was expanded to include a story which, founded on facts, nevertheless was fictional in treatment. Each of them introduced to the documentary film the elements of humour and drama expressed in personal terms. They marked an important step away from the impersonal technique of such films as *Weather Forecast* and *The Song of Ceylon*, and offered a much-wanted breakaway from the so-called 'journalistic' style of *March of Time*, a style that strongly influenced certain makers of British documentary films.

But the recently shown G.P.O. film *North Sea*, produced by M. Cavalcanti and directed by Mr. Harry Watt, goes much further in humanizing its subject. It is a story of the radio-communication service between ship-and-shore off the east coast of Scotland and of the difficulties experienced by the trawler *John Gillman* in a gale. Whereas two years ago it would have been a film primarily about a storm, today it is a film primarily about human beings and their reactions in a moment of emergency. Acted throughout by real people, it is a remarkable example of how ordinary persons can be directed for the screen. So natural are these fishermen and their families and the radio-operators at the Wick Radio Station that it is difficult to imagine professional actors doing the job better or even as well. Like a director of a feature story-film, Mr. Watt made 'tests' of his 'actors', used careful discrimination in 'casting' and recruited some of his players from the local Employment Exchange. Not all the characters played their real parts. The skipper of the *John Gillman*, for example, is played by the bosun; the skipper's 'wife' by the wife of a local baker. Thus, although the main incident of the film is based on fact, the characters and details are wholly fictional. As in a story-film, dialogue is used throughout. The ubiquitous commentary of many documentary films is happily relegated to a twenty-word sentence at the end.

North Sea may well claim to be considered as the most progressive step in British documentary films since Basil Wright, Watt and Cavalcanti made their by-now internationally famous picture of the Postal Special, *Night Mail*, in 1936. It would be wrong, however, to estimate *North Sea* in terms of documentary perspective alone. By its fictional element as well as by its characterization and in spite of its relatively small cost of production, it claims to be measured against the story-films of the studios. Its place of showing should be the cinemas, not the lecture-halls of the country.

Since the passing of the Films Bill (1938), the executives of the British film industry have seemed doubtful as to what policy to pursue. *North Sea* suggests a lead. It offers an example to those who apparently have access to money to spend in rebuilding our film industry as a medium to interpret the best sides of our national life without false sentiment. *North Sea* is more than a good British documentary film.[1] It is a film that makes most other film-making look dull. It sets a target for the future. If shown abroad, it could do much to inspire respect for that habit of meeting emergencies with calmness which is so characteristic of the British people and which is so well depicted in this film of bravery at sea and at home.

—The Times, *June* 28, 1938.

[1] Historically, the realist tradition of story-documentary later associated with Ealing Films stems from *North Sea*, as also did some of the major war films by the Crown Film Unit. Harry Watt's development from *North Sea* to *The Overlanders* was an important contribution to British cinema. It is disappointing that his later work has not pursued the same course.

The British Case (1) *(1940)*

Before me is a film trade-paper, full of brash advertisements. It pledges every new film will be a smash-hit at the box-office. It tells what's doing in our British studios (where any room is left to work). There's a story about Disraeli and How the Empire Was Built; there's another about spooks and spies; they are remaking that oldster *The Ghost Train*; and of course there's Mr. Wells' *Kipps* and Mr. Shaw's *Major Barbara. This England* sounds like a saga from generation to generation and *Once a Crook* tells of 'a released convict turned publican and intending to go straight until menaced by former associates'. Someone's making *Love on the Dole,* after being held up by the censor for three years. Of all these films, only one is about the common folk. But why *Love on the Dole* now when *Love in a Shelter* would perhaps be more apt? With the whole nation defending its front door-step, with our leaders (we hope) planning attack, are these the only screen stories we can find in the gravest hour in our history?

Much fuss has been made about the documentary—or real-life—films which our Ministry of Information has sponsored. The emotional five-minutes of *Britain Can Take It* has had more publicity than most £100,000 features films. But, good as it is, *Britain Can Take It* is a very impersonal film. Well as it serves its aim to show Americans that London is not the rubble-heap that Dr. Goebbels claims, this little film has nothing of the human story of London. Others of these short films have been good, but for the most part they've been cold, impersonal descriptions of things happening. They've shown the background of Britain at war but not the foreground of human stories, those thousands of personal stories that happen every time a bomb drops, a fighter roars up, a communiqué is issued, or a troopship leaves. Each of these dramatic stories is typical of hundreds of tangled sets of emotions and feelings that, taken together, make up what they call the Nation's Morale. Am I wrong when I say that these qualities of bravery and resilience, of patience and endeavour, are qualities admired by all the non-combatant world? Aren't *these* the film stories to be sent abroad to counter Nazi scorn for an 'effete' democracy?

The short documentary films are doing fine within their cramped ten minutes. But American screen audiences, and for that matter British, too, are used to having big events and big themes presented to them in human terms. By all means let's use real backgrounds but let's find the human stories that every day emerge from them.

For the past few weeks I've been working in a mobile canteen in a much-bombed area in the East End. I go down there at nights because it has been a means of keeping in touch with people who night after night are living a new kind of life of hardship and bravery. There are dozens of other areas in London where this is going on—in the shelters of Kensington and Kensal Green, Hampstead and Hoxton. But to me this nightly experience of the East Enders has in it the very essence of human stories.

Here under these railway arches, lying out in ones or twos or a whole family group, on mattresses and blankets and coats, is a new kind of community living. In each arch a single-shaded lamp throws down a circle of light leaving shadows in the corners where the tired are already asleep. Here is a scene which only Dickens could have put into words but which is live and real for the modern movie-camera. Away from the arches, with their card games and cocoa, in the pub on the corner, are those who up till the last minute to closing-time sing and talk and dance. A boy pianist 'swings' the tunes they like most and they are not war tunes. By day he works in munitions. In these smoke-laden, music-filled bars is a spirit that I have not seen in the West End on the few nights I have been there since the Blitz. Here are people who are working harder than ever before in their lives, people who no longer sleep in their homes (if they still have them) people who have known now over ten weeks of almost unbroken night bombing. Until this pub is hit, as many have been hit, it will remain full. If it is hit, the survivors will find another.

Through the curtain and outside the swing-door, the night is either soaked in rain or brilliant with moon. Now you can hear the bombers. The flashing points of light are shell-bursts. The street is empty save for unclaimed cats. Each gap in a row of houses, houses which should have been pulled down years ago, hides a story. The family may have moved higher up the street; it may have been split up, the mother and children evacuated to the country, the father and sons remaining at their jobs; it may have been wiped out except for one survivor who now lives in the shelter by night and the factory by day.

Long before dawn we drag the canteen to its parking-place beneath the railway arch that spans the street. One by one they come out of the shelters, blowing into their hands for warmth. Maybe they bless the rain-sodden night; it's kept 'him' away. But it's meant drips from the roofs and puddles on the floor. Cups of tea we pour by the dozen. Sandwiches, biscuits and cheese. Yet the thing we 'sell' most is the time. Always that fear of being late at the factory, the workshop, the wharf. Men and women about to go to work. Men and women just getting home from work. And each line of dialogue has its story.

'If I hadn't stopped in at the boozer, that one would have got me.'

'It's eight teas this morning, dear, we've got company.'

To me here is a picture a hundred times more worth making than those on our studio-floors. Here is life as it is really being lived. Here are the boy and girl who used to have the front room in which to talk over their future; now they have the local picture-house on Saturday afternoon or the shelter at night. Here is the docker who for the first time in fifteen years has no wife to get the meals and to sit in the pub corner with her Guinness. Now she's in Cornwall or Shropshire. Or dead. Here is the boy on leave, come back to find his chums and family have seen more of death and destruction by war than he has. Here are the flashes of humour, the quick repartee, the generous gesture of giving to anyone in need, that make up that intangible thing they call the Nation's Morale.

And through it all comes one stark thing; the need to win this war. All of them have this aim deep down, but not all are clear how and when it will be done. Not all, either, are clear about the future when the war is won, but those who are have one set aim in mind—never again shall there be a return to things 'as they were'.

So let our picture-makers try some human stories set among such real backgrounds as this. Let the real stories of Britain be told because *they* are the stories in which we can take pride. The Treasury has invested £25,000 of public money in sending a film company to Canada.[1] Can't it spare a little for a film of the East End, the South Bank of the Thames, the Midland towns—the hundreds of stories that are happening right on our doorstep? When on that fateful Saturday afternoon of September 7 the bombs first rained down from the sky on London, few newspapers realized that here was the new Front Line. They had sent their ace-correspondents by air to Helsinki and Oslo, but they forgot to send them by bus east of Aldgate. Ritchie Calder went alone for the *Herald*.[2] Is it to be the same with films? We've had *Convoy* and *Contraband*, but who's making *Coventry*? Instead of the Victorian *An Empire Was Built* I want to see *The People of the Shelters* and *Men Without Medals*. They would be real films of Britain.

—*November*, 1940.

[1] *The 49th Parallel*, by Powell and Pressburger.

[2] *Vide: Carry on, London!*, by Ritchie Calder (English Universities Press, 1941), a fine, eloquent job of on-the-spot reporting of Home-Front during the Blitz.

The British Case (2) (1941)

One little island off the coast of Europe fighting for its life; is this still the text by which we are selling the war to the world while the enemy is selling a New World Order? One little island where age-old traditions and heredity of possession still count for more than popular feeling and communal ownership; is this still the expression of Britain's case to the neutrals on the fence? We are being asked for an answer, for an alternative conception of living to that proposed by the Nazi and Fascist ideologists. One issue alone is involved, no more, no less: for what are we fighting? The answer, if it is being given, must be a positive philosophy for the future, must set out the whole alignment of Britain's youth to the rest of the world. It is an answer that must contain all the reasons for our endurance, our sacrifice, and our effort. It is an answer which, I imagine, keeps our foreign information services humming by night and day. Much there must be about the message transmitted by our propaganda machinery which it is clearly not politic to discuss. But if an answer such as we know *should* be given *is* being given, it cannot be sealed in the privacy of the council chamber, the sanctuary of the broadcasting closet, or the sound-proofery of the film studio.

My language is the film; and it is the message in the films we are sending, and plan to send, overseas about which I am anxious. My authority to discuss is the authority of one of the documentary film-makers who long ago realized Britain's need to master and employ the art of national projection. It was of our views that Sir Stephen Tallents wrote in *The Projection of England* in 1932: 'She (England) must in the first place project upon the screen of world opinion such a picture of herself as will create a belief in her ability to serve the world under the new order as she has served it under the old.' That has been the motive behind a hundred, nay two or three hundred, documentary films made this last ten years, and behind the comings-and-goings of the British documentary people to America and the Commonwealth and back. My anxiety is strong now because I fancy I see all the old ideas and all the old arguments of propaganda being dusted anew for another journey overseas.

Our British propaganda film service has recently been more active and come in for not a little praise. Some documentary units are working full tilt. To those of us who know something of the film propaganda problem, there appears to be more efficiency with detail and more care in production-planning than we found at the Ministry of Information a year ago. Some films are even being commissioned to suggest how changes in our way-of-living today may affect our way-of-living in the future. Most of the Ministry's films appear destined for home consumption. Little information is to hand about plans for overseas. But if they are carrying the message of our war and post-war aims to the world, surely we need to know those aims? The Ministry preserves the silence of obscurity.

Not so the British Council. Challenged on five points by *Documentary News Letter*, the Director of its Films Department replied in an interview to *World's Press News*. Forty films, we learn, will the British Council commission 'to show the world all that is good about Britain—its unrivalled countryside, its historic places, its centres of trade and commerce, the life of its people . . . the films must give a truthful and sincere picture of Britain and British life.' How closely that echoes the words of Philip Guedalla, chairman of the British Council Films Committee, when he was challenged by the Press about Britain's films at the New York World's Fair in 1938: 'Anything that is a pleasure to look at and advantageous to Britain will be shown.' To which Sir David Milne-Watson replied in *The Times*: 'The question really is, what kind of advantage is it worth while Britain seeking in democratic countries at the present time?'

I recall the fears about the British Council's viewpoint expressed by John Grierson at the time: 'On its Council sit representatives of the different political parties, but I would like to be sure that these representatives are as concerned as I am about the democratic nature of the picture we are presenting abroad.'[1]

The British Council's Film Department Secretary stated in September, 1940, that £71,800 was being spent on films—production, distribution and administration—by the Council that current year. These are some of the subjects furnished at request by the Director: Epping Forest, Dartmouth Naval College, What England is doing for the Blind, Oxford, Wiltshire Avon, Shipbuilding, Architecture, London Transport, Natural Resources and Bloodstock Breeding. Mostly the same old rehash, the same old symbols, the same temptation for producing companies to dig into their stock-footage. (*vide:* the films about shipbuilding and national resources.) More recently, at the suggestion of the British Film Institute (*vide:* Seventh Annual Report, 1940), the British Council has undertaken commissioning the production of films for the Export Groups via the Board of Trade, the Export Groups to pay at least 20 per cent of the cost. Two films are in hand, both in expensive Technicolor, one on textiles and another on pottery, while a third for the Lace Trimmings Group is thus reported in the Press: 'pictures the formation of crystals, the frost on the window-pane, and the hoar-frost on the spider's web, to show where the designs come from.' What inspiring information indeed for the sixty-odd thousand Iraquis to whom the British Council claims to show its films, or the audience which will cluster round the 16 mm. projector presented by the Council to the Director of Education, Bathurst, Gambia! I trust the Export Groups will satisfy themselves that their films will get the kind of circulation they are seeking, and that they will be shown to selected and not indiscriminate audiences.

What is the history of this Films Committee of the British Council to whom is entrusted this mission of national publicity for the British case overseas? It began with the Travel and Industrial Association's Film Department making documentaries mainly under John Grierson's advice between 1932-36. In 1937, the British Council, its Chairman the late Lord Lloyd, formed a Joint Films Committee with the Travel Association 'for the circulation of British documentary and other films in

[1] Cf. pp. 106, 242, 243.

foreign countries' (*vide:* Annual Report, 1937). Under the chairmanship of Philip Guedalla were representatives of the British Film Institute, the G.P.O. Film Unit (John Grierson, who almost immediately resigned), the Foreign Office, the Department of Overseas Trade, the Travel Association, and the Secretary-General of the Council. For the purpose of the New York World's Fair, the Joint Committee added a representative of the Newsreel Association, a trade body.

Those of us interested in foreign propaganda will remember the antics of this Committee after the Press—ranging from a full-blown two weeks' correspondence and a leader in *The Times* to leaders in most London and provincial dailies and the weekly journals—made some inquiries as to what *kind* of a picture of British life the British Council intended showing to Americans. We also remember that the so-called 'socially-progressive' British films (those that presented 'democracy in its working clothes'), such as the L.C.C. Jubilee film *The Londoners*, were shown not in the British Government building but in the Hall of Arts and Sciences by American request. The British Council would no doubt claim the remarkable success of its New York film-shows. So also would the documentary group. Judgement depends on which pictures of Britain came nearest to presenting the democratic case, that for which we are fighting today, *and* for which America is now sending aid.

At the outbreak of the war, the Films Division of the Ministry of Information was placed under Sir Joseph Ball, late Director of Publicity for the Conservative Party, who called to his aid among others, the General Manager of the British Film Institute (a member of the British Council Films Committee and also late of the Conservative Central Office), the Secretary of the Newsreel Association (late Secretary of the F.B.I. Films Group and a Governor of the British Film Institute), and the head of the G.P.O. Film Unit.[1] When Ball was replaced by Sir Kenneth Clark, after a four months period distinguished by inertia, the first two of these gentlemen also left. The late Secretary of the F.B.I. Films Group was given a new appointment as Director of the British Council Films Committee. A few months later it was this same new Director who was to ask one

[1] Not Mr. John Grierson. He had resigned that post in 1937.

of our most respected Sunday film critics if 'they were not sick if they saw a programme of documentaries', while the General Manager of the British Film Institute, a Treasury-financed body, later used the Institute's official journal to abuse the work of the M.O.I. Films Division. A few months afterwards the G.P.O. Film Unit's representative at the M.O.I. was transferred elsewhere in the Civil Service, but he still retained his seat on the British Council Films Committee.

The whole of this matter could well be dismissed as domestic musical-chairs if it were not for the shocking fact that the British Council Films Committee has the authority to determine a part of the British propaganda film service overseas. Its Secretary, for example, sums up the audience-interest of Latin America —some eighty million people—as being 'concerned mainly with the display of sex' (*sic*). It distributes a composite newsreel, *British News*, made up of excerpts from the five newsreel companies, which has 'given Britain a vast amount of publicity in the U.S. and other countries' and in which '. . . a considerable amount of advertising for British goods is incorporated'. I wonder just how representative of British opinion and outlook is this newsreel? I remember being exhorted in the East End, while dragging a canteen around at dawn in the Blitz, to smile because the newsreel cameraman had implicit instructions to film only people 'laughing at their jobs'.

This Films Committee has not one member professionally skilled in film propaganda, nor does it, to the best of my knowledge, solicit any advice from acknowledged experts in the field. It announces ostentatious plans for the distribution of Empire films overseas and the setting up of an Empire Film Committee but has it, in this connection, taken the advice of, say, the Imperial Relations Trust, which has had made first-hand investigation of this vast problem?

What attitude, may we ask, do these people, either collectively or singly, hold towards the democratic ideas of the future? In what way do they assess the common feeling towards the world for which we are supposed to be fighting? What past achievement or experience have they to qualify them either to commission the making of films with Treasury and/or commercial money, or to select the subject-matter for propaganda films for showing to neutrals and to the Commonwealth peoples at this critical stage in our nation's history?

Soon, if not now, the Dominions and Colonies as well as the neutrals—among them the audiences who supposedly see British Council films—are going to ask whether Britain's representation of the democratic case for the future is honest or not? If not honest, then they will demand an unequivocal representation of British popular feeling. Some of us do not think that the British Council films offer that representation. The neutrals and the Commonwealth peoples are of necessity concerned with what kind of a world Britain will wish to see if we win the war, and what our attitude will be towards a new deal for the peoples of all nations. Some of us doubt if the British Council Films Committee has even thought of this; or if it has, its films suggest rather that it favours a return to the *status quo* which we, as well as the neutrals and Commonwealth peoples, know can never be.

The Ministry of Information may not outlive the war. The life of the British Council is not so prescribed. No one concerned with the democratic cause can fail to subscribe to the aims and objects of the British Council, some of which have been efficiently and imaginatively carried out. It is because the good work done by the Council as a whole stands out in contrast to some of the activities of its Films Department that an urgent reorganization of the latter's policy and personnel appears necessary if the films it commissions are to represent overseas the real feeling of the British people.

—NEW STATESMAN & NATION, *March* 4, 1941.

Documentary is Neither Short Nor Long (1946)

As British documentary comes out of the strenuous demands of the war effort, it is faced like all the media of expression with problems of its own. Some of these are internal, matters of economics and organization; some are trade, matters of equipment and matters of distribution; some are political, matters of sponsorship and information needs; and some, ideological, where documentary finds common ground with other creative forces.

In this brief comment on the position in which British documentary film-makers find themselves today (1946), I should first note some of the limitations under which our films are operating. Distribution bulks biggest. Before the war, documentary distribution was mainly a matter of *ad hoc* arrangement. The non-theatrical field was only just being developed and not on lines which would repay expenditure on production for many years; indeed, much of its distribution was free. The theatrical field of the cinemas was a question of making a film first, arguing with the trade that it was worth showing afterwards. Certain pictures, notably *North Sea, Night Mail* and *The Future's in the Air*, had quite wide commercial bookings, but they did not recover what they cost to make owing to the low prices paid by exhibitors for such films. Others—*The Song of Ceylon, Today We Live* and *The Londoners*—had insignificantly few showings, achieving their international reputation largely in the Press and at film society and specialist cinema showings. At no time in the 'thirties was a British documentary film ever produced on the normal commercial footing of making back its production cost, plus a profit, from showings in the public cinemas.

During the War, with very few exceptions, the distribution of our films was not our headache. The Ministry of Information arranged its own theatrical distribution contracts with the trade through the Kinematograph Renters' Society, and built up its own very successful non-theatrical free distribution through the Central Film Library.

Target for Tonight, *Desert Victory*, *Western Approaches* and other famous feature-length documentaries received a wide commercial distribution in the cinemas earning considerable revenue. It is impossible to say if they earned their capital outlay because of the difficulty of assessing their accurate cost, due to the complex inter-departmental relationships during production—Service rates-of-pay, allocation of Government-hired studio-space and so on. In any case, a cash return was not the reason for which they were made.

Today, the Central Office of Information has replaced the Ministry of Information but we have yet to know if or how it will distribute its films in the cinemas, or what the trade's attitude will be to Government films now that the compulsory motive of 'national interest' is gone. The Board of Trade has received an offer from the Rank and A.B.C. circuits to accept for distribution a certain number of 'independent' films.[1] Will Government-sponsored feature documentaries come within this offer? If the trade refuses adequate cinema release for Central Office of Information films (assuming they will be as well-made as during the war), what action will the Government be prepared to take to get its films shown? It may develop widely its own non-theatrical machinery, but important as this is for a specialized service of information, it cannot offer the size of audience available in the cinemas without a very large capital expenditure, and at the risk of wholly alienating the exhibiting side of the film industry.

It should be remembered, moreover, that the most commercially successful of the Government's war films were those of the combat fronts, *Desert*, *Tunisian* and *Burma Victory*, *Target for Tonight*, *Coastal Command*, *Journey Together*, *Western Approaches* and *The True Glory*. The public wanted to see these films because they were dramatized actuality, with all the physical ex-

[1] Cf. p. 265.

citement and dramatic action of raid and battle and shipwreck.

Technically very well-made, they were not in the traditional line of peace-time documentary and, with some exceptions, they were not made by technicians from the prewar British documentary group.

Except for two, all the directors of those wartime successes have now moved out of the Service and Crown Film Units into commercial feature production. They have migrated as individuals, not as a group, which means that their influence on behalf of the documentary idea over commercial production will be fragmentary. I stress this point because I think that the documentary people are going to find some difficulty in making the subjects of peacetime Britain exciting enough to reach feature-length and to get cinema distribution willingly offered by the trade to the Central Office of Information.

The makers of what we may call the social and informational documentaries have very largely been engaged during the war in producing for the non-theatrical field. Their films have seldom been more than half-an-hour in length, the great majority being two-reelers. When they have been made specifically for the cinemas, as in the case of the 'five-minute' and 'fifteen-minute' Ministry of Information films, the distribution was free by arrangement with the trade, and not on the commercial terms of the Ministry of Information feature-length documentaries. In my opinion, many of these non-theatrical pictures could well have been shown in cinemas, being of infinitely better quality than the great majority of commercially-rented short entertainment films. Ralph Keene's series *Pattern of Britain*, many of Realist's films and such pictures as *Nightshift* and *Life Begins Again* deserved wide public showing. But the Ministry of Information was notoriously weak in its trade relations where films other than those of the *Desert Victory* type were concerned. Its renting arrangements for pictures like *Our Country*, *Cyprus is an Island*, *Today and Tomorrow*, *Silent Village* and *Diary for Timothy* left much to be desired. The Ministry of Information was least successful in its presentation of films. It too easily accepted the trade's negative reaction to anything but orthodox entertainment.

I do not blame the renters concerned. They are only fighting the battle with exhibitors which some of us knew so well before the war. It is worth recording, at this point, that there is no British company today producing *and renting* short films on their own account.

The foregoing remarks on the quality of non-theatrical production do not imply, however, that the makers of these short documentaries can necessarily immediately fill the gap left by the exodus of feature documentary directors into commercial production. Having had some experience at producing feature-length documentaries on social themes, I can say with honesty that it requires very considerable ingenuity to create dramatic suspense and narrative value to enable you to reach the 45-minute length. Such films are also growing more and more costly to make, calling for direct dialogue, studio-work and possibly professional actors. This is a very real personnel and economic problem facing British documentary.

Although films for the wartime Ministry of Information were considered 'in the national interest', technicians being given deferment for their making and several million pounds being spent on their production and distribution by the Treasury, it is worth stating here that the civilian production companies making them were given no priorities of any value, no access to new equipment, and no special production facilities. In 1938-39, thirty to forty documentary films would have been reckoned a total output. Between 1941 and 1945, well over 500 films must have been made for the Ministry of Information alone by a handful of independent documentary companies. That figure does not include the output of the Ministry's own Crown Film Unit or films for the Services. These films had no priority during production over entertainment films, advertising films or newsreels. Units were left to use what technical facilities they could themselves find, to train new technicians if personnel could be got, and to interchange staff and equipment among themselves. They emerge from the war, therefore, with perhaps an increased skill of film-making, more units and more technicians, but with equipment sadly the worse for wear, increased costs of raw stock, laboratory processing and other facilities, and wages that have considerably risen.

In internal organization, the documentary film-makers set

up their own organization a year ago (1945), the Federation of Documentary Film Units, and that body has already done much good work. It will, I hope, among other things gradually destroy the belief that all documentaries are necessarily short films. This common misunderstanding has, in my opinion, done the documentary movement much harm. It arose originally when the Association of Short Film Producers was formed to act in trade matters on behalf of the short film-makers, including advertising and cartoon film companies. It has been subsequently found that, what some of us foresaw in the first place, the policies of all short film-makers are by no means compatible. The motive underlying the manufacture of advertising and publicity films, for which screen-space is hired to the advertiser, cannot remotely be linked with that underlying documentary production. Similarly, the commercial outlook of the short film companies attached to major feature production companies is impossible to reconcile with the policy held by the independent documentary units.

From 1935 until the spring of 1940, the unity of purpose of British documentary film-makers was expressed through the Associated Realist Film Producers group, which later worked in close co-operation with Film Centre when that body was set up in 1937. The Associated Realist Film Producers was discontinued in the war years because most of its membership was scattered, but before long there arose the need for another body to express the documentary outlook. In 1945, after more than six months' discussions, the new Federation was started, working again in friendly co-operation with Film Centre and its consultancy services.

Further confusing documentary with short films in general is the Association of Cine-Technicians' Short Film Agreement, which lumps all films running to 3,000 feet or less under one heading, making certain wage exceptions where documentary films of more than 3,000 feet achieve cinema-release and where advertising films are made for hired screen-space.

I have long been puzzled as to why a technician who works on a documentary film of more than 3,000 feet in length should be paid more than if the film was under 3,000 feet, when in either case the film may have commercial showing. I can see the

Association of Cine-Technicians' difficulties here, and sympathize with them, but point out at the same time that one day documentary production must have its own agreement, as have the newsreels, irrespective of length and not based on the distribution characteristics of its films. The separation of film product into long and short categories is purely a legal convenience originating from the Board of Trade and defined in the various Cinematograph Films Acts.

In sixteen years documentary has been developed as a method of film-making and an approach to the use of the screen totally different from other types of production. It is, and let us be proud of it, a powerful aid to adult education, although its form may be drama. Documentary must always stand on its own two feet as documentary, no matter if it is 2, 4 or 8 reels in length, theatrical or non-theatrical in release. Documentary is not one thing when it is 2,999 feet and another when it is 3,001 feet. It is, in famous words, indivisible.

The economic structure of documentary demands more consideration than it can be given here. It is for the most part forgotten that what may have been achieved by the British documentary makers since 1929 has been done on the most slender resources. The prewar economic basis of all documentary production in Britain was founded on resources less plentiful than those devoted to a publicity campaign for a single American feature. It is sometimes said that the documentary film is the main British contribution to the world of the cinema. If that is the case, it has cost the nation little and the film trade nothing. If anything, the latter has gained, because the documentary influence is clear to see in such commercially successful fiction films as *Millions Like Us*, *The Way Ahead*, *The Way to the Stars* and *In Which We Serve*.[1]

When the Empire Marketing Board set up its small production unit in 1929, from which most of our senior documentary people have stemmed, money for production and money for wages was negligible, a matter of a few thousand pounds a year. Well into the days when the Post Office took over the Empire Marketing Board Unit, production costs were of the slimmest.

[1] And later the output of Ealing Studios and such highly successful films as *The Dam-Busters*, *Reach for the Sky*, and *The Colditz Story*.

Documentary is Neither Short Nor Long (1946)

Film-making was hardly a respectable way for the Treasury to use public funds. Attacked as 'unfair competition' by the trade,[1] this Government production of films now famous—*Night Mail, Weather Forecast, Industrial Britain*—represented expenditure which would have shown little profit if the trade itself had tried to make such films. Apart from this small Government sponsorship, the films commissioned for public relations by such bodies as Shell-Mex and B.P., the Gas Industry, Imperial Airways and the Orient Line, were produced on equally modest budgets. The point is that the full contract money went on the screen. Technicians received a weekly wage that compared unfavourably with what could be obtained on the feature side of the industry. To compensate, they believed in the pictures they were making. Films were produced for the sake of making good films and as a sincere contribution to the social progress of the time.

Documentary's main accomplishment, therefore, has been made possible only by sponsorship from outside the film industry. It is most important that this fact should be widely-known and its implications understood. The production cost of a documentary film, plus the overheads of the company making it, plus any profit that may be required, total a contract price which a sponsor is prepared to pay for a film about a given subject. In return the film is his, copyright and all, to do what he likes with. He may require cinema distribution because of the size of audience-coverage it can offer; bookings at a thousand cinemas can mean that a good many millions of people see the film. He may require specialized non-theatrical distribution, for which he may set up machinery to handle it himself, as several national industries did before the war, and gradually create a film library. But in either case, the sponsor is not primarily interested in the cash returns from the hiring of the film; he is concerned that audiences, either specialized or general, should see his film.

In this way a unique method of documentary film finance has grown up; a handful of small independent producing companies, operating with relatively small capital, carrying out contracts for production and arranging distribution as and when the films are completed. At no time has there been any serious effort to

[1] Report by the Select Committee on Estimates. July 2, 1934.

market documentaries as commercial products because it has always been reckoned that trade renters would not increase their miserable hire-charges because exhibitors would jib at being asked higher rentals for what they still call 'fill-ups'. Only if a documentary runs into the Board of Trade's 'feature' category, that is over 3,000 feet in length, will an exhibitor pay a higher rental, and then not sufficient to offset the increased costs of production for a longer picture.[1]

More money has been available for production as the years have passed, or else documentary could not have become so much more technically elaborate. During the war, the Treasury gradually increased the contract prices of the Ministry of Information films in proportion to the mounting costs of production. But this greater sum of money for production has only meant an increased turnover and provided temporary economic security. Documentary has existed for a good many years now on a remarkably small working capital, which has restricted its control over equipment and facilities for sound-recording and studio floor-space.

It is possible, of course, depending almost wholly on the distribution factor and what steps the Government may take to aid the position of the independent producer, that documentary may not always rely on sponsorship for its production. Sponsorship, whether governmental, industrial or otherwise, can be constricting to creative independence.

Sponsorship is not, one hopes, likely to decrease at any rate for some years ahead in Britain. There should be a big demand for documentary from the Government on the informational and educational levels. Let it be known, however, that the Government's method of commissioning its films during the war has been adequate but not so imaginative or so efficient as it might have been. The method has worked, but not without endless disputes and a loss of time and energy. A film tended too often to become a file and not a film.

Finally, there are the ideological problems lying ahead of documentary. None of us will deny that a common purpose underlies the true documentary conception. Many deviations

[1] The British Film Production Fund (the Eady Plan) has subsequently helped somewhat in this matter.

have been made from it; some necessitated by the war, others because of personal differences in interpreting documentary principles. For myself, I cannot see that the social motives which underlay so much of our work in the 'thirties have changed. A new Government,[1] more representative of popular thought, has replaced that which stood for a privileged minority. A new world organization of nations[2] has replaced the hog-tied League. New machinery is being set up to coordinate and plan in world terms for fundamental securities.[3] There is more need than ever before for a clear interpretation of issues, for explaining governments and organizations one to another and to the peoples they represent. There are still many, many social problems to be solved, many miseries to be exposed for action, many inequalities to be spotlighted and many constructive causes to be made widely known. In all the countless fields open to it, on the international as well as the national level, the documentary ideology can be carried forward in these next years provided that its creative workers maintain that integrity of purpose which has distinguished their contribution up till now.

There are those who talk of documentary merging with the fictional feature film, but they should watch that they do not confuse methods of working with ideological purpose. It matters little how a film is made, if it is made well. Its purpose is another matter. Documentary and commercial features serve different purposes. It will be hard to fuse the two unless the whole basis of theatrical distribution is changed. If the Government itself exercised some ownership over a proportion of cinemas in the country, so guaranteeing screen-space for its own product, and perhaps that of independent producers, then documentary might enter into feature production both for sponsors and on its own financial risk. That is where the next big development in documentary could lie.

—*Extracts from a privately circulated Memorandum, August* 9, 1946.

[1] The Labour Government of 1945.
[2] The United Nations.
[3] The U.N. Specialized Agencies *et al.*

Information Services and Documentary Film-Makers (1947)

At a time when the information service between the British Government and the people it represents ought to be operating on a smooth and imaginative level, there is reason to believe that relations between the newly set-up Central Office of Information and the makers of documentary and informational films are unsatisfactory.

If it is accepted that documentary is a valuable medium for the public expression of information in relation to Government policy, as well as in the service of public education in general, then it would seem that the Central Office is neither using the film medium efficiently, nor has it secured the confidence of the makers of documentary films.

The following brief survey of these relations may interest those concerned with the needs of public information:

1. *Background.* Since 1929, the British documentary film group has been devoted to the service of public information. It has served successive governments and national organizations and the films produced and the distribution methods used have been in the public interest. In its pursuit of public service, it has avoided the normal considerations of commercial film production. Several hundred creative film-makers and technicians have been trained in this tradition of discipline and service. This applies equally to the Government's own film unit, Crown (late G.P.O. and E.M.B. Film Units) and to the dozen or so independent companies devoting their work to documentary and educational film production.

During the war, the machinery of the documentary movement was used almost exclusively by the Ministry of Information and the Service departments. Relations between these companies and the M.O.I. were cordial and on the whole film-makers believed in the films they were asked to make. From an economic point of view, these companies came to rely almost wholly on Government contracts, with the required profit limitations. No commercial market was available to them for speculative production owing to the restrictive circumstances of distribution within the British film industry.

In April, 1946, the Central Office of Information took over certain functions of the wartime Ministry of Information, including the commissioning and distribution of films. In August the documentary producers, through their representative body, the Federation of Documentary Film Units,[1] expressed to the C.O.I. their concern at the delays and confusion attending many of its films. The C.O.I. expressed concern, promised improvements, and suggested regular consultations between representatives of the producers and itself. No such meetings were called. In November, after repeated requests, the Documentary Federation wrote again to the Director-General[2] requesting action. As satisfaction was still not forthcoming, a meeting was held of over fifty senior creative technicians of the documentary film companies and the following resolution was adopted:

'This meeting of technicians is alarmed at the state of affairs revealed in the document presented and endorses the observations made in it. The meeting empowers the Documentary Federation to embody in the document all amendments agreed by the meeting and requests it to despatch the document on its behalf to the Lord President of the Council[3] without delay.'

The document referred to in this resolution was a statistical analysis of the commissions received from the C.O.I. by the eight film companies represented by the Federation in the period April to November, 1946. Relevant excerpts from the preface to this document were:

[1] I had the honour to be its Chairman at the time.—P.R.

[2] Robert Fraser, now Sir Robert, and Director-General of the Independent Television Authority.

[3] Mr. Herbert Morrison, who was the Minister responsible to Parliament for the Central Office of Information.

'The documentary film-makers have been as anxious to contribute to the successful operation of the new Government information services in peacetime as they were during the war. The record of Government film production since April 1*st, however, does not measure up to the past achievements nor to the demands of the moment. No major film, comparable with those produced during the war, has been completed. Delays and obstructions have been increasingly characteristic of the commissions which the documentary units have received.*

'This decline can be attributed to a number of causes, which in our opinion require urgent investigation.'

Among observations offered on the statistical analysis was:

'The total time lost by key-technicians only (i.e. directors and cameramen) as a result of delays and cancellations is 375 *man-weeks in* 8 *months! The number of key-technicians involved has been* 55, *making an average of over* 6 *weeks lost per technician. This figure does not include the time lost by producers, executives and other technicians involved in the productions.'*

It is perhaps worth noting that about this same time, when questioned in the House about the C.O.I. film output, the Financial Secretary to the Treasury replied: 'I can assure my hon. Friend that the relationship of the Films Division of the C.O.I. with the trade is happy, intimate, cordial and continuous.'

As a result of the submission of this document to the Lord President's Office, the Director-General of the Central Office called a meeting between representatives of his office and the Documentary Federation. It was stated that within the next few weeks each of the companies present would be notified as to the extent of film programmes that each would be asked to carry out by the C.O.I.

Subsequently, some but not all of the companies concerned received letters from the Central Office outlining what films they would be expected to make during the current year. These were not contractual commitments but were taken in good faith as a basis on which to plan forthcoming productions and personnel. Six months later few of these proposed subjects had materialized as hard contracts; in the case of one major company, of over 20 reels promised, only one reel had actually been contracted!

At the infrequent meetings of the Producers Committee, set up by the C.O.I. as a result of the last meeting with the Director-General, every opportunity was taken by the documentary representatives to express their apprehension at the continued delays and financial hold-ups. It is now felt that the relations between the documentary companies and the C.O.I. have deteriorated still further.

2. *Quality and Subjects of Films.* It is frequently said by our critics, here and overseas, that British documentary films lead the world, but there is little doubt that the quality of this work has not been maintained in the past two years. It was noticeable at the recent Brussels Film Festival that the British entries in the documentary class excited scant attention; in 1936, our films won all possible awards and were the main topic of the day at Brussels. No films of the calibre and importance of *Desert Victory*, *Target for Tonight* and *Western Approaches* have been produced in Britain since the war. A large proportion of the C.O.I. film programme has been devoted to the specific needs of Government departments which the Central Office exists to serve, designed either for limited non-theatrical distribution or for one-reel release in the cinemas. These small films are capably made and serve their narrow purpose. At the same time, they fail *to inspire the imagination and full creative initiative of our documentary producers. The fact that C.O.I.'s production programme is not conceived on a national level nor geared to the realities of Britain's position in the world has brought about a sense of frustration among the technicians which, together with the delays and financial arguments associated with so many C.O.I. films, has done much to undermine the goodwill of the documentary movement.*

In March, 1946, a Working Party had been set up representative of the C.O.I. and the main documentary producers, including the Crown Film Unit, in order to expedite the immediate production of three major documentary films, which, it was represented, had been urgently called for at Cabinet level. Eighteen months later only one[1] of these films, on the inter-

[1] *The World is Rich.*

national food situation, had been completed. Its production was a procession of hold-ups and financial arguments which more than once brought its makers to the point of resignation. The other two films were abandoned after considerable public money had been spent and many months of senior technicians' time wasted. The Working Party itself continued to meet only as a result of repeated requests by its documentary representatives. At times, it seemed as if senior officials at the C.O.I. had no interest in the film as a medium for public information, although some officers of a lower rank in Films Division must be exempted from this criticism.

Thus, although film-makers must be prepared to accept responsibility for the technical quality of their work, they cannot be blamed for the uninspiring character of the subjects and themes they have been commissioned to make by the C.O.I. *As the major sponsor of documentary films, the C.O.I. must be held responsible for the lack of drama and vitality that regrettably characterizes its current product. British documentary is in danger of resting on its past achievements and is failing to maintain its lead in this branch of the medium.* A widely representative film-makers' meeting held recently in connection with the newly-formed World Union of Documentary expressed great anxiety on this point.

—*Extracts from a privately circulated Memorandum, August,* 1947.

The British Case (3) (1956)

When, nearly five years ago, the Tory Government killed with one swift blow the Crown Film Unit,[1] it did more than break up a loyal group of fine film-makers. It aimed a blow against our vital and permanent need for good British public relations with the world at large.

From 1929 to 1952, the Empire Marketing Board Film Unit—which later became the G.P.O. Film Unit and finally the Crown Film Unit—stood for a progressive, creative and continuous output of films that was the envy of many other countries. From *Drifters* to *Daybreak in Udi* (an Oscar winner) through *Night Mail, North Sea, Target for Tonight, Fires Were Started, Western Approaches* and many others, there stemmed a tradition of official film-making in the public service that made an incalculable contribution to Britain's prestige overseas. It was thrown away overnight, while Parliament was not even sitting to raise a voice in protest. Even Tory high-ups, such as Lord Waverley and Lord Woolton, privately admitted the folly of the act—after it had been committed. No face-saver could be found.

True, Crown was not the only source of outstanding documentary films. Other units had made memorable pictures for the Ministry of Information during the war, and for its dreary successor, the Central Office of Information. But the destruction of Crown was accompanied by a drastic cut in the making of all documentary films in the national interest. It was symptomatic of the official blind spot to the influential role played by films in foreign relations. It swept away all the carefully built-up demand in overseas countries both before and during the war years to see more of these pictures of the British people and their outlook and beliefs. With no new films to replace the old favourites,

[1] *January*, 1952.

our embassies and information centres could no longer fulfil the genuine desire that had been created. That kind of inestimable goodwill cannot be quickly regained.[1]

Granted the vital need to show Britain to the world in terms of film, the old argument arises as to what kind of a picture should we show? Eighteen months ahead in 1958 lies the World Exhibition at Brussels, with more than fifty nations taking part. Our official exhibit is planned to contain an imposing cinema. What films will be shown in it, who will choose them and who will make them? Will British films also make a contribution to the cinema in the United Nations Building? It is not too early to seek answers to these questions. Good films take time to plan, write and produce—even assuming that money is forthcoming to make them!

On my return from the U.S. in 1938, some of us in the documentary film movement campaigned for a widely representative series of films to be sent to the British Pavilion at the New York World's Fair of 1939.[2] It was a golden opportunity to present the real British point of view to the Americans. Soon, however, it became clear that the only films to be sent over by the officially-appointed Selection Committee were to be pretty pictures of Ye Olde Englande, presumably to whip up potential American tourists. This was in spite of the fact that the ideological theme of the World's Fair was The World of Tomorrow!

Having lived for several months with ordinary down-to-earth Americans, I was as convinced then as I am now that what they wanted to see from us were real-life films of our up-to-date, day-to-day existence. Bearded Beefeaters and Ann Hathaway thatched cottages did not speak very convincingly for Britain in the year of Munich. But they were the main products of the British Council's whimsical outlook towards foreigners. When a group of films depicting Scottish achievements in education, industry, agriculture and cultural heritage was ignominiously ignored and then rejected by the Stuffed Shirt Selection Committee, the issue came to a head. A devastating attack on the outmoded Victorian attitude of the officials was initiated by us in

[1] *Vide:* p. 246 *et seq.*
[2] *Vide:* pp. 106, 222, 224.

almost every national daily and weekly journal, culminating in a brilliantly satirical leader in *The Times* which inspired a notable crop of letters. To a small extent the Stuffed Shirts gave way but the memorable part of the whole affair was that the best and most socially-significant British films were shown in New York by special invitation—not in the official British Pavilion but in the Hall of Arts and Sciences where they evoked enthusiastic response!

The Stuffed Shirts of twenty years ago are no doubt now in cosy retirement but new ones are in incubation all the time. (Today they wear curly-brimmed bowlers.) To some official minds Chelsea Pensioners and the Tower Bridge are still the only symbols by which Britain should be known to the world. Do the peoples in the vast awakening nations of Asia, Africa and Latin America as well as the Commonwealth care tuppence about Ye Olde Englande? They want to know about the things that really make Britain tick. They want to see 'democracy in its working-clothes and with its sleeves rolled up' (Grierson's phrase of the late 'thirties), not the fancy-dress relics of a senile British gentility standing aloof from a world of 'Wogs'.

We have, if we take careful stock, a fine record of achievement in social matters that could stimulate the respect of peoples abroad. What has the Welfare State meant to the people of Britain in the past ten years? How has the unseen social revolution of the post-war years affected our lives? What are the vast contributions made to the fabric of the community by the Trade Union and Co-operative movements? Britain may no longer be the Workshop of the World but we are still a rich source of scientific research and endeavour which reaches out and touches the peoples of the world at a thousand levels. We have still the 'know-how', if not the peak in productivity.

And in creating such an overall picture, we should not ignore the many human problems that arise in all social reform. People overseas are just as interested to see how we are grappling with the problems of education, old age, delinquency, housing, civic affairs and industrial safety, to say nothing of the nationalization of some of our industries (to name only a few of the basic problems that confront all democracies today) as they are in seeing our achievements.

Impressive pictures of Calder Hall being built and of its historic opening ceremony by the Queen serve only a narrow purpose. What really matters to the countless millions abroad is how will unlimited nuclear power in years to come affect *their* standards of living and *their* struggle for greater happiness?

In the years leading up to the war, official Britain was slow to grasp that our democratic way of life needed the widest and most imaginative demonstration and explanation overseas if the counter-propaganda of the totalitarian régimes exposing the effeteness of democracy was to be fully challenged.

During the war we began to awake. Some of our most successful films for the Ministry of Information to be sent abroad were constructive pictures of our post-war aims. In 1943, Britain was the only country in the world to forecast by film the vast global problems of food supply and population increase that would arise when the shooting-war was over. *World of Plenty* was a world success because it carried a hope and a promise in war that fundamental issues would be faced when peace should come. That was why, inevitably, there was dislike of the film in high-up circles where big business lurked behind the arras, both in Britain and America. I remember a famous American writer saying, after a run-through of the rough-cut of the film, 'This is the most important film of the war. It is not politics; it is humanity.'

How quickly all that is forgotten! In the past ten years, official Britain has done little to propagate its ideas. I blame equally the governments of Labour and Toryism, as well as the established Whitehall bureaucrats whose machinery and budgets can make such films possible. As a result of a parochial pinchbeck policy in Westminster and Whitehall as well as at Baker Street,[1] the projection of Britain abroad in film has been wilfully neglected. What little has been done has been financially starved. Information needs are always the first to be slashed by the Treasury.

So who speaks in film today for Britain to the world? Is it the British Council, the Foreign Office, the Central Office of Information, the British Overseas Fairs associate of the Federation of British Industries, or who? The Brussels Exhibition in 1958 is only one example of a shop-window in which

[1] Offices of the Central Office of Information.

to show that of which we are still proud. Has anyone shaped out a well co-ordinated policy, stimulated a series of new and finely-made films in our imaginative documentary tradition for showing there? Or are the new Stuffed Shirts relying, as their Dads did, on those hardy perennials—the Trooping of the Colour, the Changing of the Guard and Stratford-Shakespeare's birthplace to dope the millions in the awakening countries in a continued 'belief' in the British *status quo*? Propaganda, information services, public relations—call it what you will—they are a desperately important part of our future standing in the world.

—REYNOLDS NEWS, *December* 16, 1956.

Postscript

To be parochial first, comment has been made on some of the problems of British documentary in the Foreword. Here let me just say that a copy of Dr. Charles Hill's White Paper on Overseas Information Services,[1] which asks for more money naturally, reached me in New York at about the same time ironically enough as it became known that the film section of British Information Services in the United States was to be shut down on the grounds of economy! This example of the left-hand and right-hand proverb strikes me as wholly symptomatic of Whitehall's so-called policy for information services.

In a decade when imagination, efficiency and co-ordination resulting from professional experience in the techniques of national projection have seldom been more needed to present an overall picture of the British people to the world (as well as to themselves), there has never been a bigger muddle or lack of a central policy. Aware dimly that all was not well with this rather ungentlemanly business of publicity—public relations had been blamed as one of the weaknesses at the time of Suez!—Mr. Macmillan announced as part of his new administration that the erstwhile Radio Doctor (Dr. Hill to the ill-informed) would co-ordinate all official publicity and information services at home and abroad.[2] The White Paper to hand is the first result, emerging we are told from a cosy week-end at Chequers.

It avoids, of course, all major problems of policy. It restates all the old platitudes—'We have brought to a fine art the working of democratic institutions. We have high standards of justice, tolerance and truth. . . . We are the centre of a unique Commonwealth of free nations,' bleep, bleep, bleep. It recognizes that such a medium as television exists, and it asks for a

[1] Cmnd. 225. H.M.S.O. July, 1957.
[2] *The Times*, January 25, 1957.

29. (a) The Stanlow Story (1953), *directed by* Douglas Clark. (Shell Film Unit)

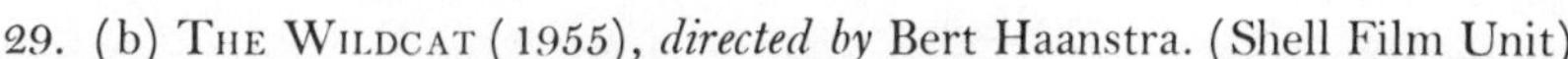

29. (b) The Wildcat (1955), *directed by* Bert Haanstra. (Shell Film Unit)

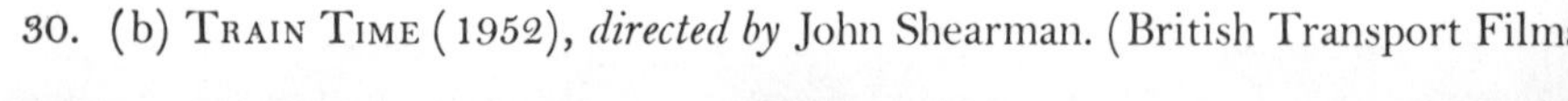

30. (a) Berth 24 (1950), *directed by* J. B. Holmes. (British Transport Films

30. (b) Train Time (1952), *directed by* John Shearman. (British Transport Films

couple of million pounds more. It goes on bleeping that 'functioning is no less important than form, and more needs to be done to ensure that quality is high' but it contains no single constructive proposal as to how such aims are to be achieved.

On the one hand, we have the picaresque spectacle of the Home Secretary, Mr. R. A. Butler, asking for the projection of Britain overseas to take the shape of 'the smallest of the great nations and the greatest of the small' (who on earth thought that one up?), while on the other hand, Lord Hailsham, then Minister of Education and now Lord President of the Council (as well as Chairman of the Tory Party) utters the acrobatic slogan 'We have to take off our hats to the past and our coats to the future'. There the vital matter now rests. The basic principles on which national projection of integrity must be based (so brilliantly set out by Sir Stephen Tallents in *The Projection of England* over a quarter of a century ago) are evaded.

That the film service of the American branch of British Information Services should have now been shut down is a perfect example of false economy. Dating from the unofficial efforts twenty years ago,[1] the regular supply of British documentary and informational films to the American public had come to be regarded by many Americans as a valuable and much sought-after service unstained by the tarnish of official propaganda. The only thing wrong with it in recent years was that it was starved of good new films from Britain, mainly as a result of the cutting-down on informational film-making by the Tory Government in January, 1952. In an economy drive, urged on by the reactionary sections of the Press, official information services are always one of the first sufferers and films—being something associated with glamour and Hollywood—are the first of the first.

The fact that this film service in the United States had actually reached a self-supporting basis of operation has obviously been taken by some civil servant investigator bent on economy (and with no knowledge of public relations) as a reason for saving public money and turning the films over to local commercial distributors! That this imaginative method of creating and cementing Anglo-American goodwill has been discontinued

[1] Cf. page 209n.

after so many years of patient and careful cultivation is a typical example of Whitehall's lack of understanding of the need for a *psychological* basis for official public relations. As so many Americans said to me this summer, 'The fact that your B.I.S. had the best library of documentary films in the United States was in itself a smart piece of public relations; the fact that we can still get the films—or rather some of them—from commercial sources destroys the very reputation which has for so long been carefully built up by the British and accepted and even demanded by us.'

This deplorably short-sighted action is still further evidence of that complete absence of continuity in policy, techniques and personnel which has undermined our information services at home and overseas since the end of the War. It is a demonstration of the effeteness of amateurism in a highly-professional field. It does not impress me that the Radio Doctor asks (in that fine sand-paper voice) for more money; that is not the first answer to improving the information services of a country that is a baffling mystery to most of the world's population.

Apart from this urgent matter of national projection, what must be stressed in this brief postscript is the world spread of the documentary idea—a kind of World Documentary Movement.

It is said that our British documentary itself is in the doldrums, and there is some truth in that. But to evaluate the documentary concept as a whole means that we must take in the vigorous developments in a country like India—alert with documentary, educational and non-theatrical film activity albeit in an embryonic stage—the impressive achievements of the now adult National Film Board of Canada (newly-housed in magnificent new headquarters in Montreal)—the steady output from official production sources in Australia and New Zealand—and, what amazed me when I heard it recently—that there are now over 30 units of documentary or informational film operation within British colonial territories in spite of the fact that the Tory Government closed down the Colonial Film Unit in London!

New Ghana takes over the lively Gold Coast Film Unit;

Malaya's Film Unit celebrates its tenth birthday. On a non-governmental basis, Burma-Shell in India and the Iraq Petroleum Company in Baghdad and the Shell people in Australia are only three examples of indigenous film units having been set-up with the technical and inspirational help of British and Dominion documentary film-makers.

All of this immense spread of the use of the film for serious non-entertainment purposes stems from the work of a handful of film-makers and practical idealists at the humble E.M.B. Film Unit in a London mews nearly 30 years ago. And they in turn adapted techniques from the Russians in the '20s and took inspiration in poetic guidance from the great pioneer, Robert Flaherty.

In New York recently I was impressed by three Puerto Rican documentaries. Seeking information, I found out that they were only a part of a remarkable project in 'community education', which has been going on for over seven years, by the Division of Community Education in the Department of Education, San Juan, Puerto Rico. Producer and educator, writer and artist have been working together towards a common end with Government backing to develop audio-visual techniques within a total creatively conceived programme. They are using some if not all the instruments of mass-communication—stories, articles, films, posters, wall-newspapers and many kinds of graphic illustration—to interpret such basic themes as the Rights of Man, the Rights of Women, and the Scientific Approach. I want to quote from a memorandum prepared about this exciting and stimulating project which demonstrates the common sense and intelligence of its promotors:

'Community education is *not* the purchase of a sound-truck fully equipped with all the latest projection-equipment, commissioned to ride into the hills, the plains or the desert to show films to the people on subjects someone not in the audience considers important that the audience should see. It *isn't* a Walt Disney cartoon on the effects of impure water followed up by a simple, attractive poster of Indians in their native dress. It *isn't* a loud-speaker set up in the plaza exhorting the people to follow the directions of the mechanical voice. It *isn't* flip-cards, flannel-graphs, film-strips, puppets or any of those useful inventions. It is *none* of these and *all* of these. It is all of these when they are so closely interwoven into the fabric of the whole that the fabric would be torn if they were removed. When the writer, the film-maker, the graphic artist and the educator are one, in complete harmony on purpose and the means to achieve this purpose, then and only then will the above media be used successfully in a community education programme.'[1]

Here is an example of a small nation with tremendous social problems to solve going about it in a modest but at the same time brilliantly intelligent way by using the modern mass-media and creative techniques of this electronic age.

In spite of the scope of this world achievement in the use of the cinema for serious ends, perhaps indeed because of it, I repeat the suggestion made in the Foreword—that the documentary concept itself has got confused. It has become bedevilled by its close associations with sponsorship, upon which it has had to lean too long and too heavily for permanent good health. British documentary—and almost all of documentary after it as well as Flaherty before—has been developed on the economics of governmental, industrial or public corporation sponsorship. Documentary served the need, it was always said and rightly, of public information and social awareness. On the other hand, we should remember that documentary produced as a normal part of the film industry in Western countries has seldom been economically practicable because of the belittling attitude of the exhibiting side of the industry to all short films. But documentary cannot, and must not, be defined by the source of its financing! Documentary is a concept, an approach to the use of the film and other media, as I underlined in my *Documentary* book some twenty-two years ago. That is what I mean when I say earlier that the ways of the documentary and of the story-film in one of its many *genres*—the realistic—may be converging.

[1] I am grateful to Mr. Fred G. Wale, of the Division of Community Education, for access to this memorandum which was prepared for Unesco.

IV

THE CONSTANT CRISIS

NOTE

To the man-in-the-street British films must seem to have been in a state of permanent crisis almost as far back as can be remembered. That is indeed the fact. From the end of World War I until today, the production of British feature films has boomed and slumped, prospered and declined, until it would appear that no action, governmental or otherwise, can place this side of the film industry on a secure and prosperous basis. And as the making of films has become more and more entangled with the rising control of accountancy and monopoly-ownership, so has the freedom of the independent film-maker of feature pictures become more and more curtailed until today it scarcely exists in Britain.

To give a kind of background to this passage of events, this section has been prefaced by a survey of British feature films which was prepared for the Venice Film Festival a few years ago. It will serve, perhaps, to remind us of names of people and titles of films that emerged over the period under review.

British Feature Films at the Venice Film Festival (1932–52)

If the British contribution to the world art of the cinema over the past twenty years was to be judged by the British films shown at Venice, it would present a very unbalanced picture. This unfortunate state of affairs is not necessarily due to the organizers of the Film Festival, nor wholly to the methods adopted by the British trade bodies which have selected the entries. It is due to several causes and raises problems that must be faced by the responsible officials of any international film festival.

In the first place, many critics will agree that the most vital and aesthetically interesting period in British feature films was during the years 1942 to 1947. This was an all-too-brief era when British directors came near to expressing real-life on the screen and their films interpreted something of the feelings of the British people at the time. The realistic approach which had almost exclusively been associated with the British documentary movement in the 'thirties became of great influence. As the distinguished critic, Dilys Powell, wrote: 'We have seen too how even in the film of simple fiction, the demand has grown for knowledge and understanding. The British no longer demand pure fantasy in their films; they can be receptive also to the imaginative interpretation of everyday life. The serious British film has thus found an audience as well as a subject. If it preserves its newly-found standards of conception and technique, it will find not merely a national, but an international audience.'[1]

Of these years, 1942–47, four were during the war and thus few of the important films by which British cinema must be judged overall were ever seen at the Venice Film Festival.

[1] *Since* 1939 (Phoenix House, London), film chapter by Dilys Powell.

Carol Reed's *The Way Ahead*, Charles Frend's *The Foreman Went to France*, Noel Coward and David Lean's *In Which We Serve*, Harry Watt's *Nine Men*, Frank Launder and Sidney Gilliat's *Millions Like Us*, Asquith's *We Dive at Dawn*, Powell and Pressburger's *The 49th Parallel*, Thorold Dickinson's *Next of Kin* and Frend's *San Demetrio, London*—none of these appeared before the critics and distinguished audiences who gather at Venice. It was a misfortune of war. Writing of this key-period in 1944, Richard Winnington, the most discerning and knowledgeable of all British film critics, said: 'Our contribution to an art which pierces the mass-human mind and touches the mass-human emotions more potently than any other before has outstripped in quality and truth all that the vast organization of Hollywood has lately produced.'[1]

A second reason why a number of outstanding British films have not reached Venice is obviously because they have been presented first at other film festivals and have thus been ineligible for entry. This is inevitable and will affect any nation's entries so long as we have more than one international film festival in a year. Thus we find that, to our surprise, such famous British films as David Lean's *Brief Encounter* and *Great Expectations*, Ealing's *Dead of Night*, Thorold Dickinson's *Queen of Spades* and *Gaslight*, Jack Lee's *The Wooden Horse*, McKendrick's *Whisky Galore*, Carol Reed's *The Third Man*, Sidney Gilliat's *The Rake's Progress*, Bernard Miles's *The Chance of a Lifetime* and Robert Hamer's *It Always Rains on Sunday* never reached Venice. This is regrettable.

A third reason is because of the quite understandable difficulty of a national trade organization being able to discriminate between commercially successful films and films of high artistic merit. It usually ends in a compromise selection. There is no doubt that if a British company believes it has made a film which will have a good chance of commercial success in overseas markets, then it will try very hard to have it screened at Venice. If it should be fortunate enough to be presented with an award, that honour can certainly help in the subsequent commercial distribution of the film. But with cinema being the great unsolved equation between Art and Industry, such potentially

[1] *News Chronicle*, April 17, 1944.

successful commercial films may not be of the highest aesthetic quality. We know how rare it is that a film from any country succeeds in both purposes. In looking at the publication 2,000 *Films at Venice:* 1932-50,[1] I find a number of British films which cannot possibly have been entered for any serious film festival on the grounds of either artistic or technical virtues. I refrain from giving their titles: they are best forgotten.

Thus my approach to British cinema as represented at the Venice Film Festival in the past twenty years must be conditioned by the above-stated factors. Otherwise it would be a dishonest and unbalanced point of view.

In surveying the films which were submitted, it is convenient to separate them into two distinct groups—prewar and postwar.

The years from 1932 to 1939 in the British cinema were mainly distinguished by the fact that few films produced then were in any way characteristically British except that they were made on British soil. We should recall that this was the period when, following on his remarkable international success of *The Private Life of Henry VIII* (1933), Alexander Korda filled his studio-citadel at Denham with a scintillating galaxy of talent from Europe and Hollywood. At the Gaumont-British studios, at Associated-British at Elstree and at independent companies, much the same took place. It was a fixed belief of the time that for a British film to be successful in the international field, it must be made by a cosmopolitan team of film-makers. The authors of film books sometimes print impressive still-photographs from the romantic films of this period which give an entirely false impression. It is a truism that the best stills pictorially often come from the worst films. Beautiful design in costumes and settings can incline to static cinematography and wordy story-telling.

It was indeed a cosmopolitan era for British cinema! Looking back at the names responsible for the expensive and often technically excellent films of that time, you will find the following array of talent (excluding stars and actors, that is): the Korda Brothers, Max Shach, Lajos Biro, Kurt Bernhardt, Jacques Feyder, Paul Czinner, Georges Périnal, Otto Kanturek, Franz Planer, Erich Pommer, Paul Stein, Mutz Greenbaum,

[1] By Flavia Paulon (Soc. Poligrafica Commerciale, Rome, 1951).

Andrei Andreiev, Lothar Mendes, William Cameron Menzies, Josef von Sternberg, Count Toeplitz, Gabriel Pascal, Karl Grune, Frederich Feher, Eugen Schuftann, Tim Whelan, Victor Schertzinger, Eugene Fremke, Berthold Viertel, and Ernst Stern—many of them distinguished artists.

Of the 'British' films exhibited at Venice during that period of the 'thirties, I find only six which in my opinion as a critic and a film historian should have been shown: Flaherty's *Man of Aran*, Korda and René Clair's *The Ghost Goes West*, Pommer and Whelan's *Farewell Again*, Michael Powell's *The Edge of the World*, Asquith's *Pygmalion* and just possibly Wilcox's *Victoria the Great*. Of these, the two best were of the documentary school. I do not find Korda's own film *Rembrandt* (one of the most sensitive things he has done) nor any of Hitchcock's fast-moving thrillers which were a bright feature of the Gaumont-British group under Michael Balcon's producership—*The Man Who Knew Too Much*, *The Thirty-Nine Steps*, *The Secret Agent* and *The Lady Vanishes*. Berthold Viertel's modest film *Little Friend*, Brian Desmond Hurst's *On the Night of the Fire* and Carol Reed's *Bank Holiday* were serious omissions.

The middle and late 'thirties of British feature films were summed up in Sir Michael Balcon's words: 'Over-boosted, over-costly films inexpertly made by unprofessional newcomers immobilized numbers of technicians and artists and studio-space during production and earned a bad reputation for British films on their release.'[1] The great financial débâcle of the British film-making industry in 1937-38 is too well-known to dwell upon.

*

Coming to the post-war period, British representation at Venice was better. In 1946, the huge Rank Empire which had grown up in the war years was still making possible some good films that were as characteristically British as those of the war period to which I have referred. Dickinson's *Men of Two Worlds* and Asquith's *The Way to the Stars* were hangovers from the realist approach, the latter being perhaps Asquith's best film. *Henry V*, produced by Olivier, made a world impact

[1] *Twenty Years of British Films* (Falcon Press, London, 1947) by Balcon, Lindgren, Hardy and Manvell.

and started all over again the argument for and against putting Shakespeare on the screen. The fourth film shown at Venice in 1946 was Korda's colourful *The Thief of Bagdad*, although it had been made six years earlier. If this old film was considered eligible for showing in 1946, it was a thousand pities that Carol Reed's *The Stars Look Down*, Thorold Dickinson's *Gaslight*, the Boulting Brothers' *Thunder Rock* and John Baxter's *Love on the Dole*—all made about the same time as the Korda picture and far more important—were not also entered. 1945 and 1946 also saw the production of David Lean's two best films—*Brief Encounter* and *Great Expectations*—but, alas, neither was seen at Venice.

The next year saw the first examples of Ealing Studios' work at the Festival. Since the early years, Sir Michael Balcon had quietly developed at Ealing a semi-realist style of modestly-costed films that owed much to the documentary method. Indeed, several of his film-makers graduated from the documentary group, including Harry Watt and Cavalcanti. Criticism may be made of this new school of work from Ealing, but at least it must be agreed that it was more characteristically British than the product of other studios. Basil Dearden's *Frieda* and Harry Watt's Australian subject *The Overlanders* were outstanding in Britain's contribution that year, as was also what many critics consider to be Carol Reed's best picture, *Odd Man Out*. It was certainly one of the most intelligent and sensitive films to be made in Britain.

1948 was the year in which the Rank Empire stood at its summit and from its studios to the Festival went Olivier's *Hamlet* and David Lean's *Oliver Twist*. They were both highly-stylized, formalistic conceptions, proving at least that the technological side of British studios was vastly improved. From the Rank studios also came Powell and Pressburger's ballet film, *The Red Shoes*, about which critical opinion has remained divided. Carol Reed—now under Korda's wing, be it noted—made *The Fallen Idol*, another example of craftsmanship that was making Reed world-known as a director.

But just as in 1937, the writing was on the wall. The Rank Empire was about to run into gigantic financial losses and to curtail its production activities to a minimum. The lesson provided by the films made during the war—so obvious to some of us—had not been learned. The Rank group repeated at Pinewood and Denham the very same mistakes that Korda had made ten years before. They failed to realize two absolutely basic things: first, the spending of huge sums of money does not automatically mean good quality films; second, big sums of money spent on British films does mean that they can only be regained eventually from success in the American market, which has always been a very highly-speculative proposition. Thus now Sir Alexander Korda, with fresh sources of finance, was able to collect round him one by one most of those film-makers who had been given such lavish opportunities by Rank, namely: Carol Reed, David Lean, Powell and Pressburger, Launder and Gilliat and others from the Rank fold. But yet again the temptation to spend big money proved too great! *Anna Karenina* and *Bonnie Prince Charlie* were very costly adventures, and Korda found that he was soon in need of a £3,000,000 loan from the newly set-up British Government's Film Finance Corporation! Once more film-history repeated itself.

From 1948 until today (1952), British feature film directors have tended to shy away from the interpretation of the living world around us. There have been notable exceptions, of course, especially from Ealing Studios, but there has been a tendency for subjects to become more and more literary and for directors to become involved more in style and technique than in what they were saying. In their search after technical perfectionism, directors lost touch with the pulse of ordinary everyday life. Romantic fantasy seemed to be the aim, which is a curious sociological comment when we realize that Britain itself was in the grip of post-war austerity!

In 1949, of the British films seen at Venice, Robert Hamer's beautifully-made *Kind Hearts and Coronets* undoubtedly headed the list. The Rank Empire's *The Blue Lagoon* and Korda's *The Elusive Pimpernel* revealed an escape into empty romanticism. Ealing Studios' epic approach to *Scott of the Antarctic* was too ponderous to stir us deeply and Emlyn Williams's *Last Days of Dolwyn* was too slowly theatrical in style. Again two outstanding British films did not go to Venice—Carol Reed's *The*

Third Man and Thorold Dickinson's *Queen of Spades*, both excellent examples of acting and craftsmanship.

In the last year with which this survey deals (1950) we find again some return to the semi-realist style. Dearden's *The Blue Lamp*, Gilliat's *State Secret* and the Boultings' *Seven Days to Noon* were fast-moving melodramas which, as Hollywood and Hitchcock know, are an honest part of cinema. Dmytryk's *Give Us This Day*, an essentially American story made nevertheless in a British studio, was painstaking but, like Powell and Pressburger's version of the Mary Webb novel, *Gone to Earth*, it never really became alive or convincing. Perhaps our best contribution of the year was Jay Lewis and Roy Baker's submarine film, *Morning Departure*, which reminded us of the war period. We should again note that four important films—Jack Lee's *The Wooden Horse*, Wilcox's *Odette*, Bernard Miles's *The Chance of a Lifetime* and McKenrick's *Whisky Galore*—were not included in the entry.

Thus it will be seen that while some outstanding British films of the two periods before and after the war reached Venice, there was a large number which did not. It would be most unwise, therefore, for any critic or historian to attempt to form an honest overall judgement of British feature cinema by studying only the entries to the Venice Festival. With a few notable recent exceptions, the British feature film was at its best, its most vital and its most human during the years 1942-46.

—Abridged from TWENTY YEARS OF CINEMA IN VENICE (*Edizione Dell' Ateneo, Rome*, 1952).

NOTE

Towards the end of World War II, the production of British feature films might have appeared to outside observers to be in a prosperous and secure state. Audience attendances at cinemas were at the highest level ever recorded. Some outstanding films had been, and were being made. British films were no longer pale copies of Hollywood models. They stood on their own feet—so far as the home market was concerned. So long as sensible economics prevailed and the reason for success was accurately analysed, all seemed set fair.

At the same time, observers within the industry had become seriously alarmed at the increasing monopolistic structures by which the production-distribution-exhibition of British films were being interlocked. They feared that the freedom of the independent producer—usually the most imaginative of the species—would be more and more curtailed, dependent as he was on the booking-powers of the three main cinema-circuits (two controlled by one organization) for a fair showing of his product.

With this in mind, together with the importance of the cinema as a reflection of national life and as an interpreter of national ideas at heart, Sir Stafford Cripps, President of the Board of Trade in the Labour Government of 1945, *invited me to prepare in my own time a memorandum for his study on the Government and the Film Industry. It was intimated that the Government had under consideration the setting-up of a Film Corporation.*

This memorandum was presented in December, 1945, *and is now published for the first time. It predated by four years the first big post-war crisis in the industry and also anticipated the unhappy relations which were to arise between the Central Office of Information and the British documentary film movement.*[1] *Mr. John Grierson was also a signatory to the Documentary Film section of the memorandum.*

[1] Cf. pp. 227 *et seq.* and 236 *et seq.*

The Government and the Film Industry (1945)

I. BACKGROUND

Since the end of World War I, the British film industry has been in constant trouble. Two Acts of Parliament and a Cinematograph Films Council have been unable to solve its major problem—the organization of a healthy, creative and economically sound production of films in regular supply. The three sides of the industry—producers, distributors and exhibitors—have seldom found common agreement, unless the three have been merged into one vertically-integrated group. Thus, on the one hand, there has been a continuous dependence on imported Hollywood films with which the British exhibitor has occupied his screen up to 80 per cent of its showing time; while, on the other hand, British production has boomed and slumped in the manner described in the Lord Moyne Committee's Report (1937) and the Board of Trade's *Tendencies to Monopoly in the Cinematograph Film Industry*[1] (1944).

During the recent War, however, a new monopoly controlled by Mr. J. A. Rank has virtually dominated all British film interests except those held by the Associated British Picture Corporation group. Under this control some good and important British films have been made. At the same time, disquiet is felt in many quarters that so much power vested in one group is an unhealthy and precarious state for an industry which can so widely reflect the characteristics and opinions of a country's people.

In these twenty-five years of haphazard existence, the produc-

[1] Often called the 'Palache Report', after Mr. Albert Palache, the committee's chairman.

tion of British films has done less than justice to the reflection of British ideas and thought to people overseas. In most markets, including the Commonwealth, the Hollywood film has had precedence. The qualities of the cinema as a great instrument of public education have been ignored by the industry's exponents. Small attempt, except in the field of documentary films, has been made to use this powerful medium as a British contribution to world thought. It has been a characteristic of the industry always to produce its films supposedly for the largest possible number of people and hence gain the biggest returns. Seldom have the social responsibilities attached to such an influential medium been accepted by the controllers of the industry. If the same disregard for social responsibility were to obtain in the publishing and broadcasting fields, Parliamentary and public concern would at once be expressed.

The cinema has grown up as a cheap and convenient form of community amusement, and until now the interest of various governments has been confined to its commodity value and its yield in entertainment tax. There is, therefore, an urgent need, accumulated over twenty-five years, for a new Government to adopt a fresh attitude to the film industry, not only in regard to its economic and trade aspects but also in respect of its national and international importance in the public service.

II. INDEPENDENT PRODUCTION IN BRITAIN

The national need is recognized for the increased production of feature films in Britain on an independent basis.

This need exists for the following reasons:

(i) More British films are wanted to decrease the number of American films now imported to fill screen-space in British cinemas, and so to reduce the export of British money to the United States.[1]

(ii) British film production is at present dominated by two vertically-integrated cinema-owning groups,[2] and by

[1] In 1946, it was estimated that 72 million dollars were remitted to America as earnings from Hollywood films exhibited in Great Britain, representing over half of Hollywood's net earnings.—*The Economist*, August 30, 1947.

[2] The Rank Organization and the Associated British Picture Corporation.

American-financed production required in the United Kingdom to meet the legislation of the Act of 1938. This is an unhealthy position in a creative industry.

(iii) The export of more British films overseas would aid our monetary position and help to make understood more widely the British viewpoint in world relations—economic, political, cultural and sociological.

In recognition of the above needs, it is understood that a proposal is now being considered by which a Government Film Corporation might be set up to provide finance and studio facilities to makers of independent feature and documentary films, and to secure proper distribution for such films to cinemas in the United Kingdom.

This proposal very rightly implies an acknowledgement of the fact that a healthy, creative film production industry does not necessarily spring from a few big companies owning studios, machinery for film distribution and circuits of cinemas. It recognizes that a steady flow of good films can result from a number of small independent units, without ownership of studios, provided that finance and studio facilities, together with fair access to cinema screen-space, is guaranteed by Government action.

The success of such a Corporation would depend upon various factors, of which the main would appear to be:

(i) The terms of selection by which production projects will be considered for acceptance for manufacture by the Corporation. Corporation officers will require to be selected according to their knowledge of public taste, of film production methods and of adult education, as well as their ability to see the information policy of the Government interpreted in dramatized feature production. It should be in the Corporation's power, moreover, not only to consider and approve production projects submitted to it, but also to initiate production according to the needs of the Government information service. It should have the authority to commission scripts from writers for feature films and to put these scripts into production through reputable independent Corporation facilities.

(ii) The Corporation's films must be as good as, or better than, films produced by ordinary commercial practice. To achieve this end, the services will be required of first-class producers, directors, writers, actors and technicians. The Corporation must offer greater freedom of subject-matter and more opportunity for technical experiment than exists under normal commercial production. Although there is reason to believe that some of this personnel might welcome and avail itself of the proposed Corporation's facilities, some arrangement may have to be made for part-release from contractual commitments.

(iii) The proposed Corporation should bear in mind that one of the most important essentials of good production is continuity.

Film production is dependent on efficient teamwork between creative talent, experienced technicians and skilled operatives. Continuity of production is a necessary security on which to base teamwork. This can have effect in three of the Corporation's activities: in the full-time employment of the technical floor-staff at any Government controlled or owned studio; in the security offered to small units of creative film-makers working together from film to film; and in the steady flow of product to the screen so that audiences become familiar with and desirous for a better type of film.

(iv) It is fundamental that films produced through the Corporation should be regarded from the start as potential financial successes. It would be most regrettable if the Corporation were to be considered merely as a subsidy to production or if its films were not meeting a consumer demand. This policy should not, however, deter the Corporation from facilitating experimental production from time to time. A major brake on commercial British production has always been the lack of opportunity for creative experiment, whereas Hollywood has sometimes fostered experiment, even at the risk of financial loss, knowing that successful experiment can influence trends in film-making for several years ahead.

(v) An important part of the Corporation's production plans should be the institution of a carefully worked out Training and Apprenticeship scheme, which the industry has always lacked.[1] The Association of Cine-Technicians Union should be consulted in this matter and would no doubt welcome such a proposal.

(vi) Costs of production should be geared in relation to receipts *obtainable from the home market.* It might be possible to reduce actual production cost by instituting a method whereby key film-makers and actors could be paid on a working salary basis and receive a royalty on takings after the production and distribution costs of a film had been recovered. Any such method would have to be the result of agreement with the Screenwriters' Association and the Association of Cine-Technicians. Advance production costs might again be lowered by allowing studio running costs to be reckoned as indirect charges and divided proportionately among a year's productions. The Finance Officers attached to the Ministry of Information Films Division could no doubt make useful recommendations in this direction.

(vii) If it is assumed that the Corporation can get independent films produced in this way, there remains the problem of securing adequate screen-space for exhibiting such films.

It is understood that the three big British cinema-circuits have offered to book the proposed Corporation's films in place of a proportion of imported American films. This offer is to be welcomed. It should not be regarded, however, as anything but a temporary and partial solution to the problem. Acceptance of such an offer and its terms of agreement should be subject to scrutiny. A Corporation film could be rented out with another film produced by one of the organizations making this offer, with the result that it might be difficult to assess the relative allocation of percentage takings on the two films. It would not be to the trade's interest, presumably, to allow a Corporation film to gross more than, or even perhaps as much as, a normal commercially-made film.

The question of publicity would also need careful safeguarding. It should be remembered that the Corporation's films could represent a powerful competitor to the monopoly companies, not only in cinema receipts but in utilizing the services of

[1] And still lacks in 1957!

technicians. For these reasons, it is urged that other and more long-term methods of distribution be investigated by the Corporation. It has been suggested, for example, that as from a specified date exhibitors should allot a minimum amount of screen-space (to be adjusted every year to the volume of Corporation production) to the showing of Corporation films. Exhibitors' programmes would thus be governed by two quotas: the quota of imported films and the Corporation quota. The balance would be filled by independently-financed British or British-American films. Another method, based on less compulsory action, is proposed in an Appendix attached to this memorandum.

III. AMERICAN FILMS IN THE UNITED KINGDOM

While the production of more good quality British films is the most desirable way of lessening the number of imported American films, it is recognized that it will take years of intense British production before American films will be reduced to occupying even 50 per cent of British screen-time.

One immediate way, however, to reduce the import of American films would be to legislate so that cinemas reverted to a single-feature programme, supported by short films, thus lessening the number of feature films required by the cinemas in the United Kingdom.

Evidence from exhibitors suggests that such action would not result in decreasing attendances, but that it would mean more full houses per day and less public time wasted in queueing.

Reversion to a single-feature programme would also abolish the current trade practice of distributors splitting their share of cinema takings between two feature films shown in the same programme; the independent producer invariably suffers if the other film is made by a company with which the distributor is associated.

A single-feature programme would, moreover, be of great help to British producers of short films, not only documentary films but short-story films which would provide excellent opportunity for training new talent.

It is widely agreed that American 'B' films, which usually make up the second feature in programmes, are an undesirable element in British cinemas. If the present renter's quota under the 1938 Act were to be substantially raised, and if a single-feature programme were to be introduced, it would aid in reducing the import of such 'B' films which, it is understood, do not represent a large revenue from British cinemas. American distributors in Britain would tend to import only their films which have the highest potential earning capacity and to cease importing those with the lowest.

A further way by which the production of films in Britain could be increased has been suggested in some quarters. American renters should be compelled to spend a high proportion of their earnings from American films in this country in the financing of films made in Britain to meet their renter's quota needs, which may be raised. It should be recalled in this connection, however, that American interests have never had the desire to participate in the making of films in Britain except under legal compulsion. Where such participation has occurred in the past, it has been undertaken either with a deliberate intention of discrediting British-made films, as in the 'quota quickie' films under the 1927 Act, or with the idea of making American films 'on location' which, after fulfilling their legal purpose for renter's quota in Britain, can be distributed overseas as products of American and not British skill (e.g., M-G-M's *Yank at Oxford*, *Good-bye, Mr. Chips* and *The Citadel*).

IV. BRITISH FILMS OVERSEAS

The recommendations under this head made in the Palache Report are to be supported. It is hoped that the proposed Corporation would be empowered to implement them.

At the same time, it is felt that the problem of securing adequate screening for British films in the United States is long-term, unless some reciprocal trade agreement can be negotiated between the two Governments.

It is believed, however, that the present policy adopted by the Rank Organization of spending a larger sum on the cost of production than can be recovered from the British market, in the belief that this extra expenditure will help to gain access to American screens, is unsound. There is no evidence whatsoever available that an expensively-made British film will secure distribution in the cinemas of the United States more readily than a reasonable cost production. Provided the desire should be held by American cinema-owners to play British films because of public demand, it is the subject and character of the film which would decide its selection and appeal, not its extravagant method of production.

Lacking any reciprocal agreement, it might be considered that legislation could be brought about whereby an American renter in the United Kingdom is compelled to guarantee distribution for a British film in the United States and the Dominions in return for being permitted to distribute a specified number of imported American films in the United Kingdom. An elaborate system of checking bookings and takings overseas would need to be introduced to prevent such an agreement from being abused.

V. CONDITIONAL BOOKING AND FILM RENTALS

The Palache Report dealt frankly with the problems of Conditional Booking (page 17, para. 53 *et seq.*), by which is meant 'block-booking', or the renter's insistence that an exhibitor should book one or more films he does not want in order that he may have a film he does want. This was made illegal by the 1927 Act, but nevertheless the practice is believed to be still in operation. It is extremely harmful to British film production.

While recognizing that it is very difficult to abolish this practice, except by actual control of cinemas by the Government or by municipalities, because it is more than an exhibitor's business is worth to disclose any attempt on the part of a major renter to impose 'conditional booking' upon him, nevertheless it is felt that the Board of Trade should look more closely into this matter with a view to taking effective action.

Film rentals are another feature of distribution and exhibition that demand inspection. The Palache Report is also outspoken on this matter. It should perhaps be considered that a fixed maximum percentage should be permitted as the renter's share of an exhibitor's takings. This matter will obviously arise in connection with distribution arrangements to be made for the Corporation's films.

VI. DOCUMENTARY FILMS

Apart from the considerations set out below, it is assumed that the Government will continue its sponsorship of factual films, at present directed through the Ministry of Information Films Division and the British Council's Films Department, and that there will be a Films Division of the proposed Central Office of Information to commission films from the independent documentary units and to administer the Crown and Colonial Film Units.

The production needs of the proposed Central Office of Information may not, however, fully utilize the production capacity of the documentary units, nor may the terms of authority of the Central Office of Information embrace the whole scope of documentary and educational films.

Any proposed Government Film Corporation, therefore, must take into consideration the special needs of the British documentary film movement.

For sixteen years, and especially during the war, the majority of the financial sponsorship of the independent documentary units has come from the Government, originally through the Empire Marketing Board and the G.P.O. and later through the Ministry of Information and the British Council.

This sponsorship has been maintained spasmodically and only the Government's own units at Crown and Colonial have had continuous security.

It should, therefore, be a first step of the Government Film Corporation to safeguard and develop the economic security of the independent documentary units, which have so far preserved their immunity from the monopolistic control that grips the feature film side of the industry.

Under Government sponsorship, documentary film-makers require a measure of protection from officials and 'subject-experts' who know little of the actual conditions governing the making of films. The status and confidence of documentary producers are being progressively undermined by this official ignorance.

The documentary group of units derives a proportion of its finance from local government and quasi-official bodies and from large corporations. The Government Film Corporation could help greatly in developing this field of sponsorship in an articulate manner, in particular by establishing a planned system of production and a planned system of distribution supplementary to the planned policy for independent feature production and distribution.

Few documentary film units have established access to distribution in the public cinemas except during the war by Ministry of Information arrangement. A large number of short films shown on British screens are supplied by the major American companies, being either their own Hollywood product or cheaply-made British shorts acquired from the less-reputable 'quickie' producers. In many cases, it is attempted to make these short films a condition of feature film booking, especially with the three main circuits.

The Government Film Corporation in securing a guarantee of distribution for its independent feature films should also take steps to achieve a similar security for suitable documentary short films.

The Government Film Corporation should plan a number of feature-length documentary films, say twelve a year, through the appropriate members of the Federation of Documentary Film Units and the Crown Film Unit, and guaranteed circulation should be secured at circuit theatre prices. These films should be considered apart from commissions which may be placed by the Central Office of Information.

The Corporation could be of great service to the documentary group of units by encouraging still further the expansion of specialized distribution, e.g. through the Trade Unions, Co-operative Societies, etc., and by aiding the activities of such bodies as the Scientific Films Association and the Film Societies.

The Corporation could aid greatly the development of the documentary group by instituting a public relations and intelligence service devoted to documentary films. The methods of presentation, press-relations and publicity used by the Ministry of Information Films Division during the war left much to be desired. Ministry of Information films were successful more often in spite of the Films Division's presentation methods than because of them.

The Corporation should be active in introducing a Training and Apprenticeship Scheme into documentary production in conjunction with the Association of Cine-Technicians and the Federation of Documentary Film Units.

In consultation with the proposed Films Department of Unesco, the Corporation should initiate travelling scholarships for documentary technicians to other countries and vice versa.

The Corporation should keep in review the progress of educational, cultural and scientific films.

The Corporation should further draw up a plan for production and distribution in which the requirements and responsibilities of the Central Office of Information, the Ministry of Education and the Foreign Office are specifically blue-printed and the productive capacity of the commercial production companies is allowed for.

The Corporation should use the proposed Unesco Films Department and a *properly reconstituted* British Film Institute as agencies for relationships with foreign educational groups.

The Corporation should maintain the closest contact with any Films Office set up by the United Nations and facilitate the theatrical and non-theatrical distribution of U.N. films within the United Kingdom and the Commonwealth.

APPENDIX

Proposal for a Distribution Plan for a Government Film Cororpation

1. It is assumed that independent good quality British feature films will be made through the proposed Film Corporation, and that, in the first year of production, some ten films might be produced. Immediate screen-space could presumably be found for such films by acceptance of the trade offer described in the preceding memorandum (see page 265). It is felt, however,

that the Corporation must work out a long-term and more permanent method of distribution.

2. Various proposals to solve this problem of distribution, which is fundamental to the whole concept of a Government Film Corporation, have been made. They range from nationalization of the cinemas, or placing cinemas under municipal management, to control over a proportion of the space required by law for British films in each cinema. Most of such proposals, however, depend on the use of compulsory methods which, in the field of leisure and public education, are the least desirable.

3. The situation should be recognized, moreover, that poor as is the quality of some feature films offered today to the public, audience attendances still remain higher than at the outbreak of the war, although the restrictions on other ways of spending money should be borne in mind. This suggests that at least many people are satisfied with the films offered to them, although there may be many others who would pay to see a better type of film if it was available, among them possibly many people who do not go to the cinema at all or only occasionally.

4. It is characteristic of the film industry that production companies aim to make their products appeal to the largest number of people. Few, if any, attempts have been made to appeal only to a section of the public, as is the case in publishing, broadcasting and the theatre, and to gear production costs accordingly, mainly because the industry has never troubled about specialized forms of distribution.

5. There is considerable evidence today, however, derived from the increasing formation of film societies, from the experience of the Ministry of Information's Regional Films Officers, from the wide success of non-theatrical distribution, from the Press and from discussion groups and public meetings in all parts of the country, that a certain section of the national public would support a better quality type of film, both long and short, if there were the cinemas in which they could be exhibited. The film trade presumably does not reckon this section of the public profitable enough to cater to, and even if it were, methods of salesmanship and advertising would require drastic overhaul.

6. It is to this section of the public, which it is suspected is much larger than the trade supposes, that the Corporation might well look for the initial return on its cost of production on both feature and short films.

7. If this principle is accepted, the following proposal is made:

(i) In every city or town in the United Kingdom, which has a population of approximately 50,000 inhabitants or more, there are four or more cinemas.

(ii) The Corporation should acquire, either by outright purchase, or by renting for five years, the use of one cinema in each such city or town, increasing the number of such cinemas in proportion to the population. In Manchester, for example, three might be the appropriate number; in London, twenty.

(iii) A minimum of 500 such Corporation-controlled cinemas should be the aim. Choice of cinema should be governed by suitability of site and seating capacity. The latter should average 750 seats. The cinemas thus selected would range over both circuit and independently-owned halls.

(iv) These cinemas should be placed either under the direct control of the Corporation, or under the management of the municipality (for which statutory powers would be needed), but in either case their programme booking would be controlled by the Corporation.

(v) Existing advance bookings in every case would be taken over so that Corporation films could be gradually introduced as and when their production was completed. As and when existing bookings allow, programmes should be changed to a single-feature plus shorts make-up. First priority of feature booking should, of course, be given to Corporation-produced films, but for some long time there may be insufficient of these to supply a regular programme. Second priority on booking, therefore, should be given to European and occasionally to American films not considered by the trade to be of wide appeal. Programmes need not necessarily be restricted to a week's booking, but be permitted to run as long as economically justified.

(vi) These cinemas should charge normal admission prices, but the entertainments tax should be payable into the Corporation's fund for production, to be earmarked perhaps for experiment. All box-office takings would be remitted direct to the Corporation, which would establish its own machinery for meeting the running costs of the cinemas.

(vii) In addition to observing the normal opening hours of the locality, these cinemas should be made available at appropriate hire-rates in the mornings and on Sundays for specialized performances to meet the increasing projection demands of municipalities, educational bodies, universities, schools, cultural and scientific societies and specialized groups of all kinds that are using films more and more as part of their activities.

(viii) Care should be taken in the staffing of such cinemas to see that managers are of the right personality and possess the necessary local knowledge to build the cinemas into centres quite different from the ordinary commercial cinemas in the city. The public should be led gradually to expect a higher quality of entertainment combined with public education than the ordinary cinemas provide. At the same time, every city and town of any size would be assured of good projection facilities for any educational or cultural use of the screen over and above those made available on 16 mm. by any Government Information Service.

8. In this way, it is suggested, the Corporation would have an assured market for its independently-produced films which would ensure at least a recoupment of production cost. If, however, the Corporation's films reach the quality and desirability believed possible, their market is not limited to the Corporation-controlled cinemas. They would be available to independent exhibitors for normal booking, but only after the programme needs had been met of the Corporation's cinemas. Bookings obtained in this way, both at home and overseas, would represent a surplus over production cost and would be utilized in the way proposed above.

9. This proposal, it is suggested, would cause the trade less dislocation than any proposals to nationalize cinemas or control

a proportion of screen-time. It would represent the least interference with the industry on all sides, but at the same time it would both stimulate creative film-makers on the production side and supply the growing demand among the public both at home and overseas for a better quality film without asking the trade to take the financial risk.

NOTE

The reasons why no action was taken on the foregoing memorandum will no doubt one day become public. At a later date, the proposal for a Fourth Circuit of cinemas under some form of public control was much discussed and it became a main plank in the trade unions' joint policy for the film industry.[1]

So far as documentary was concerned, the mournful record of the Central Office of Information has been seen in the memorandum quoted on page 236.

The permanent 'crisis' in which British film-making was to exist, even when bolstered with large sums of public money, up till today is spotlighted in the following articles. Not one of the several constructive proposals put forward here, or elsewhere by others[2] *concerned with the welfare of British films, was adopted during subsequent years.*

[1] *British Films: Trade Union Policy*, 1956, A Joint Statement by the Association of Cinematograph and Allied Technicians, British Actors' Equity Association, Electrical Trades Union, Film Artistes' Association, Musicians' Union and the National Association of Theatrical and Kine Employees.

[2] For example, Mr. Nicholas Davenport writing in the *Financial Times* and other journals.

The Chance Before British Films (1948)

A NATIONAL FILM BANK

After a period of uncertainty and nervousness, the British film industry would now appear to have before it the biggest opportunity it has ever had. For the first time since World War I, British film producers stand in a position from which they can go ahead and prove that this medium can be *both* a means of entertainment for the community and a form of great creative expression. This Government, more than any of its predecessors, has taken the trouble to try and understand this quarrelsome, complicated and adolescent industry which has grown up in a few decades to become a powerful factor in the national economy. The leaders of this industry have now no excuse for not going ahead and grasping what they have never held, a leading part in world film production.

Several decisive actions have been taken to bring about this new position. The Cinematograph Films Act of 1948 has recently set the unexpectedly high quota figure of 45 per cent for British feature films to be shown in British cinemas, thereby greatly angering the Americans because of the resultant restricted screen-space for Hollywood films. The Act also stipulates that a minimum of eighteen British feature films a year made by producers independent of the major groups (controlled by Rank and the Associated British Picture organization) should be given a fair distribution over the cinema-circuits owned by Rank and Associated British. The new four-year agreement signed between the British Government and the Motion Picture Association of America permits the latter to take only £4½ million out of Britain as revenue from Hollywood films instead of the £16-£18 million annually in recent years, further amounts being dependent on what British films are allowed to earn in the United States. The Americans are encouraged to invest their additional earnings in the production of films made here, such 'British' films being reckoned as British in the American market. This may cause awkward moments in the claims on British studio-space, artistes and technicians, and the latter's union is sticky about the admission of foreign technicians unless arranged on a reciprocal basis.

Finally, after months of rumours and evasive replies to questions in the House, the Government has announced that it will find £5 million of public money over five years to finance British film production. The President of the Board of Trade (Mr. Harold Wilson) has been as good as his promises, made both in the House and to the technicians at their annual meeting last April. But it is one thing to set up the machinery for a National Film Finance Corporation, with cash in hand, and another to see that the money is used to put on the screen some really good British films that will earn back at least their cost of production and add to the reputation of British cinema at the same time. It is not so simple as may be supposed.

Mr. Harold Wilson has not made this finance available direct to producers, although the major intention is stated to be to help so-called independent producers—meaning those who are not financially associated with the major producing groups of Rank, Korda and Associated British. Like the City's film financiers before him, Mr. Wilson has argued that it is no use financing production if distribution for the completed product is not forthcoming. He has, therefore, compelled the independent producer to submit his plans for production to a distributor who, in turn, can approach the Film Finance Corporation for a loan to be made on a commercial basis. Money will not be advanced, it is said, for any one particular film nor will the Corporation attempt to control the kind of pictures to be made. If productions so financed via the distributor eventually lose money at the box-office, the Corporation will expect repayment from what other assets the borrower (presumably the distributor) may have, which can only be his profits from other films. This means, in effect, that the distributor will have to approve a producer's story and his probable cast before applying to the Corporation for working capital.

To make an analogy, it is as if the Government, anxious to improve the quality and quantity of British literature, were to give the book wholesalers a large sum of money with which they in turn would commission authors to write—not what the authors felt impelled to write, but what the booksellers and wholesalers thought would sell best. True, it is said that during the five years which the £5 million is to last the Corporation will eventually deal directly with producers, but the fact remains that to begin with the distributors will determine the quality and type of films made. Thus has Harold Wilson met the many demands that have been made, especially by the film trade unions, for a Films Bank.

Much has been said and written in all this controversy about the independent producer and his plight, and the public has perhaps been led to believe that there exist some dozens of brilliant producers, with the necessary teams of technicians and equipment, to say nothing of the stories, waiting to spring into action the moment the Film Finance Corporation unleashes some cash. In point of fact, the independent producers of feature films have been those in the main concerned with a product which has scarcely brought anything valuable to the reputation of British cinema. All along, reference to independent producers should have been to 'would-be' independent producers. It is possible, for example, that some of the producers and directors now working with the major studio groups may like to break away into independent production, and there are probably a few documentary producers who would like to expand their activities into feature production but who have lacked the capital and distribution. But before doing so, it now transpires under the new plan that they will have to reckon with the fact that the films they want to make will have to secure a distributor's approval before the Film Finance Corporation can be tapped.

It should be noted that there are very few British distributors apart from those who are an integral part of the big producer-renter-exhibitor groups (and the latter have no reason to wish to encourage independent production which offers competition to their own product). Thus any new independent producer, who may have had considerable experience in film-making with other companies, finds himself dependent not on his own belief that he can make the kind of film which the Film Finance Corporation is supposed to want made, but on what a small handful of Wardour Street distributors believe will be box-office.

Now it is an established fact that the more influence distributors (the middlemen of the industry) have had over production, the more films have tended to become stereotyped and have conformed to believed proven box-office standards. Distributor control over the making of films inevitably leads to extreme caution, to resistance to new ideas, to obsession with box-office values judged by a teen-age level of audience objective. Is it on these standards that £5 million of public money are to be invested in British production? If it is, then we can look forward dismally to more such films of the *No Orchids for Miss Blandish*, *Idol of Paris* and *The Wicked Lady* type. Is this the kind of British film the Government wants to back?

On the other hand, now that the feature quota has been fixed at 45 per cent, it is more than likely that these independent producers of lurid pictures may not wish to avail themselves of Government finance via a distributor. Mr. Wilson may be spared his blushes. Assured of a distribution by quota needs, private finance may well be forthcoming to produce this type of picture which has an audience waiting for it among the more illiterate of the 25 millions who go to the cinema once a week.

Thus it begins to look as if Mr. Wilson's £5 million will be needed for more speculative purposes than financing the kind of film stories which the Wardour Street distributors would like to see made. Where it is surely required most is to make possible experimental and new types of production which the industry so badly needs but which are difficult to finance on orthodox lines. Mr. Wilson has made it clear that he is not concerned to find public money to discover 'if Mr. X is a genius', but at the same time he has no justification for making it easier to perpetrate more semi-pornographic pictures. Thus we come down in the end not to finance at all but to what really matters most, the creative policy that is going to guide British film-making in the opportunity that lies ahead. That is where the by-now famous £5 million could be of the greatest use.

With the chance of British films earning hard money from the

American market becoming less certain than ever, it is now imperative for our producers to use every effort to reduce costs of production. We may, happily, see an end to lavishly made costume pieces and elaborate spectacles taking months to shoot, because such subjects were chosen in the belief that they would appeal to American audiences as well as to British. It is public knowledge that Mr. Rank lost £2 million on such 'prestige' ventures and he is unlikely to pursue this unprofitable policy now that access to the American market is more difficult than two years ago. Korda, also seeking the American audience, has yet to announce how his three productions, *Anna Karenina, An Ideal Husband* and *Mine Own Executioner*, costing perhaps some £1 million or more in all to make, have fared in the United States.

Both Korda and Rank still have considerable sums locked up in such expensive pictures as *Red Shoes, Oliver Twist, Bonnie Prince Charlie, Esther Waters* and *London Belongs to Me*, all of which will presumably depend on speculative American earnings for them to show a profit on their production and distribution costs. These films may well represent an investment of over £2½ million. Thus economy in production, not only in methods and production time but in the type of film made, has become immediately pressing. With it comes an opportunity for British film-makers to regrasp the realism and indigenous quality that distinguished some of their films during the war before the mirage of the American market caused a fake-internationalism to be the aim.

A great deal has been written by the critics about a group of modestly-produced films made during the war years, of which *The Foreman Went to France, The Way Ahead, Millions Like Us* and *We Dive at Dawn* are probably the best examples. These films had an honesty and freshness about them that was liked both at home and overseas because it was recognized as part of everyday experience. They were unmistakably British films in character, style and environment, whereas more recent pictures such as *Caesar and Cleopatra, Anna Karenina* and *Black Narcissus* might have come from any cosmopolitan studio. For the first time in many years British film-makers found an approach to the screen which was their own and not an imitation of Hollywood or an attempt to achieve some mythical international style which has prostituted so much British talent since the days of *The Private Life of Henry VIII* in 1933.[1]

This realism of a few war films, so much admired by foreigners, has only been carried over into post-war British production by Sir Michael Balcon at Ealing Studios in such successful films as *The Overlanders, Hue and Cry* and *It Always Rains on Sunday.* These films, far from imitating Hollywood, have been made with the home-market primarily in mind and, in the long run, will probably be far more financially remunerative in proportion than the extravagant pictures mentioned above. If they are given a fair chance of overseas distribution, they will do well. *The Overlanders* must already have made a substantial profit from the British and Australian markets alone. It is to be hoped that Ealing will meet with equal if not bigger success with its new films, such as *Scott of the Antarctic* and *Eureka Stockade.*[2] A return to down-to-earth realistic subjects that have some connection with life as it is lived today is the only sane production policy for British producers to follow in the opportunity that lies ahead.

This will depend, however, not only on the policy laid down by the studio executives but on the initiative of the creative film-makers themselves. With the immense sums of money they have had at their disposal the past few years, British directors, cameramen and other technicians have developed their skill immeasurably. No one can deny that films such as *Great Expectations, Odd Man Out, A Matter of Life and Death, Red Shoes* and *Hamlet* are technically well-made. The quality of photography, the set-design, the music, the model and trick-work in British studios these days is high. But so it is in other countries.

Cinema as an art and as a mass-entertainment has reached a stage where technical ability by itself is not enough. What matters now is the use to which this technical excellence is put. Are our young directors and writers going to be satisfied to use their talent in putting on the screen subjects and stories aimed at a teen-age audience, or are they going to measure up

[1] Cf. p. 123.

[2] Unfortunately neither came up to expectation.

to the challenge offered them from abroad by such directors as William Wyler, Rossellini, Dmytryk and Elia Kazan with their films *The Best Years of Our Lives, Open City* and *Paisan, Crossfire* and *Boomerang*? The fact remains that no British director since the war has made a film to place beside these titles so far as significant subject-matter is concerned. And, moreover, each of these films was a commercial success. They were entertaining, but they were also genuine contributions to adult thinking and world affairs. They were not made for 'prestige'. They were well and honestly made because their makers believed fundamentally in what they were trying to say on the screen. That is the test. That is the only vindication of cinema.

Now to return to Mr. Wilson's £5 million. If there is any justification at all for investing public money in British film production, it must be more important than satisfying the pubescent taste of a few Wardour Street distributors. Should not this money be made available to productions which will have some valuable contribution to make to national or international affairs, whose commercial success cannot perhaps be guaranteed in advance? The new Films Act legislates that eighteen independently-made feature films a year must be accepted for distribution by the three big circuits dominating British exhibition. Let twelve of those eighteen films a year for three years be capitalized by the new Film Finance Corporation. Let the Committee to be set up to administrate the finance, said to include several persons with a knowledge of film trade affairs,[1] be the body to which producers apply. In this way, without relying on the policy perspicacity of the major studio groups, we could at least be sure that those creative British film-makers who really want to use their skill to say something in the world during the next three years can be given the chance of adequate finance and fair distribution at least on the screens of the United Kingdom. Let that inspiration and encouragement be forthcoming and it is a certainty that our best film-makers, writers and acting talent, will avail themselves of the position. Britain will have done something towards taking its great film opportunity.

—World Review, *October*, 1948.

[1] This was not substantiated.

The Film Crisis (1949)

A speaker in the House of Commons recently said, 'Things which make sense in other industries make nonsense in this industry, and it is extremely difficult for many people to grasp the situation.' He was perhaps expressing a view that is, unfortunately, widely held about the film industry.

To those unversed in film politics, the situation which now obtains in the British industry must appear incomprehensible. Parliament has fixed a high quota, 45 per cent, for British feature films and a National Film Finance Corporation will shortly have £5 million to loan for production, of which over £1 million has been allocated in advance. Yet 20 per cent of British feature film technicians are said to be out of work and fifteen out of twenty-six studios are standing idle!

During the second reading of the Cinematograph Film Production (Special Loans) Bill (December 2nd), the President of the Board of Trade gave some vital figures which are most relevant. 'There are at present,' he said, 'about 30 million attendances a week in this country at nearly 5,000 cinemas, and . . . we understand that some 8 million people go to the cinemas twice a week or more. The gross annual receipts of the cinemas are at present running at the rate of about £108 million a year —over £2 million a week. The yield of the Entertainments Duty alone is some £38 million.'

These statistics at least enable us to estimate the size of the home market for British feature films and so to relate current production costs to possible revenue.

Of the £108 million taken annually at the box-office, £38 million goes to the non-contributory partner in the business —the Treasury. Of the remaining £70 million, some 40 per cent, that is £28 million, is believed to be paid in film-hire by exhibitors to distributors, the other £42 million going in cinema operating costs and exhibitors' profit. Of the £28 million paid for film-hire, an average of 25 per cent is probably taken by the film distributors or renters (the middle-men). From the £21 million left, something must be deducted for advertising, the cost of copies of films in circulation, and also a share is required for the supporting programmes (newsreels, shorts, second features, etc.) This is a difficult figure to assess but £3 million would perhaps be a conservative estimate. Thus some £18 million is likely to be left as the net revenue from all feature films shown on British screens made by American, British and Continental producers. Of this amount it is estimated that between £7½ and £8 million is the British share, which has again to be divided between the Rank, Korda and Associated British production groups and the various so-called independent producers.

Feature films today are costing anything between £100,000 and £200,000 a piece to produce, if we omit the 'prestige' films of the *Oliver Twist, Bonnie Prince Charlie* and *Anna Karenina* type, which are nearer the £¾ million figure. £7½ million would permit seventy-five films to be made at the lowest cost of £100,000 each. The British Film Producers Association promised the President of the Board of Trade seventy feature films in the quota year October, 1948–September, 1949, which presumably Mr. Wilson anticipated when he fixed the quota at 45 per cent. From present trends, their average cost is likely to be nearer £150,000 than £100,000 a piece, totalling some £10½ million *or £3 million more than the home-market is estimated to be worth*!

Most film men would agree that the revenue from overseas is highly speculative. The American market has been virtually closed as a retaliatory measure to the 4-year Anglo-American Film Agreement and the 45 per cent quota of British films on British screens, but even if it is opened again (and there are signs of this), earnings are never likely to be considerable unless a complete change of policy is adopted by the American motion-picture industry. Revenue from the Far East today is negligible, partly because of frozen currency. The Commonwealth and Dominion screens are helpful and a small amount is usually expected from those European countries where currency is not blocked. But the most hopeful estimate of overseas revenue in present conditions would not balance the £3 million gap, although the producers are asking for Government help to bring into this country takings which are frozen.

Possibly these figures may explain why film producers are asking the Chancellor of the Exchequer for a proportion of the £38 million taken as entertainment tax to be returned as a rebate on those pictures which are successful? The more successful a film, the bigger the rebate, is the proposal. A sum of £20 million is said to be being asked. This request amounts really to a subsidy, and is being made in spite of Mr. Wilson's repeated statements that the Government has no intention of subsidizing the film industry.

They may also explain why the big producing companies may be shy of putting new finance into this year's production, preferring instead to wait for revenue to accrue on capital already invested in production over the past two or three years. Expensive films like *Great Expectations* (1946) may only now, two-and-a-half years later, be showing a profit. Films like *London Town* and *Caesar and Cleopatra* will presumably never show a profit. It could be several years before it is known if *Oliver Twist* or *Hamlet*, both made last year, will eventually pay for themselves. (These 'classical' films, like Disney's *Snow White and the Seven Dwarfs*, may have a long earning life in contrast to the ephemeral life of the usual feature film.)

They may explain again why all but two of the commercial banks, National Provincial and the Bank of America, are said not to be continuing to advance loans for production.

Thus whereas only a year or two ago there was a cry about the shortage of studio-space in which to make British films, today only eleven out of twenty-six are working. About 8,500 operatives are believed to be at present engaged in production, which is, however, probably more than were in employment in 1939 when 103 feature films were produced. It is possible that there are more men to-the-job today than before the war, but then it should be remembered that technical quality has improved and production methods have grown more involved.

The Association of Cine-Technicians, which represents the technicians engaged in production, is understood to be pressing the Board of Trade to use compulsory powers to requisition vacant studio space, presumably in the hope that the National Film Finance Corporation will make available loans for production. But no matter how skilled may be the cameramen, art-directors, editors, sound-recordists, unit managers and their numerous assistants, a successful film depends primarily on its director, writer and main actors to say nothing of the producer. Has the A.C.T. (a trade union) a programme of films ready to go into production, with good subjects, scripts, directors and casts available?

A great deal of criticism has been made of the difficulties met by independent producers (that is, those without their own studios or who are not financially dependent on the big production groups) in getting adequate distribution for their films when they are made. That the various methods of film exhibition and distribution require examination against the background of the economics of the industry as a whole is recognized by the fact that Mr. Wilson has a committee of investigation now sitting on these matters under the chairmanship of Lord Portal. Its findings and recommendations will be of immense importance to the future of the industry. It is frequently represented that the charges made for distribution by renters are excessive, 20 per cent to 25 per cent of a film's earnings being not an uncommon demand.

All parties are agreed with Mr. Wilson that production costs must be brought down, but no one seems prepared to accept the reductions. From top to bottom in the industry, wages and salaries are well above those in other industries, but who is willing to accept the first cut? Proposals are made that highly-paid film-makers and players might take a 'living wage' and expect a share of a film's profits, but in practice the industry's complicated methods of distribution make this difficult and open to dispute. Confidence would probably be absent on both sides. The Rank Organization's much publicized 'Independent Frame' method of production is viewed with suspicion both by operatives, because it will eventually mean a concentration of production into less studio-space than now, and by the creative makers of films because they believe it reduces film-making to a mechanical operation leaving little room to exploit the real assets of the medium. 'Independent Frame' and back-projection processes may have a contribution to make, but it is hardly likely or desirable that complete films made in this way will ever wholly displace normal production methods.[1]

Reduction in costs can undoubtedly be made without damaging quality (and would include cuts in abnormally high salaries in certain quarters), but it would be quite impossible for such reductions to bring back production to prewar figures. Ingenuity, improvisation and imagination, on the other hand, have never done the industry harm where and when they have been used, which is seldom.

These are only a few of the many aspects of the inexplicable film crisis, to which everyone in the industry has a solution. It would not be difficult to inspire a temporary spurt in production by several methods, but it would not touch the root of the problem. The major thing for the industry to avoid is being panicked into making a large number of mediocre films at small cost. That would do irreparable harm and only result in falling revenue. Films of all types are wanted, but quality must be more apparent than of late. When it comes down to frank analysis, the industry is not rich in top-rank film creators. It has a big pool of skilled technicians and a fine array of acting talent upon which to draw, but it is weak in really gifted directors, writers and producers who are the prime creators in this difficult and sensitive medium.

Finance is not the only problem: a more efficient use of what talent is available, perhaps to be achieved by a production council on which the creative element is strongly represented, and a more realistic policy of subject-planning, could both help to alleviate the crisis.

Above all, the cancer within the industry is lack of confidence. The technicians lack confidence in most of the producing concerns (they have not forgotten 1936); the producing concerns lack the confidence of the financiers (who also remember 1936); the exhibitors are frightened of public taste changing and play

[1] 'Independent Frame' vanished almost as quickly as its foolish head was raised, at a cost to Mr. Rank of which one shuddered to think.

for safety with established methods of appeal. Parliament alone is confident that the £5 million it is voting for production will not be lost![1]

—THE SPECTATOR, *February* 11, 1949.

[1] From October, 1948 to March, 1957, first as the National Film Finance Company and later as a Corporation, it helped to finance 374 feature films and eighty-one short films. On March 31, 1957, its advances from the Board of Trade stood at the maximum allowed figure of £6 million. Its net deficiency on the same date amounted to £3,598,086. Its total of amounts written off and provisions was £4,812,461. (Annual Report, May, 1957, Cmnd. 176.)

A Plan for British Films (1949)

This present two-year 'crisis' in British film-making is not a national one. Cinema everywhere is faced with a struggle for survival. Star-spangled products are no longer certain successes. Ask Hollywood! With television round the corner as a competitive entertainment, the cinema has got to be stripped to the buff to rediscover its universal appeal.

Film is art plus industry. Neither can survive without the other. The industry can commit suicide: cinema will exist so long as there is a camera and a piece of negative. The crisis has been reached because the basic attractions of the film have been forgotten by its exploiters. Britain can seize this chance for revitalizing the cinema as can no other nation. As in the war years, we are in the unique position of coming to the rescue of cinema. But it cannot be done without Government action and aid. The complete nationalization of the industry as in Czechoslovakia will not help us. The jungle cut-throat rivalry of Hollywood is no answer. Only a sane, balanced, intelligent relationship between State finance and control, individual creative contribution and the best efficiency of private enterprise can crack the crisis. Britain alone can do this with harmony.

One of the disappointments of the Labour Government has been its failure to grasp the basic problems of the British film industry; its promising initial interest was not pursued. Despite a new Films Act to safeguard British screen-time, a Film Finance Corporation with £5 million to spend in production, and a limitation on the export of earnings of American films in the United Kingdom, the Labour Government has ignored the fact that making films is a creative act first and an industrial process second.

Seeking to encourage British production, the Government has already spent a lot of public money putting on the screen mainly what the distributor—the middle-man—wants. It has bolstered up trembling concerns and given out a handful here and a handful there to 'keep things going'. It has not touched the roots of the problem. Money alone is not enough. Money plus encouragement of new ideas and talent is what is wanted. To give distributors such control over ideas and talent is a deplorably reactionary step for a so-called progressive government.

The great weakness of the Film Finance Corporation is that there are no creative people in it; no one with any first-hand knowledge of film-making. Can it not see that pumping money into the industry, even with guarantees of this and that, only encourages the old mistakes to be made over again?

A major difference between the film industry and other industries is that when film executives make ghastly blunders, they seldom get fired. They always get 'another chance'. One permanent result is that the confidence of technicians and workers remains impaired. I am convinced that the operative manpower in the film industry will work hard and loyally to make more good British pictures if—and only if—there is absolute confidence that employers are capable of creating a healthy and progressive production industry that will give continuity of employment. Unhappily, there are few producer-employers today who command that confidence.

It is too late to cry 'We told you so'. But the fact remains that the fate which has overtaken so much of our production today was foreseen and stated at least three years ago. Nobody at the helm listened and they are not today's sufferers. That is the recurring tragedy of the film industry.

Drastic methods are needed to stop collapse. Nothing positive for the future can be done by patching. Direct action by the Government is inevitable. That means participation. How can it be done with immediate effect but with least upset?

1. *Production*: Leave to their own devices those studios whose personnel is fully occupied. Let them go full steam ahead with their schedules, without Government aid if possible. Of the remaining studio-space, divide off ruthlessly the efficient and up-to-date from the war-worn and not-so-good. Divorce the running of these worthwhile studios from the actual producing companies. Put them under a Government Studio Corporation

with experienced management. Make them available at reasonable rentals calculated on a non-profit making basis to visiting production units. The latter should pay rent and overheads only when they are actually using the studio services. Make these studios simply into well-run servicing plants not in any way connected with the success or failure of the films made in them. Their job is to provide the material industrial facilities needed to make films.

How are the films to be made? We must be quite cold-blooded about this. A film is basically made by three people—the producer, the director and the writer. *Crossfire*, a favourite example of a good film which was good box-office, was made by Producer Adrian Scott, Director Eddie Dmytryk and Writer John Paxton. Stars, cameramen, grips and carpenters—they all contribute but, stripped down, a film is the conception and creation of a three-man team, occasionally a two-man team when the producer is also the writer or the director. How many such teams or units exist in Britain capable of making top-quality pictures? Fifteen, perhaps? How many could be formed tomorrow by creative people who are either 'resting' or browned-off on work about which they couldn't care less? Another twelve at most. Some twenty-seven unit-teams in all. For our purpose less, because some of these teams are already under obligations for some time ahead. Say fifteen teams could be found, each a small, self-contained unit with its own policy and control. It is these teams who will determine how many good British films can reach the screen next year. I suggest not more than thirty. Not the money nor the studio-space nor the quota—but these key film-makers will decide our output.

2. *Subjects*: Once and for all let us get away from the fetish for adapting West End stage plays. Adapt good novels if you like, but don't make pre-publication a prerequisite of a script. Get the young writers out and about. Give them a fair weekly wage and give them subjects to explore and write up. With careful briefing and intelligent producer guidance, some first-class stuff will come in. Free the writer from distributor dominance, and subjects will flow in.

3. *Finance*: If ordinary capital remains shy as at present, then the Film Finance Corporation must operate further. I imagine

that there's not much left of the original £5 million, but Mr. Wilson suggested that he might get more. But, and again this is fundamental, this public finance for production must go direct to the people who make pictures and not, as has largely been the case to date, to the middle-man who advances it to the producers. This practice has meant that the distributors have virtually decided what subjects are made, by whom and with what actors. The Finance Corporation must face up to the position that if it aims to save the industry, it cannot avoid financing projects put to it direct. To do this, it needs expert help. There must be found, I suggest, three or four persons with between them a first-hand knowledge of film-making and a sense of public taste who will serve as a Production Committee to the Corporation. They should be selected and appointed by the President of the Board of Trade. One member should sit three years, the others changing every two years by rotation to assure variety of viewpoint and continuity of policy. There are such people, both in the film trade or closely associated with it. Their sense of public duty could be appealed to for them to relinquish their present posts and put their ability and experience at the service of the public, the Government and the industry. This small committee could in actuality plan a great part of the future of the British film industry, that part which does not go ahead under existing arrangements.

The tastes of this committee must be wide. All kinds of films are wanted from slapstick to Shakespeare, the criterion being that they must be the good of their type. The aim should be to encourage talent, foster new ideas, create the conditions for creative film-making which at present do not exist. These few people must carry the confidence of all who make pictures and have the future of the industry at heart. It is not impossible.

4. *Distribution:* The Film Finance Corporation has insisted it backs no project unless it has a guarantee of release. But it overlooks the existence of the Films Act, 1948. If films produced and financed along the lines indicated above do not get a release through normal channels (and remember exhibitors need to fill a 40 per cent quota), then surely release must be obtained through the clause in the Act that lays down that each of the three big circuits must distribute a minimum of six films per

year from independent sources? In fact, if the Corporation finances a subject direct, this should guarantee its acceptance as one of the eighteen stipulated by the Act. The Corporation must appoint reputable accountants to see that the producer (and the Corporation!) gets a proper share of the film's earnings. It might even be necessary to set up a Government-controlled distribution agency, operating on a non-profit making basis, to ensure that as much money as possible flows back into production.

5. *Costs:* Obviously the home-market and the Commonwealth should be the first aim. Budgets should not exceed £125,000. Producers, writers, directors and actors should be asked to take a proportion of their salaries in deferments, that is to say, from takings after actual costs plus loans have been repaid. If they were assured of a fair deal from distributors, I think these key-people would accept this, especially if the distribution concern was under Government control. They might have to wait for their money, but they would get it.

None of the above proposals, practicable though they are, solves Mr. Rank's or Sir Alexander Korda's problems. They are not meant to. But they are a bare outline of a plan that, if worked out carefully by the right people, could give new hope and encouragement to the hundreds of film-makers of all grades who are desperately anxious not only to have jobs but to put British films where they belong—at the top. It must be done before more skilled labour and brains dissipate into other industries or get thrown on the scrap-heap. It must be done, or something very like it, if the Government places any value at all on a healthy, progressive and hard-working film production industry. We have had lip-service enough; let us now have action.

—THE LEADER, *November*, 1949.

A Policy for Films (1949)

THE BRITISH INDUSTRY'S CRISIS

The slump in the British film industry, the decline in production, and the increase in unemployment are not symptoms of a situation that has arisen overnight. The recent statement of the Rank group merely brought things to a head. On all sides the Government is expected to do something more constructive than it has so far done.

Before proposing action, however, the President of the Board of Trade is presumably studying the report of the Plant Committee, which inquired into the distribution and exhibition of films against the background of the whole industry. Last December Mr. Wilson told the House: 'I do not think we shall get a real settlement in the financial side of the industry or any real economic stability in it until we have the report. . . .' The Rank group's financial statement has no doubt disappointed Mr. Wilson because only in July last year he was looking forward to a long period of prosperity in 'an industry which is absolutely essential if we are to solve our long-term balance-of-payment problem'.

This is the third attack of self-afflicted paralysis that the industry has had in thirty years. It may never recover from a fourth. It may not recover from this one unless the problem is tackled at the roots. What must be avoided is a patching up of unsound structures. For a large proportion of the entertainment tax to be given to producers without precise knowledge about how it will be used is unthinkable. Nothing suggests that it would be well spent so long as two-thirds of the industry—the exhibitors and distributors—maintain conditions which make successful production virtually impossible.

The Film Finance Corporation, scarcely a year old, must

already have used a good proportion of its £5,000,000 in 'keeping things going', but it has proved that money alone is not enough. Money and encouragement of new ideas and talent are needed, plus opportunities for those with creative ability whose frustration has been almost complete.

The status of the Film Finance Corporation under Lord Reith is now more important than was at first intended. If the industry is to have more public money (and it is hard to imagine it saved without), the Corporation must have more control over the spending of it. That distributors must, as at present, approve of a producer's story, his director, and the chief actors is no guarantee of a good film. If the production side of the industry is to use the talent now lying unused, is to find new ideas and policies, and to recapture the public's fading interest, some method must be found by which the Corporation can directly participate in production. To do this it must be qualified to judge film subjects and have a first-hand knowledge of the industry's potential talent—abilities it does not at present possess. Its staff must have the industry's future (both economic and artistic) at heart as well as at pocket. The basic fact has been ignored that making films is a creative act first and an industrial process second. The inability of the accountant-mind alone to build the delicate bridge between sound economics and creative talent is the weakness of the industry. It is significant that the only producer to show consistent success, consistent within the limits of entertainment, is Sir Michael Balcon, himself a practical experienced film-maker, in whom his team has complete confidence.

Only an intelligent balance between State finance plus control over means of production and individual creative working can crack the crisis. It is the kind of partnership for which the British, more than any other people, have a genius.

Mr. Rank has said that his group made demands on the industry's creative talent that were beyond its resources. It is more accurate to say that available talent has not been always used to the best effect and that other available talent has been neglected. The number of producer-director-writer teams we possess which can make top-quality films determines British output. At present it is fewer than thirty a year. Independent teams of this kind, and not large organizations, should be backed by public money if any is forthcoming. It is vital that their skill is used to the utmost in conditions for film-making that at present scarcely exist.

The belief that the three branches of the industry—production, distribution, and exhibition—should be separated is not new. The Palache Report of 1944 had strong views on the matter. If producers are to get a fairer share of cinema revenue it is hard to see how the Government can avoid securing more remunerative distribution arrangements for British films. Some control over the cinemas beyond that of the present quota may even be needed. Two steps could be taken, one short-range, one long. A distribution company might be set up to rent Government-aided films at a minimum handling charge, and at least eighteen such films a year could secure circuit exhibition through the Cripps Selection Committee established in 1946 but never yet used. More distant, a new circuit of cinemas might be formed by putting under a Film Corporation, publicly controlled but not State-controlled, a proportion of the cinemas at present contained in the three main circuits plus certain independent houses.

As an immediate measure the best-equipped of the studios now empty or soon to be so should be run on a non-profit-making basis by the Film Corporation and kept quite separate from production finance. Producers with public backing should be able to rent this space only as and when they need it. If the Film Finance Corporation has a planned production programme certain studio space can be kept fully occupied by a flow of films guaranteeing regular employment to the many technicians and operatives needed in film-making. The unions have lost faith in the industry's big producers to solve their problems.

The 40 per cent quota of British films will not be met, except by the production of a high proportion of rubbish. Apart from financial difficulties, there is not enough good talent in and around the studios. But to increase this talent for the future a strong case can be made for instituting a single-feature programme in British cinemas and for the supporting short films to be predominantly British. These provide admirable training for future film-makers and the Film Finance Corporation should aid such production.

A Policy for Films (1949)

These proposals, which are a minimum requirement, do not mean nationalization of the film industry. They mean control over a part of the means of production, distribution, and exhibition while permitting more freedom for creative initiative than exists in the industry at present. They leave free organizations such as the Associated British Pictures group, with its circuit of cinemas, and Ealing Studios, to pursue their own policies with private enterprise, and permit the Americans to produce here with blocked takings from their films: though this only provides employment of a kind and does nothing to help a British film industry which so desperately needs help.

—MANCHESTER GUARDIAN, *December* 2, 1949.

'We're not monopolists, are we?'—J. Arthur Rank to Joseph A. Rank.
Drawing by Richard Winnington published in the *News Chronicle*, July 27, 1946.

By Guess and By God (1952)

The mystery of J. Arthur Rank differs as to who seeks an answer. To someone who has been film-making, writing about film-making and trying to follow the jungle of film politics for nearly twenty-five years, this biography[1] does not hold the key. I am not greatly interested in how much personal money Arthur Rank has put into British films and cinemas; that is his own affair. I am not greatly concerned, as is Alan Wood, in solving the equation between Rank's Methodist beliefs and actions and his monopolistic empire that embraces every branch of cinema and much of television and radio; that again is a personal matter. Stemming from a Methodist family myself, what has always puzzled me is this—how did this shrewd, likeable, hard-working, unostentatious Yorkshire businessman come to surround himself with advisers and executives most of whose first-hand experience of film-making was as lacking as his own? Very few whose services he bought have been associated with British film production, and their record was not inspiring. Early on, Mr. Wood states the known fact that about 400 feature films a year can supply not only the needs of a middle-size town in England but also all the towns in the world by simply duplicating copies. Hollywood is equipped to make all 400. 'So any British film,' he adds, 'which found a world market was taking screen-time away from Hollywood and threatening its profits. That is why the British film industry . . . has always been fought with unremitting hostility by Hollywood interests.' All the more inexplicable is it that Arthur Rank should have chosen among his top executives men whose main interests till then had been marketing Hollywood films and who had little knowledge of British film production!

Baffling, too, was Rank's ill-considered invasion of the

[1] *Mr. Rank*, by Alan Wood (Hodder and Stoughton, 1952).

American market by his 'prestige' films. No heed was paid to Korda's expensive and unsuccessful American campaign ten years earlier following the unique success of *Henry VIII.* Although operative in British films since 1934, Arthur Rank's 'advantage of ignorance' (as Mr. Wood calls it) did not prevent him from repeating the mistakes of his predecessors. Belatedly did he realize that wide distribution for his films in the U.S. was a mirage and that the real audience lay in the American specialized art-theatres. Others could have told him that before.

Writing an easily read and fascinating story, Mr. Wood quickly assures us that 'on almost every conceivable point, my views are directly opposed to those of Arthur Rank'. Rank emerges clearly as the honest man who fell among thieves, the biggest thief of all being the Labour Government.

Why did Rank go into films? To this eternal question, the book gives many answers. 'The lure of films,' writes Mr. Wood, 'may be in the love of gambling for its own sake; it may be the fascination of an amusing hobby; it may be the delights of dictatorship or the attractions of glamour; it may be lust for power or lust for film actresses; it may be sheer disinterested idealism.' He omits, oddly enough, that there are people who devote their lives to films because they believe in and love films as one of the greatest mediums of expression. Rank's public-relations experts say that he went into films 'to help the nation'. Mr. Wood is convinced, however, that Mr. Rank's own explanation is right: 'I am in films because of the Holy Spirit.' Later he qualified this to: 'I am doing this work for God and my country.'

This may be the reason for Rank's many personal acts of generosity, some of which are here recorded. Maybe it was the motive behind the children's films and *This Modern Age*, both to his credit and sad losses when the economy drive set in. Maybe it is why he has, to the best of our knowledge, never sought redress against the Yes-men and lip-servicers who hung around him. But it is still hard to accept that the Holy Spirit triumphed over the business acumen of Joseph Rank's son when such astonishing projects were undertaken as the David Hand animation set-up (£500,000), destined to failure from the start as a second-hand imitation of Disney; the Independent Frame process at Pinewood (£600,000), much overrated by Mr. Wood; and the fantastic madhouse that spawned *Caesar and Cleopatra* (£1,278,000) as well as the musical monstrosity *London Town* (nearly £1 million). Of the latter, Wood says that Rank did not discover till too late that the Hollywood director specially brought to England to make this musical-to-end-all-musicals had never made a musical! Could he not have consulted a year-book?

Perhaps it is all too easy now to look back at Rank's mistakes; one should also remember the successes, whatever they cost. To be always recalled are *Brief Encounter*, *The Way Ahead*, *Great Expectations*, *Odd Man Out*, *Millions Like Us* and for some people *Henry V* and *The Red Shoes*. 'In America,' Mr. Rank is quoted as saying, 'they like to make pictures about things that might happen once in twenty centuries. We like to make them about reality.' How tragic that he did not stick to that belief! Were *Christopher Columbus*, *The Wicked Lady*, *The Bad Lord Byron*, *The Blue Lagoon*, *Captain Boycott* and dozens more about reality?

What this book brushes aside are the many warnings to which Arthur Rank could have paid heed if he had so wished. As early as 1945 the valuable Arts Enquiry report on *The Factual Film* (not apparently known to Mr. Wood) had a section on British feature films which was widely circulated in draft. It foretold most of the events that subsequently overtook the Rank Empire. When his big production programme of 1947-48, to meet the sudden need for British films as a result of the Dalton duty, failed so disastrously, Rank announced: 'Our plans to meet an unexpected and critical situation were too ambitious. . . . We made demands on the creative talent in the industry that were beyond its resources. . . .' As *The Times* said in reviewing the P.E.P. report on British films: '. . . the trouble with the creative talent is that it was left to those whose primary concern was with business to define what constituted it. The definition may have left many reserves of the real article untapped and untried.'

What has never been recorded is that in 1946 a largish group of directors and writers associated with most of the outstanding wartime feature-documentaries offered their services as an integrated production unit to Mr. Rank to make moderate cost story-films. Their offer was rejected. Most of the group have since become individually successful in feature production.

Mr. Wood's statement that, 'The trouble with British film production after the war was not only that it ran out of money: it ran out of ideas with the same group of directors repeating themselves' is only true if related to the fact that the Rank Organization did little to invite talent into its studios at that time. To blame, as Mr. Wood does savagely, the A.C.T. union is a gross distortion of the facts.

The real villain to emerge from the book is the Labour Government. From the setting up of the Plant and Gater Committees in 1948 until it lost power last year, the Labour Government only tinkered with the industry's problems. Never did it tackle the basic problem of the dominance over production held by the distributors and circuits. So that today, despite the National Film Finance Corporation's £6 million largely loaned to producers via renters, despite the Eady Plan, production is still essentially controlled by non-creative interests. 'All businesses,' Mr. Wood quotes John Davis, for so long Rank's right hand, as saying, 'are fundamentally the same. The engineers, technicians and creative workers look after the product. The accountant co-ordinates the whole on sound lines.' But it is the banker and the accountant who have the final say today in the stories, directors and casts of the majority of British films.

Considering that Mr. Wood is not of the film world, there are few errors in the book. Less than justice is paid to the Ministry of Information Films Division under Jack Beddington for its great influences over feature films during the war, especially in bringing documentary and feature film-makers together and for its part in the birth of *The Way Ahead* and *Millions Like Us*. The estimate of *The Chance of a Lifetime* is not that held by many; the reason for its commercial failure may not have been that given by Mr. Wood. And the P.E.P. report has finally disposed of the fallacy that it is the entertainment tax which strangled the British film industry.

Little can now be gained from muck-raking over the successes and failures of Arthur Rank. How can the damage be repaired? As Mr. Wood says, 'With the appointment . . . of a former cinema manager first brought into production to advise on what the box-office wanted, Rank's film career had reached full circle. He had gone in to fight the battle of producers against distributors and exhibitors. . . . Now he had ended with an exhibitor in charge of his own production.' Sir Michael Balcon, named by Wood as Rank's chief critic in 1943, is now a director of Odeon Theatres and adviser to the Film Finance Corporation's group at Rank's Pinewood.[1] The Rank Organization itself, after drastic economies and merging, is slowly retrenching. Is it too late for Arthur Rank to learn from his mistakes? If he seeks the help of those whose integrity for good film-making is known, if the pick-ups that still linger are shed, he could rise again as a producer wiser by his experience if he really believes in the cinema as an expression of life, as well as an industrial machine.

—TRIBUNE, *September* 19, 1952.

[1] Balcon resigned from the Rank Organization in 1956.

Films and Dollars (1952)

Before the end of September (1952) the American motion picture industry will know how much of its British earnings it can continue to extract in dollars. To the Americans the matter is important. *Variety* has estimated that 'remittances from Britain for the year ending September 30 will probably be considerably larger than the total net profit from world-wide operations of the ten top (Hollywood) companies for a twelve-month period. British remittances will account for about 20 per cent of the approximately $125 million expected from the entire foreign market.' For television has not yet wooed away British audiences so much as it has American.

In January, the Chancellor of the Exchequer stated that our current rate of expenditure on American films is £9 million a year. The annual earnings of American films in the United Kingdom total £14 million. The frozen balance of £5 million can, by the Anglo-U.S. Film Agreement, be spent in thirty-three ways, including, of course, the making of American films here. When the Agreement was signed in 1948, American companies were permitted to remit £17 million per annum, at that time a quarter of their earnings. But a revision of the Agreement in 1950 added to this figure any moneys due to American companies from the Eady Producers Fund for their British-made films, plus one-third of the sums invested in such films, making a new remittable total of about £26 million—the £9 million referred to by the Chancellor. Another trade-journalist in New York, however, remarks: 'American films expect to earn 40-42 million dollars in the British market during the year . . . leaving no major company with unused frozen assets.' Add, too, the revenue from the sale of the Hollywood companies' British-made films in world markets.

It is true that this last activity provides casual employment for British actors, technicians and operatives, and that studio overheads are maintained. But the films are scarcely 'British'. Can anyone accept *Ivanhoe*, *Robin Hood*, *Captain Hornblower*, *The Mudlark* or *Treasure Island* as anything but Hollywood interpretations of British stories? Because *Quo Vadis?* was filmed in Italy, does anyone regard it as an Italian film? National character and feeling in a film are due to its creative originality and way of thinking, qualities that come primarily from the producer, director and script-writer, who for these films are mainly brought from Hollywood. The movies qualify for the quota, and for Eady Fund bonuses, because 80 per cent of the total labour is costs paid to British subjects. But these British employees are not the people who creatively shape the film. A proviso should be made in future that at least the director and/or script-writer should be British, preferably both, and that only one American star be imported. As it is, these expensive films are marketed across the world as American presentations.

Whatever new settlement is reached between U.S. film interests and the Board of Trade, it is inseparable from our own film production problems. Every additional British feature film that can be made and screened means one less from Hollywood. Though this should have given a strong incentive to British producers, the reverse has so far been true. For all the £6 million of public money loaned for production by the National Film Finance Corporation, and the return to producers of £3 million from the Eady Fund, the number of British feature films produced in the past three years has dropped from eight-one to sixty-four a year. In five years employment of film-makers (excluding artistes and musicians) has decreased from over 7,700 in 1948 to around 3,700 in 1952. Only about half of our production facilities is fully employed.

At the same time, 771 of Britain's cinemas did not meet their feature quota obligations in 1950-51. It is said that the big circuits tend to regard the 30 per cent quota as a maximum, not a minimum figure of British films to show. British exhibitors in general favour a large import of American films because, as the General Secretary of the Cinematograph Exhibitors Association wrote in *The Times* in January, 'Exhibitors usually pay a higher rental for British films than for American films.' The American industry can afford to do this; save for the top budget films, its production costs are largely recoverable in the U.S. market. Yet, as Sir Michael Balcon said recently, 'the work of British producers comes much nearer to satisfying the tastes of British audiences than that of their American counterparts.' Independent British exhibitors obviously like to have a large number of American films available so that they can play off one renter against another, while the big circuits presumably have obligations to the major Hollywood companies—A.B.C. with Warner Bros. and M-G-M for instance, and Rank with 20th-Century Fox and Universal-International.

Yet though we must somehow stimulate British production, we must not repeat, in the Johnston-Thorneycroft talks, the grave mistake of 1947, when a customs duty of 75 per cent of the estimated value of imported films was imposed—a step that led to a Hollywood boycott. We want to see the best American films. But before we complacently accept an annual drain of dollars, perhaps to the tune of £14 million, it is the Government's duty to look for means of reducing it. Our own production potential is not fully utilized as it is, and we could also reduce the total number of films shown. Three years ago, as the Plant Report pointed out, many good films, American as well as British, could be given longer booking periods than is at present trade custom. 'It is only a quite exceptional film which . . . is seen by as many as one-half of the potential cinema patrons in the United Kingdom. Similarly, it is exceptional for a feature film to be shown in as many as one-half of all the cinemas in the country.' Distribution and exhibition methods today are wasteful, and a reorganization could reduce the volume of imported films.

So far as British production is concerned, there is general agreement among our producers that unless the Eady Fund is continued after 1954, we are unlikely to sustain even the present level of film production. But opinion is more divided about the National Film Finance Corporation. It is true that the Corporation has taken the padding out of film budgets, and has enabled the industry to produce some films that would not otherwise have been made. But no professional film-maker is impressed by the purely statistical claim that screen-time shot per day has risen by 40 per cent or that the number of production days has been halved. The type and quality of films matter as much as the figures that delight the accountants. Rigid budget control has led to an increasing number of static, all-dialogue studio-bounded films, but it is very debatable whether this kind of photographed stage-play, which is so similar to a television production, will continue to attract audiences to cinemas. The visionary producer today would get his units out and about, filming against real backgrounds with a freedom of movement that television cannot as yet attain.

No one will claim that British film production can or should be expanded rashly. But it could be expanded today without any loss of quality. . . . We cannot tell what the optimum level of British film production may be until every reputable producer, director and script-writer either has continuous work or the prospect of it. But we do know that we are at present below that level.

Whatever temporary financial arrangements may be made with the U.S. film industry in September, that is the problem that really faces both the industry and the Board of Trade. A successful British film policy must start from the premise of full employment, rather than be based on the common interest of American producers and British exhibitors.

—New Statesman and Nation,
August 30, 1952.

Forgotten Lessons in Realism (1952)

The British feature film was beyond question at its best during the war years. Today, when production proceeds like a rudderless ship, it is perhaps worth looking back at that exuberant period to seek the reasons. Early in the war the director of the Ministry of Information Films Division[1] brought together some of the liveliest directors and writers of feature films with some of the principal documentary producers and directors to exchange ideas. Their informal discussions were, without doubt, one of the three causes for the realist approach being adopted by the makers of feature films. The second was the influence, first, of Mr. Cavalcanti and, later, of Mr. Harry Watt, who had made the famous *Target for Tonight*; and the third was that many young men with a documentary training were making their talent felt in the Service film units. From its earliest co-operative effort in September, 1939, the Crown Film Unit, with such films as *Squadron 992*, *Coastal Command*, *Fires Were Started*, *Western Approaches* and many more, succeeded in expressing in terms that could be understood by all something of the real character of the British people.

All the important feature films of the period—*The Way Ahead*, *Millions Like Us*, *The Way to the Stars*, *San Demetrio*, *The Foreman Went to France*, and even later, *Brief Encounter*, revealed that in this realistic approach which combined understatement with warm understanding, the British film had developed a characteristic for the first time. Léon Moussinac's famous dictum, '*L'Angleterre n'a jamais produit un vrai film anglais*,' was no longer true; indeed, it had not been since Carol Reed's version of Dr. Cronin's *The Stars Look Down* in 1940. Historically there is no question that this influence can be traced to the documentary movement in the 'thirties, with its

[1] Mr. Jack Beddington.

ardent desire to make films as a contribution to the way of our time.

It is now well-known that this special characteristic, which won for us so much esteem overseas, has largely disappeared from British film-making. With the exception of a few films like *Whisky Galore*, *Mandy* and *I Believe in You*, feature production in general has eschewed those very qualities which brought it repute in the war years. It is true that *The Sound Barrier* and *Cry, The Beloved Country* treat contemporary themes with some success, but again they are exceptions. The need to reduce costs, the closer watch over budgets and schedules, necessary though they have been, have also been the excuse to restrict the choice of stories to photographed stage-plays whose filming almost entirely in the studio is easier to check and control than filming on location. Satisfactory as this must be to the accountant turned producer, it is strangling to creative development, as anyone familiar with films made for American television must be aware. In fact, such photoplays are so remarkably akin to the televised play that people may not much longer be coaxed away from the little screen at home to the big screen in the local cinema. The film is still the widest open window on to the world, but its producers appear busy pulling the curtains.

The documentary film has also had its troubles since the war. Relying as it always has on sponsorship and not box-office returns for its production finance, the documentary film-makers have found their major sponsor—the Government—less and less inclined to use the medium in its more ambitious and dramatic aspects. A good number of training, instructional, and informational short films has been made competently in the past six years but now many of these have ceased except as requests from private industry or one of the nationalized boards. The Crown Film Unit is disbanded. The Transport Commission's Film Unit continues producing for a prescribed purpose. The Shell Film Unit pursues its distinguished career of specialized films of a scientific and mechanical nature, unsurpassed for their craftsmanship. But the talents that produced the famous documentaries of the past, that created such a prestige around the world, mainly lack adequate outlet.

A few documentary directors of repute have been struggling

along in feature production, their ideas not understood and their abilities largely dissipated. An occasional film like *The Wooden Horse* is no compensation for its director being idle for two subsequent years. The promising director of *Western Approaches* has yet to be given material worthy of his skill, although his *White Corridors* was impressive. The writer-director of those two inspiring human documentaries, *The Undefeated* and *David,* is allowed to languish. Mr. John Grierson at his Group Three, with resources provided by the Film Finance Corporation has made only one film out of five that develops the realist principle. *The Brave Don't Cry* is a notable effort, but even it suffered from being anchored to the studio with which the Group is burdened, where floor-space must be kept filled and overheads paid when, maybe, the very stories it should be making do not need the artificial make-up of studio contriving.

It has been said that today there are no stories with the urgency and vitality of the war years. That is hard to believe. But certainly they will not be found by sitting at a studio-desk reading the proofs of the newest novels, nor by attending first nights at West End theatres. The stories are there—among the people and in the everyday events of this country. They will not come to the writers; it is the writers who must go out and look for them. That again is difficult, because what is called 'pre-production money' is hard to come by and most film-writers today are in no position to speculate. There is little encouragement of original screen-writing by feature producers. They appear to prefer the ready-made success in theatre or novel form.

In the uneven pattern of British film production today there is need for a new focus point where the realist qualities of the war films may be joined with the experience of the documentary people to make a series of feature films at moderate cost that will express the strength of character and determination of the British people. Realism does not necessarily imply a strictly factual approach. It can mean the interpretation of the ordinary man's dreams and wishes. Realism may be the basis for fantasy, or comedy, or drama. It is no use to make these films piecemeal, or to hope that they may emerge singly from existing producer groups. As the Crown Film Unit and other units and studios have shown, it is the loyalty and teamwork of a group of creative directors and writers, with their attendant units of technicians and craftsmen, working through a producer whose devotion to a cause inspires confidence, which are needed to provide the renascence. No great foresight is required to propose a maxim for British producers—'Show in the cinema what television cannot show in the home.' This may lead to spectacular costume romances and musicals at which the British have never been good and at which Hollywood excels, but it could also lead to a rediscovery that the whole world outside the cabined studio is the real stuff of the cinema.

—The Times, *September* 25, 1952.

Postscript

'The British film industry today is more lively than ever.' So says a half-page advertisement in today's *The Times*.[1] I hope this is true! If by 'lively' it is meant that more films are being made than in recent years, so much the better for the many people employed. But if by 'lively' the copy-writer implies that British films have suddenly discovered a new virility, a spate of fresh creative talent, an unexpected impulse to use the screen to reflect and interpret the real outlooks and ideas, characters and relationships of the British people in this momentous decade, then I think he is guilty of overstatement, or shall I say he is wishful-thinking? A glance at current production-schedules in our studios reveals in the main the same old line-up of stock subjects.

Since the last piece in this book was written five years ago, sundry events affecting the future of the British film industry have occurred but none of them fundamentally brightens the outlook for a better use of cinema as is found in other countries. A new Cinematograph Films Act was introduced into Parliament in April, 1957. It makes the old Eady Plan into a permanent official body to be known as the British Film Fund Agency which, through a levy imposed on cinema-exhibitors' takings, will make repayments to the producers of British films to encourage further production. From the same levy, the Fund will also provide finance for the Children's Film Foundation, which is an admirable thing. The Act also extends the life of the National Film Finance Corporation for a further ten years, hoping that it will pay its way; and, as expected, it continues until 1960 the compulsory inclusion of a set proportion of registered British-made films in cinema programmes as pre-

[1] October 29, 1957.

vious acts have done. In the meantime, the U.S.-Anglo Film Agreement has been renewed.

Superficially, this formidable array of legislation gives the impression that economically the future is set fair. M.P.s of all parties no doubt preen themselves. But nothing has been done to improve the position of the independent film-maker who is, and still will be, as dependent as ever on obtaining a distribution-guarantee for his film before he can raise the money to make it—even from the N.F.F.C.—and the distributor will, as before, call the tune on subject and script, director and main cast with a circuit-release first in mind. We are still in Britain a very long way from attaining the freedom and scope for genuine independent production that has revitalized the whole motion picture world in the United States and to which I referred in the Foreword.

It has been noted by foreign observers of the British cinema that its front-office executives show a marked antagonism to individuality in film-making and for that reason few of our films have the stamp of personality as does a film by, say, Wyler, Kazan, Clouzot, Clair, Zinnemann, Bresson or George Stevens. This, of course, is true and the cause of it, I suggest, is that individuality fits awkwardly and perhaps unreliably into an industry which is being run more and more by minds trained in figure-work but unfamiliar with what the Americans call 'creativity'. Both talents are essential to film-making which is an industrial art, but alas, they are seldom possessed by one individual. A mutual trust must be established between two individuals, a trust that is based on a respect for their particular talents. All too often, the man-of-figures brashly invades the province of the creative partner, while the latter is too timid or frankly disinclined to encroach on the province of the former—even if he were in the position to do so, which he is not. Thus, in almost all cases, the individualist film-maker in feature pictures in the British cinema is a misfit. He gets in the way of the machine. He's a real Outsider.

A question much asked recently is, Why are the British unable to present at any of the various international film festivals a feature picture that can be fairly set alongside the best work of other nations? The awards and prizes and critical acclaim which we do get from time to time are almost always given for work produced outside the main commercial activity of the industry. (E.g. *The Bespoke Overcoat*, *Every Day Except Christmas*, *Together*, *Daybreak at Udi*, *Thursday's Children*). These are products from the specialized field at which we British frequently excel. But feature films from other nations which are singled out for merit are not always freak offbeat productions and certainly not often produced outside the framework of their national film industry. Bresson's *Un Condamné . . .*, Wyler's *Friendly Persuasion*, Zinnemann's *A Hatful of Rain*, Bergman's *The Seventh Seal*, all award winners at 1957's festivals of high standing, were made as a part of commercial film production in their respective countries.

The fact is, and I repeat deliberately words used earlier, that we have learned less in Britain than in any other country, including the United States, about how to equate art with industry in the cinema. In spite of a Films Bank, of continued Films Acts since 1927, of levies for production, of protective quotas in cinemas—we still haven't found the structure in which individual creative talent can express itself freely and say something worth saying about contemporary life. Little encouragement exists for screenwriters to write what they feel urged to write instead of what they *think* a producer *thinks* will satisfy the distributor—upon whom rests final decision. Too many of our film-makers are absorbed in the purely technical problems of film-making; too few hold a viewpoint about life and are prepared to fight to express that viewpoint.

It is arrant nonsense to say, as has been said in the Press this year, that the contemporary issues of the British people are not so dynamic filmwise as those of other countries. What are we—a nation living in a vacuum? The colour-bar, old age, Anglo-American relations, capital punishment, juvenile delinquency, jazz clubs, labour relations, automation, scientific discovery, colonial relations, national service, foreigners in Britain, industrial management, technological development, the spoliation of the countryside, youth movements—the list is endless from which virile, exciting, dramatic stories could be derived. Instead, we keep turning back to the heroics of the last War, and to more suburban middle-class comedies, more dreary musicals (our most unsuccessful *genre*) and the ubiquitous crime-thriller.

That is why I cannot, much as I should like to, agree with our advertisement-writer when he says, 'The British film industry today is more lively than ever'. The industry hasn't been 'lively' in a real sense since the end of the War. In ideas, imagination, originality and freedom for talent both old and new to create, our feature film industry as a whole is frustrated. It will remain so until something drastic is done to provide real freedom of opportunity for the independent and progressive film-maker.

But let us also bear in mind the fact that the whole industrial and economic structure of cinema is changing, and changing fast. Methods of production, distribution and, yes, exhibition are changing—rapidly. The mass-impact of television as the new major source of public entertainment, as yet only felt in comparatively few countries, will ultimately alter the whole role of the cinema, including the British cinema. And it can only be to the cinema's—as well as the world's—overall benefit.

INDEXES

Index of Films

Index

Index

x

Index

Index

Index of Names

Index

Index

Index

Index

General Index

Index

Index

Index

Index

Index

Index

Index